The Book of Sorrows

P9-BYL-849

BY THE SAME AUTHOR

The Book of the Dun Cow

The Book of Sorrows

Walter Wangerin, Jr.

Harper & Row, Publishers, San Francisco

New York, Grand Rapids, Philadelphia, St. Louis
London, Singapore, Sydney, Tokyo, Toronto

A hardcover edition of this book is published by Harper & Row, Publishers, Inc.

THE BOOK OF SORROWS. Copyright © 1985 by Walter Wangerin, Jr. All rights reserved. Printed in the United States of America. No part of this book may be used or reproduced in any manner whatsoever without written permission except in the case of brief quotations embodied in critical articles and reviews. For information address Harper & Row, Publishers, Inc., 10 East 53rd Street, New York, NY 10022.

FIRST HARPER & ROW PAPERBACK EDITION PUBLISHED 1989.

Library of Congress Cataloging-in-Publication Data
Wangerin, Walter.
   The book of sorrows.

   Summary: In the aftermath of the terrible conflict with the dreaded Wyrm, Chauntecleer, Pertelote, and the other inhabitants of the Coop try to piece together their shattered lives until Wyrm once again insinuates himself with dire consequences for all.
   [1. Fantasy] I. Title.

PS3573.A477B6 1985   813'.54 [Fic] 78-22475
ISBN 0-06-250929-2
ISBN 0-06-2509365 (pbk.)

89 90 91 92 93 FG 10 9 8 7 6 5 4 3 2

For Joanne Ryder, my patient friend

If you will hear my words,
and hearing welcome them and fight the plague,
you will find strength and lightening of your load.

Sophocles

Contents

IV. NOW, THE SERPENT WAS MORE SUBTLE THAN ANY OTHER BEAST

V. THE SUN OF RIGHTEOUSNESS, WITH HEALING IN HIS WINGS

PART ONE
SOMETHING UNRESOLVED

One
Pertelote

Two Hens, white in a yellow field, walking with that thrust of the head which suggests that they are going secretly, on tiptoe, as spies, or comic exaggerations of spies, placing their claws with infinite care—

Two Hens, made all the whiter by a deep blue sky, go east across the yellow field, walking and pausing by turns, so that they seem two separate tears trickling down the face of the field.

They are in an open space. Their voices carry, though they speak low to one another. And though they are speaking low, they've neither stopped nor taken their gaze from the land before them. They've come, and they go, with a purpose.

"There. Can you see it?"

"Where?"

"Straight ahead, a little to the left."

"That tree?"

"No. Below it."

"It's a big tree."

"A willow. We wouldn't have come so far for a willow. We've willows enough at home." She points with her beak. "See the darker green behind the tree?"

"That?" The other Hen tucks her beak against her neck, a gesture of distaste. "An ugly tangle, to my eye," she says.

"Well, that's it all the same, Jasper. It's what we're looking for."

"So far," grumps Jasper, "for such a weed."

At once the first Hen laughs aloud. Jasper glances to see if it's a mocking laugh. It isn't: Pertelote is laughing for pure pleasure, enjoying a joke. Jasper's a fat Hen, unhappy at long distances of travel.

Jasper's fatness also gives her little liking for herself. Generally she assumes that everyone else holds the same low opinion of her character, and therefore she suspects mockery. Laughing isn't loving, certainly not when she laughs at herself, and likely not when others do. And mocking wants a pecking, for pecking commands a certain respect, and respect reestablishes a certain order. That's Jasper's way. She glances at Pertelote—

But that Hen's affection is so clean and so faithful that Jasper simply cannot doubt it. God gave that hen a bright, uncomplicated eye. If Pertelote is laughing, then could it be that Jasper tells a good joke?

They continue forward, both gazing forward, one snatching glances at the other. That one tries her joke again: "Hmph! Hmph! So far for such a weed!"

And the other laughs the louder, like bells. "Jasper, you uncomplaining Hen! You're so good to have along!"

Jasper blinks and believes it.

Two Hens cross a yellow field together. The fat one has a thin pink comb, no ornament at all, mere nakedness on her head. But Pertelote's comb is sultry red and beautiful; it troubles the soul by its beauty. Her neck is a slender stalk. And at her throat there sprouts a choke of feathers both crimson and burning. This patch of color is startling in her whiteness; and though she wears it unconsciously, none who meet her can help but stare at it and wonder at her depth. *Who are you, Hen, with such blood at your throat, and such beauty?*

In the time it takes to cross the field, Pertelote chats a memory with Jasper.

"I used to sing for a grey Goose once," she says, never taking her eyes from the weed ahead, "an old Goose, swollen in all her joints, lumpish at her beak, so that it didn't close properly. But she was well skilled in every virtuous plant and healing herb. She would nod when I sang, and weep, as old Birds do; and then she'd thank me by showing me simples, teaching me their strange and vigorous faculties. She taught me, Jasper, goodness in ugliness. A weed is a weed only if you do not like it, and you don't like what you don't understand. Learn it, and suddenly it's no weed, but a medicine. And if a medicine, why, then it's the grace of God. That old Goose," says Pertelote. "Ah, the grey Goose died, killed by the Basilisks—"

The season is autumn, cool and clean. Beyond the willow, the land rises up into hills all covered in an evergreen thicket. The sun slants down behind two Hens white, in a golden field. Blue, green, golden, and here a feathered white: it's a lovely day altogether. And they have arrived below the willow.

Pertelote moves straight into the tangle of weed, dividing leaves by her breast. Jasper halts.

"Wait!"

Pertelote looks back. "You're tired?"

"No more'n seventeen miles tired," says Jasper.

"Well, it's five steps more," says Pertelote, "as slow as you want them. There's good medicine beneath these leaves."

But it's not so much the weariness that stops her as the fastidiousness of the fat Hen; that, and hesitation before the unknown. These weeds look like a foul, green slough.

Jasper says, "It stinks."

Pertelote grins, laughs, then turns away and pushes herself deeper in. Jasper gazes after her: it looks as though the smaller Hen is sinking into water.

"Do I have to come?"

"Ah, Jasper, you're a bold sort."

"A clean sorter Hen. Your leaves stink. Um, do *you* got to go into that? What if there's snakes? What lives below—?" The farther and the deeper that Pertelote goes, the higher Jasper cranes her neck and the wider go her eyes. "Well," says Jasper, "it's getting dark, now. Time to go home. Um, you want to go home? Whew! That was a chilly—"

Suddenly Pertelote plunges down and disappears.

"Awk!" says Jasper, shooting up on her toes. "Lady? Lady?"

For an instant, Jasper the Hen is utterly alone before a living sea, and the field is golden, and the dome of the sky is blue: but all is soundless. It's only herself alive. She swallows. "Lady?"

Then, where Pertelote disappeared, the sour green leaves suck down, making a depression; they jerk with sudden angry violence, slapping, whipping one another. Jasper feels a panic in her breast. There comes a popping sound, and the leaves rise up again, as still as the sea.

"Lady?" Jasper hops the fringes, patting wings to her sides. *"Lady?"*

Pertelote's head appears, smiling. "A thornapple," she calls, then sinks again, and the leaves repeat their shaking and snapping. And then it is clear what's happening: Pertelote is plucking fruit.

And Jasper is grumpy.

"Two thornapples," Pertelote announces above the leaves, wading out now. "Exactly what Russel needs for healing."

Jasper turns away with enormous dignity, showing Pertelote tailfeathers and a great butt.

Pertelote regards her. "Are you still tired?" she asks.

"I have never," says Jasper, "in all my born life came on so rank a weed as this."

"Ah," says Pertelote, "jimsonweed offends you."

"And besides all that, I do not know why my Lady brung me with her."

"Why, Jasper!" Pertelote's voice is honey. "To help me carry these." And all at once she sticks the thornapples to Jasper's tail.

"Awk! *Awk!*" The fat Hen ascends the air, beating little wings; but the green burrs hold fast, and all her dignity is gone. "I stink! I stink!" she cries to the sky, and Pertelote collapses in laughter, and the tears run from her eyes.

"Sister! Sister! Don't land sitting! Oh, Jasper!"

Almost Jasper allows the anger to shape her face; but Pertelote's laughter is so full of joy and affection, that Jasper melts to be thus important to her Lady.

"And why did I bring you along?" laughs Pertelote. "For companionship. I love you, Jasper."

That undoes the fat Hen altogether. She drops her head in embarrassment, the thornapples nodding behind her, and says, "Now don't go gawky on me."

Pertelote smiles. "One more medicine to go," she says. "And for that we'll climb the hills."

Jasper narrows her eye. "Them hills?" She points beyond the jimsonweed.

"I need juniper berries," says Pertelote. "There's where the juniper grows."

"Now?" The fat Hen has noticed the blue sky purpling, the golden ground descending, and the evening breeze gone chilly. "Ain't these two enough?"

"Thornapples will put the Fox to sleep for us," Pertelote explains. "But it's the juice of the juniper must bathe his infections. Jasper?"

"To be sure, to be sure," muses Jasper. "Of course." To be loved is all well and good. But to be caught in the cold of an autumn night, well: that's another matter.

"Jasper? Coming?"

And, moreover, on top of that, to mince one's way through a field of the foulest weed, contracting a smell, an unsociable smell—

"Sister? Jasper?"

"Whew! Ain't it a bit peaky out? Whew! Such a shiver just passed my bones!"

Now, the beautiful Pertelote, Hen of an excellent flock and wife to the loud, renowned Bird Chauntecleer, possesses wonderful powers of persuasion, greater, certainly, than Jasper's fussy resistance; and Pertelote would use them now, and Jasper would attend her even to the hills, with gratitude and a personal sense of importance—except that suddenly Pertelote glimpses motion on the hillside and soon falls silent at the sight. A dim passage of white. A shadow, pale within the juniper thicket. Then nothing.

Pertelote's mood changes. The laughter passes away, while concern darkens in her face as evening darkens the sky. Her eye she fixes on the thicket.

"Jasper?" A whole new tone to her voice. Solemnity.

Jasper is suddenly ashamed. "Well, but I didn't mean I wouldn't nor couldn't, you understand—"

"Jasper."

"What?"

"Go home."

The big Hen falls quiet. It's what she wanted, of course; but her Lady isn't even looking at her. She didn't want it this way. "What did you say?"

"Go home."

"Lady." Jasper's voice takes on a truly penitential softness, and behold: it is lovely. "Lady, I will stay with you. I didn't mean I should desert you. What would I do without you? Or, maybe, you—without me?"

For a loving instant Pertelote responds to that voice, turning from the gorse to look at Jasper cleanly, absolutely. "Oh, Jasper, what better can you do me now than to carry the apples home, and to tell my Chauntecleer that I am fine? You are a beautiful Bird. You have my love. You cannot lose my love. Go home."

"Well," says Jasper, "I've breathed in a chill, after all—"

"An excellent reason to hurry," says Pertelote. She touches her sister once, then turns her attention back to the hills, whose tops are taking fires from the sun. "Here comes the night."

Jasper makes a silly grin. "Fat Birds, thin blood, you know."

"Don't belittle yourself, my sister," Pertelote says over her shoulder, feet still, standing still, but her spirit yearning forward. "You are more healthy than any of us. Go home. Be warm."

"You don't need someone to protect you, then?"

"I need a messenger to tell my husband I love him. Go home. Go."

So Jasper backs away. "Whatever *you* say," she says. "Not my own inclinations, you understand, since I generally finish anything I start, you understand. But the darkness and the cold and the distance—" with which the Hen Jasper bolts and races westward with a wonderful stretch of her neck and a bounce of baubles behind. A healthy Hen indeed.

And Pertelote walks in the other direction, deeper east, through the dark datura toward the hills, toward the thicket gloaming before her.

The Hen is very intent, peering into the juniper as though probing with a beam of light. Yet her motion remains restrained, smooth, easy. "Ah, my hiding heart," she whispers. "Is *this* where you go every day? Is this your seclusion? Why?" It was not something, but some *one* she saw slipping through the juniper so far from home.

The sky, the whole dome of the sky, is as deep and translucent as amethyst. The sun is gone, now. Dusk flows round dear Pertelote's feet, and the Hen begins to hum. This evening can hold a hum, like the melodious ringing of a bell, as though one stood *within* the bell and the sound came down from all around. Sweet Pertelote is the tongue, and the great round sky the thing she rings.

She hums because she does not sneak. She wishes her coming to be no secret, no threat, no shock, no harmful approach. *Peace, world; Pertelote brings her love.*

But then, as she begins to climb the hill, still below the juniper gorse, she changes her humming into a song, explicit words and true emotion:

> "One Lady, she left us for spite.
> *All right:*
> Forgotten, she was, overnight,
> *All right:*
> And the morning was better without her.

"Another, she left us in sorrow,
   Poor Sparrow!
We craved her return with the morrow.
   Black laurel!
The mourning was bitter without her—"

Up and up the hill the Hen repeats her song, gently touching words that might turn angry, might turn sad; and when
she comes to the juniper thicket itself, softer and softer goes
her voice until it is stilled altogether, and she breathes a
while.

Then: "Which one are you, Chalcedony?"

She speaks only just above a whisper, with perfect assurance
one is hearing her. But no one answers. The evergreen growth
is windless.

"Are you the Lady of spite?" says Pertelote. "Are you the
Lady of sorrow?"

Evening turns. Pertelote, so seeming alone on the hillside,
is patient.

"I want you to know, dear sister, that I didn't come looking
for you. I know that your privacy's a treasure. I came on
another errand altogether, but seeing you, how could I leave
you? Finding you, how could I seem to reject you? Meeting
you must mean greeting you—"

All at once, one blue berry the size of a pea rolls out between juniper roots, dribbles downhill, and lodges in Pertelote's toes.

She whispers, "Ah. So you know why I came."

One at a time, other berries follow, bouncing into a little
heap, an offering at the foot of the Hen, and all in utter
silence.

Pertelote is inclined to weep, gazing at that pile. "Ten," she
says. "Oh, Chalcedony, you private sister of mine, so kind and
watchful, ten. Ten exactly, and the reason I came. Do you
know how much I love you?"

Slowly, like a poor flag brought sadly to half-staff, the skinny head of a Hen appears above the gorse; and so, Chalcedony is looking at Pertelote.

"Do you think," she says, "that you could go away now?"

"Because I have what I came for?" She returns the look. "Well, I could go. But how would I carry ten berries on my own?"

Chalcedony considers this, blinking in bewilderment. There are no feathers around her eyes, pink flesh only, making her seem vulnerable and undernourished—and sad. She has eyes too huge for a Hen. "'Tis a puzzle, surely," she says. "Perhaps you could take only two?"

"Perhaps. But then I'd have to return for the others. And two at a time would have me back here—what?—four more times."

"Four?" The mathematics pain this timid Hen. "Four. Well, but there's never no need you'd come in here, is there? Never no need to stand close?"

"Ah, sister, why shouldn't I? Why couldn't I," gently she whispers, "come close to kiss you?"

"*Kiss* me?"

"Are you indecent?"

"Oh, ma'am! I hope I may say I am never that!"

"Of course not. But you are hiding—?"

"Well. Well. Well." Chalcedony gazes downward.

"Are you the Lady of spite?"

"No!" Her head snaps up, her wide eyes pleading. "No, never of spite, truly. Don't never, never think such a thing of Chalcedony!"

"So, then," says Pertelote as though there's nothing left but this: "You are a Lady of sorrow, and I should comfort you with a kiss."

Chalcedony drops a second glance to something below her, immediately raising her face again. "Of sorrow?" she whispers, then bursts into hopeless tears.

"Oh, sister, sister, sister." Pertelote enters the thicket, winds her way to the skinny Hen and takes her under the wing, holding her, and Chalcedony sobs terribly, shaking tears. And she kisses her.

So the evening deepens while a skinny, bare-feather Hen spends her tears, but not her sorrow. Pertelote does not ask for causes. Pertelote understands the need of privacy and knows how to wait.

"I'm sorry, ma'am. I didn't never cry before. Not till now and I seen you."

"Well, now you may, and I cry with you, Chalcedony."

"Aye."

Finally, the sad one sighs and is still, and then it is her own sole choice: Chalcedony parts from Pertelote, stepping backward and gazing with true reverence down toward the ground. "See?" Pertelote, too, bends her eye to their feet, and there sees a faint whiteness lying in the gloom. "Do you see?"

Something, it is, most precious in the sight of Chalcedony.

"I see," says Pertelote. "An egg."

"Perfectest little egg," says Chalcedony.

"Lovely. Unblemished." Pertelote waits a careful three minutes and then asks the question that hangs between them. "But why is it here?"

"Here?"

"So far from home, Chalcedony."

"Here," repeats the thin Hen, brushing the egg with the tip of her wing. "Well," she whispers, "I couldn't never make another one since the Rat kilt the first, and that the first of all I ever made." She looks up quickly to Pertelote. "But I understood, what with the war and all, events and all, churning up my innards. No peace in me for making eggs." She sighs. "Ah, but then the other Hens went to laying again, and brooding again—but not Chalcedony, and that was a mockery around the Coop, and there was things that Jasper said. And there was children, and there was motherhood for all the Hens—but not Chalcedony. I couldn't see no reason why, excepting maybe the mockery of it all." Chalcedony looks with deep appeal into Pertelote's eyes, searching understanding for so tender a revelation. "But I said in my soul, 'Why mayn't Chalcedony also be laying an egg?' And I said—" She is whispering lowly, now: "I said, 'Why mayn't Chalcedony get a child—' "

"Ah," sighs Pertelote.

"You had young ones, right, ma'am?"

"I did. I did once."

"Then you know. You've got the understanding."

"I do that," whispers Pertelote.

"So, you see, I came away, and alone, alone, by the mercy of God, I laid this here egg—"

"Just one."

"—at the ending of the summer, and no woman never thanked God more often than did Chalcedony, sitting on her egg, with smilings and jubilations on her dear and blessed, precious. . . ."

The little Hen begins to sob again, choking on the last part of her story. Again, the beautiful Pertelote covers her with a wing.

Pertelote says, "It is the autumn, now."

Chalcedony nods. "The autumn, aye. The killing autumn."

"How many months, then? Two?"

"Oh, Lady, Lady! *Three!*"

Pertelote bends her neck to hear such knowledge and such sorrow. "Three," she whispers. "Then cry on me, Chalcedony, do. Weep your whole heart upon my breast. I know the grief, and don't I? For I had three sons. More than that, I had the gift of naming them and watching them to grow and seeing their father to laugh with them. But they died betimes. I know, sister. Oh, it is a hollow, horrible world."

"Never," sobs Chalcedony. " 'Twill never hatch, the little thing, now, will it?"

Pertelote shakes her head. "No. Never."

"Oh, Lady, why mayn't Chalcedony get a pretty child?"

"Hush. Hush. Hush, sweet sister mine. Hush. Hush. Hush—"

And so descends the evening on two white Hens hug-

ging in the juniper, the sky so sadly purple, a bruise in the universe.

Thus it was, in those days, with Pertelote the Hen.
She sought the souls of her sisters.
And when dark was dark indeed, and when silence had
embraced the Hens embracing one another, Pertelote said,
"It is not good to do nothing. Chalcedony, let's do two things.
Let's bury the unborn together. This is right, even if the baby
never showed its face. It had your love, after all."
The skinny Hen agreed to that: it had her love and all her
yearning.
"And then," said Pertelote, "let's see how two of us can
carry ten. Russel the Fox is in need of nursing. I know a
poultice made of juniper juice—"

Two
Russel

Sacred datura was a dangerous narcotic and therefore the final
physic which Pertelote attempted on Russel the Fox, the treat-
ment of last chance. Delicately she administered its seeds to
him, by gentle and watchful measures; and so she laid him to
sleep.
To sleep. This was necessary because the Fox was a compul-
sive. He talked. The gift of God unto the Animals, that they
could speak, was in Russel an addiction and a sin: he could not
not talk; and therefore the wound he'd received from the Basilisks in the war, the poisoning of his tongue and snout, had
never healed. Both summer and autumn Russel went about

with a nose the size of a popping sausage, making no sense whatever, but making it all the time, at every hour of the waking day. Language troubled his flesh, forever inflaming it; but Russel traded pain for expression, grieving every one of his friends, and talking, talking, talking.

Through the summer and the autumn together Lord Chauntecleer the Rooster was driven to distraction, because all he had for healing the Fox was the strength of his command, and a Rooster can cry *"SHUT UP!"* only so many times in a day. Russel would try. Dear God, how Russel would try. He'd roll his eyes toward Chauntecleer, boiled eggs above that horrible swelling, and nod agreement, and gaze upon the angry Rooster, and say nothing—nothing, in order to give that organ rest; nothing, to cease the aggravation, to allow the suppuration; nothing, not a word, till Chauntecleer left. And then, with a shiver of pain and pleasure, with a sigh for his weakness and pangs for his guilt, he'd speak a word, helplessly another, tragically a third and a fourth, until it was a speech he'd begun to fashion; and Russel the Fox had begun to live again, resignedly to die. Talking.

But a mute Russel is a Russel who is not. A speaking Russel *is.* Even so did he explain (aloud) his compulsion. It was the desire to *be.* On the other hand, even so do creatures scratch an itch all bloody, and still continue to scratch it, with red and dripping nails.

There was a Wolf, once, who sliced his tongue upon a flint embedded in a saltlick. Tasting blood, and finding it sweet, that Wolf licked and licked his tongue to lacerations. He gulped his lifesblood hungrily, and died.

"SHUT UP!" shrieked Chauntecleer.

"Please, Russel," whispered the Hens attending him, petting him, clucking around him and caring. "We can wait to hear you. Can't you wait to talk?"

And seven Mice sat near, in tears when their uncle persisted describing the world unto them, grieved by the great flaps of his jowls and the yellow pus they ran.

"I'll tell you a trick," said Russel, and they wept, beads for black eyes, bathed in tears. "One little trick. Just one last trick. A trick most practicable, and besides that, useful. One."

And when he named the trick, "Catching Minnows with One's Tail," they wailed, all seven of them, as though he had named the end of the world.

"For the love of God," groaned Chauntecleer the Rooster, "Russel, shut up."

Minnows!

So Pertelote the Hen had no choice but to administer the sacred datura.

She split her thornapple and persuaded the Fox to swallow its seeds as aids for meditation. That was *her* trick. His eyes grew bright a moment, then they panicked while his neck went wobbly, then they glazed; and he laid his ruptured snout upon the ground, and he slept.

And the wood was silent then. And Russel did not speak. All the Animals watched with weakened hearts, and Pertelote soaked a dry moss in the juice of the juniper and swabbed the loose, infected parts of her brother Fox, her claw a graceful instrument. Purple smearings on his gums.

Chauntecleer's eye nearly cracked with its concern.

"Is he sleeping?"

"He's sleeping," said Pertelote.

"Oh, thank God."

"Aye. There's hope for a silent Fox."

The seven Mice crept forward and patted a reddish rump. They wrapped his tail around him.

And Russel made soft snoring in his flesh.

Thus it was with the creatures in those days following the war. They struggled to survive its consequences—not only the wounds it left behind, but also the diminished circumstance of their existence, for they had no house any more.

They struggled bravely.

But at first blush, they seemed to fail. For Russel the Fox—he died.

Yet take each moment in its turn and give each day its due attention: just now the Rooster pleaded of his wife, "He's sleeping?"

And she repeated, "Aye. There's hope for a silent Fox."

Three
Chauntecleer

It happened that Russel fell asleep beneath a maple tree. Therefore, to that maple, all solitary in the center of the wood, the Animals repaired, and for a while it became their home.

Well, they had no Coop, no roof of any sort. Wyrm had made them nomads, and life was bare because of him.

Life was bare, but life was heavy nonetheless. The Animals had lost the innocence of ignorance, and Lord Chauntecleer in particular suffered the knowledge of the presence of Wyrm. He measured all his commands and all his activities against the size of that monster—and they were, all of them, diminished. He didn't plan, but that Wyrm was in the plan. He walked abroad, and Wyrm attended him. He looked on the sleeping Fox, and he saw the work of the Serpent. He watched his Hens find roost in the maple tree, clucking, gossiping with one another, trusting their souls to sleep, and he saw the prey of the Evil One. In the evening they were endangered. And the dark of the night was perilous. So then evening and night were no longer comforts to close the day. Every evening, every night arrived as another threat of the Enemy. Chauntecleer wrestled the darkness.

And every morning the prayer of the Rooster was the same: "Why?"

Why is Wyrm?

Wyrm, that subterranean Serpent! No one deserved so ruinous an evil underneath her feet. No one had defied him; no
one had sinned enough to justify his presence in the universe.
Absolutely no one. Yet, he was; he was; he existed. Long and
foul and putrifying, a single muscle, a massive, contracting
muscle in the round earth. Why? And he hated God with a
furious hatred; but he focused his spite on the Animals, and
they were the ones who suffered his cruelty, but who were
they? Animals. Plain Animals, yet he had murdered them. He
killed the Mouse's husband. He killed the Wee Widow Mouse
herself, so that her children were orphaned. He killed the
children of Chauntecleer and Pertelote, early, before the war
began. He killed their nurse. He killed fools and heroes alike,
and when the battles began, the killing was indiscriminate, the
memory now unspeakable: the beautiful Nimbus down on his
knees, his Stag's face raised to heaven, his mouth agape, his
pleading as silent as the spheres, and the screaming of others
was his answer. For the Foxes and the Otters and the Rabbits
died, killed; and Geese and Duck and Swan, Bees, Ants, Birds,
Pigs, Sheep, the meek of the earth, slaughtered, killed, for no
sinning of their own, but Wyrm, Wyrm, *Wyrm* was there;
Wyrm was seeking his freedom; Wyrm had weakened them;
now Wyrm had split the crust of the earth like a rind, and the
Animals looked down into the gorge, and the Animals saw him
face to face, that mighty Serpent, and all were horrified, and
all of them transfixed—all but one. One. Mundo Cani Dog
took him a stick and taunted Wyrm, ha! And when the Wyrm's
eye turned to see this speck, why, Mundo Cani leaped over the
cliff, ha-ha! down and down the gorge, the earth-crack,
Wyrm's hatch, and landed fighting on the monster's eyeball:
pierced it, pierced it, slashed it to madness, so that the great,
slick muscle doubled on himself, and the earth-crack couldn't
stand the spasm; it collapsed in earthquake; it thundered shut.
So Wyrm was contained. So, ha! Ha-ha to the monster imprisoned again! So Wyrm crawled the belly of the world. So. But
so *what?* He was still alive, for all of that! And he took with him

a friend beloved above all others, that humble Mundo Cani. When one went down, they both went down together. Oh, how shall we live without the gentle Mundo Cani? How can we ever be complete again? Oh, Wyrm! Oh, Wyrm!—Oh, fire and fury! Wyrm!

Mighty God, you talk to us! Tell us: *why does Wyrm exist?*

He killed peace.

He killed their deeper trust and sweet security; Hens had rather more suspicious eyes than ever they did in the past. Chauntecleer's Canonical Crows were more needful than ever before, more necessary than the rising of the sun; nonetheless, ironically, they were less believed than ever before; because of the war which came in spite of them. Because of Wyrm.

Oh, Chauntecleer crowed crows nearly baroque for subtlety, intelligence, and beauty; he went extraordinary lengths to make each Crow a something, a memorable blessing each in itself, all tender to the Chickens; but sometimes he wondered whether those lengths didn't measure a personal doubt. And could it be that the grander, more wonderful the Crow on its outside, the emptier it was at its core?

Mighty God, please talk to us. Explain it, explain—

Why is Wyrm?

It is recorded with no surprise, that the Animals under Chauntecleer's protection—even the children hatched after the war—lived grimly, chilly toward the world, spare regarding their own needs, and of no particular hope in the future. Wyrm had murdered cheer. Cold realists were these Animals of the experienced eye: as fearful of believing as they were of creeds themselves, when the object of either was invisible.

On the other hand, their tenderness toward one another grew intense. How they loved each other, when suddenly the life in the other seemed so precarious, so rare, so precious. How solicitous they were for the sick one's health, and how glad at his healing, for it was something of themselves had healed. One was in all, and all were joined to one. Well, all had the same transfiguring memory, hadn't they? And all the same enemy, and he was great and they were few. Aye, sorrow binds poor hearts, and weakness isn't ashamed to hide in the binding. They loved each other. It was nearly painful how much they loved each other: grim to the world, watchful of a Fox's convalescence—

And here is an irony certainly: what kept Wyrm within his prison (this by the cosmic ordination of the Lord God) was precisely this union of the Animals. They were his Keepers. They were themselves the spiritual netting which, when it remained a woven whole, denied him freedom in the universe. Not any individual Animal did this thing, but the dear love among *all* the Animals: community, that was warp and woof! Therefore, Wyrm's bloody bid for freedom had, for him, the final effect of cinching the net the tighter around himself, for they loved one another the more, and in loving are the weakest strongest.

No wonder. No wonder, then, that all the Animals, all wordlessly, let Russel's snoring call them to new roosts, new digs, and a new home, however temporary. Well, the Coop they once inhabited had fallen in the earth-crack, too. Where else had they to go, if not to one another?

In the evening, in the night, twenty-nine Hens sat like globes of fruit in the branches of the maple tree; and seven Mice had dug themselves a new hole at its roots; and a Weasel lurked not far away.

And Chauntecleer crowed, from the lowest branch, a soft, familiar Compline, to make this place and this particular night less alien. This is how he wrestled darkness. And the Hens tucked their heads beneath their wings. They settled down to little homely clucks, and finally to sleep.

Chauntecleer listened to the Fox's snoring. Soon he heard Pertelote's humming from beside the Fox. Two questions arose in him.

Aloud he called to Pertelote, "Is he sleeping? Is it good?" After a silence she answered, "He's sleeping, Chauntecleer. But I'll tell you the truth: I don't know how good it is. He cannot eat asleep; he cannot heal unnourished—"

In his heart was the other question, and the nettle. The Rooster had lost another treasure to the war. Wyrm had killed self-confidence. That quality lay in him like a fetus dead and decomposing, and no one knew, none; Chauntecleer himself could hardly understand his heart's oppression. Simply, silently, and with a passion almost whining, he said, "No one deserves to die any more. No more, no more, Almighty God. Not one." Then a trembling sigh and helpless eyes to heaven: "Will you come, and will you tell me clearly, why? Why? *Why* this Wyrm exists?"

Four

The Brothers Mice

Lord Chauntecleer had done a shocking thing soon after the war: He had given every one of the Animals leave to leave him, if any were so inclined. The Brothers Mice had heard this permission with bewilderment and a stinging, as though whipped with briars. This was no freedom; this was no favor to them! Had they offended dear Chauntecleer?

They went into their hole and put their noses together and said nothing. When finally the youngest, Samstag, began softly to cry, the others used his tears as a melting to utter the immediate response of their souls. "No," they said. "Oh, no. How could we leave the dear Rooster for anything on earth?" And that was that. They didn't leave. Closer than ever they stood with their friends. Warmer than ever were the tuggings of their hearts, brighter than ever the black beads of their eyes.

And now, in these latter days, it was Russel the Fox who had all their attention.

With an earnest, soldierly decorum, they stood watch at points about their uncle's body, all hours throughout the day. They ran small errands for Pertelote. They patted the Fox. Incessantly they laid tiny hands on his rude fur and stroked him, making sympathetic squeaks in their throats, like "Ah!" and "Too bad" and "Oh, dear Uncle." (*Uncle:* he liked the term; therefore, they used the term.) And Russel snored.

Day after day the Fox was kept unconscious. This was a risk, as everyone knew, the extremest test of Pertelote's medicines and trust in her judgment; but he seemed, indeed, to be healing, and Animals began to smile again, Mice especially. Pertelote had lanced the swelling then dabbed and dabbed its discharge; she'd probed and pressed it, rinsed, washed, and dressed it several times a day. Little Mice gagged at the stench a Fox could make, but manfully they stayed, and dutifully they brought her moss for sponging, thorns for surgical instruments, and choruses of support. "Who can cut like the Lady Hen? No one. Can anyone squeeze pus as good as Pertelote? No one. Ah: see? See that? Ah!" They sat around her, when she breathed so close to Russel's face, their paws crossed at their breasts, their noses high, their backs straight up: seven peppershakers of praise.

And Russel snored.

His face contracted to its normal shape. The inflammation cooled. The snoring became rather a rattling, drier and less moist. And then the mortified flesh around his snout, his jowls, and the interior of his mouth began to harden, like a scab, except that this was not a scab upon his skin; it *was* his skin. As it hardened, it shrank the further, so that his cheeks withdrew into a constant grin, and then the Mice felt silly. Every time they saw the Fox's grin, they grinned back, with quickenings of their spirits; but then they remembered that he was sleeping. He didn't see them grinning at him. And they felt silly. They went and touched the mask forming on his face —which *was* his face—and felt it to be bony. "Lady Hen," they whispered, scratching this casement, this crust, "do you think our uncle feels this?"

"If he didn't flinch from my thorn, Wodenstag, he won't feel your nail. Don't worry."

"No," said Wodenstag Mouse. "No, not my nail. Do you think he feels *this?*" He ran tiny hands all over Russel's face. "This hardness?"

"Not yet," said Pertelote gently. "But he will when he wakes up."

"Will it hurt my uncle?"

"I expect it will bother him. He won't have joy in a wooden mouth."

"Ah, poor Russel!"

"But this is the way he'll grow new skin, Wodenstag. He'll grow it underneath the scab, you see? And it won't hurt, unless he splits the scab too soon or cracks it to the quick. And how could he do that, when seven brothers watch him night and day to keep him from talking? How? I don't know how."

"Yes. Yes," said the Brothers Mice.

One evening Freitag was gazing closely at Russel's face when suddenly the right eye flew open, startling the Mouse, and he jumped backward. The eyeball turned round, here and there, though the Fox moved not another hair; it seemed to find Freitag, who instantly began to nod and smile and wave —all signs of goodwill and greeting, all from a Mouse who felt very dumb about what do you do for a sick Fox whose eye suddenly flies open? "Hello? Hello?" he whispered. "Do you see me, Uncle? Are you there? Hello?" The eye flashed a moment of recognition, then softened, and the lid came down, down over it. It closed.

"Whoop!" squealed Freitag, darting first one way and then the other, seeking any other waking creature in the world, news to tell, news to tell! "He's better! I saw it! He opened his eye! We had a talk about this and that. He went back to sleep. Isn't it wonderful? Uncle will be all right!"

Did anyone believe Freitag? Well, they went to Russel, assessed the level of his somnolence by plucking hairs from the Fox's tail, and pronounced Freitag such a lover of the Fox that he fancied his wishes real; they blessed his bright imagination; but they did not believe him. Freitag had a reputation for exaggeration.

But those who tell tales, when finally they tell the truth, are deepest cut to be *still* mistrusted. Freitag scowled. Freitag folded his tiny arms to show his personal offense: "Russel *did* wake up, and he was healthy, and he looked at me!" Then Freitag proved the truth of his assertion by the infallible method of sleeping *outside* the Mouse's hole, while all of his brothers slept inside. This was a Mouse of much honor. This was a Mouse of very high principles, absolutely to be believed. Therefore, he intended to stay out in the cold at least to midnight—at least till his brothers fell asleep.

In the end, he never went in. Proofs came as he hadn't expected, and the Mouse was granted a vision, a truth, he would rather never have known.

Russel the Fox did indeed wake up.

Freitag heard a stirring, a soft depressing of autumn leaves, and sighing. "See?" he thought, and he arose by his hole, put his body erect, trying to pierce the darkness. No one was alert but him; and if he had his way, no one would be alerted until he was sure, until he was the single messenger abroad.

The leaves suffered a sudden crunch, then silence. Several punctuated sounds followed, unhappy jerkings, and a mortal gasp, as though something had been discovered. Freitag's little hairs rose up.

Then a dark figure walked on four feet unsteadily, circling, constantly dipping its head. It was Russel, of course. It was the Fox, up on his legs. Freitag skittered to him, grinning after all.

"Uncle! Uncle!" he whispered.

The Fox swung his head in the Mouse's direction. Freitag

was excited, but close up the sight stopped him, and he became confused.

Russel wore the perpetual grin, open-mouthed, showing teeth between his whiskers. But Russel's eyes were swimming in tears, and a deep groan issued from his chest, a groan that could be shaped into no word at all, merely, "Eh-h-h-h, Eh-h-h-h," because his mouth was fixed. He kept dipping his head to scrape his face in the bend of his wrist. He ran his snout into the ground. Then he gazed again at Freitag, as though Freitag might relieve him somehow, or answer questions unpronounced, unpronounceable.

"Hello, Uncle," said the Mouse, hesitant, pushing a smile onto his face. "So, here you are!"

"H-h-h," said Russel. That's all. That's all he could produce, a rush of air. His eyes swelled even larger, still turned pathetically to Freitag. He struck his nose with a claw, so sharply that the Mouse jumped. He gazed at Freitag, tears standing hot in his eyes. "H-h-h! *H-h-h!*"

Poor Freitag. Now he didn't want to be alone with Russel. "Lady Pertelote," said Freitag, "said that it's only a scab, Uncle, and that you have to have it for a while, and then it will go away. Uncle, please be okay. She said that in time, at the right time, you would peel it off yourself, see? Please be okay. Please don't be sad. I'll come and pat you on the shoulder all night long—"

But Russel the Fox, grinning and weeping at once, turned into the night and began to move away. Freitag followed. They moved shudderingly. Russel would fall from rubbery legs; and that's when Freitag would talk and touch the Fox and tell him about glad things; but Russel always found his legs again and, extraordinarily, began to trot, his bush tail dragging earth, his poor nose low, and Freitag was driven to dash; and they went east, eastward through the wood as though Russel knew his destination.

Soon Freitag realized that the Fox was going somewhere on purpose, and the Mouse grew nervous.

"It's okay if we go back and tell Lord Chauntecleer the wonderful news, don't you think, uncle? And Lady Pertelote, too, now that you're well again, Uncle? What do you think of that idea?" called Freitag. "I myself think it's a good idea. Maybe you could turn around—"

But Russel grew more and more intent, and faster, not slower; and even his head came up in the process; and Freitag made a thousand Mouse-puffs, trying to keep pace and catch his breath. And so they went.

They came to the Liverbrook, a southward-running stream, cold in the autumn, but perfectly wet.

Straightway, Russel the Fox plunged his face underwater, standing on a level bank. He thrashed his head back and forth, back and forth, blowing, boiling water—

"Well," said Freitag behind him, "That's a good thing to do. No, I never thought of that, washing your face. You're very wise, Uncle." And after a long, long moment, while Russel crouched lower and thrust his neck and forelegs and shoulders deeper into the stream, "Don't you think," said Freitag, "you should breathe? Uncle?"

Breathe? He did. In a way that Freitag didn't anticipate.

Russel the Fox exploded from the water, barking. It was a loud shout he sent into the velvet night, and then giggles, and then true laughter, touched only at its peaks by frenzy.

"Freitag!" roared the Fox, avuncular, "I am so glad, not to mention pleased, that you are here, which is where I am, which means, with me!"

The Mouse smiled with his mouth. Not his eyes. His heart was so terribly uncertain. "You are talking," he said.

"I am! I am! I am that indeed," cried Russel the Fox. "And in a minute I will also have something to say!" he said, delighted at the prospect.

"Could we say it," said Freitag, "to Lord Chauntecleer, Uncle? What do you think about that?" And he whispered, "You shouldn't be talking, Uncle."

But Russel roared, "I know what!" and a fracture appeared

between his nostril and his lip, and it filled with blood, a thin line of blood. The blood laced into wet fur. "I know what!" He turned and climbed northward along the Liverbrook, upstream. Poor Freitag followed. At a limestone ledge, projected one foot above the water, Russel stopped. He grinned a true, benevolent grin upon Freitag the Mouse; it wasn't a scab-grin any more; but it split flesh in a hundred places. Russel lifted his paw into a histrionic pose, and announced before his audience of one: "Catching Minnows with One's Tail!"

Every split in the Fox's mouth bled.

"Uncle Russel, please," said Freitag. "I don't want to see any tricks. I don't want to hear of any tricks. I don't want my Uncle to be in trouble or in pain, and there's a reason for this, Uncle. I love you. See? Why don't we go back, now. What if we went back, now?"

But Russel the Fox wasn't listening to Freitag. He was seized by another passion. Unaware, he rubbed his nose with the joint above his paw. Unaware, he smeared blood through his whiskers, making them spiky. Unaware—because his attention was all behind himself, where he was sinking his tail into the water, "Yes!" slowly, "Yes, yes!" allowing the long fur its swimming separation. "Catching minnows," he said, breathless, glaring at the Mouse: "Catching minnows Foxes have to do with wit, good nephew, since Foxes lack other equipments, see? See? This is the true notability of the Fox: wit! See? Listen: the Fox introduces his bushy tail into the stream—"

"Uncle, please!"

"—as per you see me doing now. You see, tiny Mouse? Do you see?"

Freitag choked with anguish. Russel's mouth had begun to bubble pink. When the bubbles popped, they spattered Mouse-fur.

"Oh, yes, I see, dear uncle," Freitag squeaked. "Could we please quit now?"

"The word to love," said Russel, panting, gazing hectically at Freitag, grinning, "is seaweed. Seaweed. *Seaweed!*" The Fox spat a great gout of blood. He was bleeding inside his mouth as well. Viciously he scraped his muzzle as though it were a hindrance. Freitag held his own nose between two paws.

"Oh, God!" said Russel. His eyes began to fill with tears. "God," said Freitag. He too, was weeping. Through tears they stared at one another.

"Now," said Russel, rushing. "Now, the Fox must keep so still, for his tail, silent and waving in the current, is, don't you see, the seaweed, heh-heh! And what of minnows?"

"I didn't ask," Freitag pleaded.

"Why, minnows congregate in seaweed. There's the trick! Deception! Ha! Quiet, now. Be still. Be quiet and wait. Quiet—"

What could Freitag say?

There came, now, a moment of horrible silence. By an extraordinary will the Fox went rigid, performing his trick, and Freitag stiffened, too. But what he saw was his uncle bleeding in streams, and he heard the blood-drops potting stone below his chin, and the Fox's teeth were outlined in blood: he had savaged his mouth with talking. Yet they held perfectly still, these two, staring at one another—waiting for what? Minnows? Russel grinned, but his eyes burned and Freitag thought he would burst soon in screaming.

Suddenly Russel moved. It was a whirling movement, and a climax: he whipped his tail from the water, slapped it on stone, and minnows began to flip like silver scales; then he rose to four legs, threw his head to heaven, sucked air, and wailed at the top of his lungs, "God! God! It isn't too much to ask! *I only want to talk!*"

That was more than the Mouse could stand. Without a thought he leaped backward, spun, and shot top speed to Chauntecleer. Russel was suffering. Russel was racking himself. "He's talking! He's talking," shrieked the little Mouse. "Oh, what'll we do? He's talking!"

But that piteous cry of the Fox was the last that ever he uttered.

The Animals, when they came to the Liverbrook, found an abject creature, Russel the Fox, shamefully nudging minnows one by one into the stream; this, though every one of them was dead.

Chauntecleer seized the Fox's face in a claw. He held to the moonlight a mouth torn ragged, lips that hung in ribbons, and he cursed the Fox, and he cursed the night, and he terrified the Hens, and he said, "Why should I cry for you, Russel? No, I won't cry for you!"

But he did.

And the Mice were stricken helpless by the Rooster's tears.

Five
Failing

The day that followed was blue and beautiful—and mute. Clouds of impossible whiteness, sheer-edged against the sky, both high and eyeless, sailed heaven. They saw nothing. They were. They said nothing, knew nothing, cared nothing. They floated, and they were. It was enough to make one weep.

And the trees revealed a wild variety of emotion: umber, the burnt-brown, brooded; the Lady oak took red at the edges, a deep flame-red, while yet she kept green at her heart, and so she seemed a gentlewoman of a long experience; some of the maples burst yellow, effulgent, crying attention, demanding attention; some of the maples slurred a bright primary red, an almost unnatural red, upon themselves, like harlots laughing; some of the maples shed their leaves in the first draft and stood naked. Aspens were modest, giggling trees; but where they were, they were so many. They could afford to be modest. Pine and fir thrust green among the colors, unchanging, unwilling to change, criticizing by their contrast every other change. And the elm and the walnut, the willow, the gum, and the locust: the woods, the woods, the busy woods, the heartless forest and the trees, that whole congregation simply went about its natural business, and where was the one among them who stopped and groaned? Who stopped and acknowledged that things were *not* the same? How could the leaves turn now? How could the season turn, the world so mindlessly turn, while Russel lay sick on the ground?

Chauntecleer the Rooster strutted around Russel's Maple in a speechless fury. This was the most splendid day of the autumn. But beauty had no right to be—not now. And if it persisted nonetheless, then it proved itself heartless. Blind. Coldly cruel, deserving the spite of a Rooster.

This day smelled clean, and it nipped one's toes. It carried the breezes of harvest, the crackle of cornstalks, the promise of a distant snow. It asked vigor of the living creatures, high blood, food, and laughter—

It was enough to make one weep.

Not a Hen took pleasure in that day, nor any of the Mice. Even John Wesley Weasel maintained solemnity—for Chauntecleer could not stop pacing. He threw himself left and right, his anger hissing in his nostrils, an eye turned grimly on the whole brutish world, an eye for Russel the Fox.

Russel the Fox: no motion now, no color in him, no vigor, no promise, no effort, no good. He lay beneath his maple— a bright yellow one—with his riven snout on crossed paws, his jaws separated as though held around a vowel, his eyes perfectly flat. Pertelote had swathed his mouth in a bandage of cobwebs; he hadn't argued. He hadn't cared.

Yellow leaves fell on Russel. Chauntecleer saw that and fanned his wing at them, and yanked back his head, as if to say, *See?* Supreme contempt. Plain fury. In fact, he said nothing, but paced more viciously.

Then Russel moved, and Chauntecleer froze, watching.

A contraction, a slow wave passed up his back, from his loins to his neck; he half rose; he put his face down and shook. It looked as though he were caught in long, inconsolable sobs, as though the full understanding of his grief had finally possessed him.

Chauntecleer took one step away from the Fox, then one step toward him.

The spasms continued, more sharply, until they forced a noise out of Russel: not sobbing, not crying, but a ratchet of gas, air coming with such violence that it sounded like gunshots. Then Russel vomited a stream of vile liquid. And then he lay down again, and his face was in his vomit.

Chauntecleer exploded.

"Aw, Russel! Can't you *try* to help yourself? Who's going to care if you don't care for yourself?"

The Rooster had pitched himself forward toward the Fox— to do what? To hit him? The better to scream at him?—when Russel raised his brow and rolled his eyes to Chauntecleer and looked at him. He gave his friend one glance of inexpressible sadness, as if to say, *Don't you know?* and then he gazed again into infinity, and that was all.

But that glance broke the heart of the Rooster.

"No, no, oh, no," pleaded Chauntecleer. "I don't mean you any more pain than you have, Russel, no, no. I'm sorry. Ah, my friend, I am so sorry."

All of the rage of the Rooster melted away, leaving humility only, a painfully humble Chauntecleer.

So it was Chauntecleer himself who put his neck below the Fox's chin and lifted him from the vomit. And it was Chauntecleer who wiped the Foxface clean of its filth, slow strokes, merciful strokes, loving, penitential strokes and licking where that was necessary.

Chauntecleer kept the Fox's bed, thereafter, with leaves soft and warm and deep. Chauntecleer nursed him more tenderly than a Hen might. And Chauntecleer never left him, neither in the day nor in the nighttime. And the Rooster never, never lifted his voice again against the Fox, but always crooned and

muttered kindness—and pleaded forgiveness, and constantly
prayed poor Russel's forgiveness.

But Russel spoke no more.

So that is the way that it went.

When Russel would not eat, Chauntecleer suffered—and
fed him. He whispered loving words to him; but among those
words he apologized: for Russel's lack of appetite; for having
to push fermented apples into his mouth; for manipulating
Russel's jaws in a mimic of chewing; for everything, for the
humiliation of having to be fed.

But the Fox didn't speak. The Fox did not so much as turn
his eyes toward Chauntecleer. So the Rooster's heart grew full
to overflowing, and his pain found no relief. When the Fox
discharged a thin, hot liquid from his bowels, Chauntecleer
was almost grateful; the more loathesome the task, the more
shriven the Rooster. He sought slavery. He wanted no help
from a single Hen. He wanted *not* to sleep. He grew somewhat
feverish himself. But Russel grew no better.

The Fox's mouth simply surrendered to infection. It didn't
even swell this time. Ulcers opened and ran constantly; and
the flesh around them corrupted, died, and fell away; and the
gums softened. The stink was unendurable. Yet Chauntecleer
came near with food, and still he moved the jaws into a chewing motion. As Russel declined, Chauntecleer's help took a
certain desperation, and his happy words became more hectic,
his apologies more miserable, his gestures almost antic. He
jerked the jaws together.

But Russel wasn't talking any more. Russel was com-
municating absolutely nothing, not even pain. Therefore, the
Rooster could not know, until they actually fell out onto the
ground, that he'd been breaking Russel's teeth from their
sockets, and some of these the Fox must have swallowed, but
here were three that dropped between the Fox and the
Rooster: teeth!

"Ah, Russel!" wailed poor Chauntecleer. "Russel, forgive
me. Oh, my brother, I am so sorry, so sorry. I never meant to

hurt you. Why do I hurt so many creatures? Russel, please believe me, I didn't know what I was doing—"

It was precisely at that moment that a light seemed to warm in the Fox's eyes. Chauntecleer looked and looked in them, wanting with all his heart to believe that his brother was looking back. "Are you there?" he whispered. And for an answer, O dear God, the Fox actually put up a thin paw and brushed the Rooster's beak, just bumping the tip of it.

"Well!" said Chauntecleer. He coughed. He cleared his throat violently. "Well!" He had an abundance of water, suddenly, inside his head. And he wanted to laugh. But laughter would squirt this water everywhere. "Well!" he thundered, top of his lungs. "So! Okay! Tell you what. Don't go away. Because listen: I can chew for you, right? Right! I'll be right back!"

Gone was Chauntecleer the Rooster at high speeds, searching the Hens. Because where Hens were, there were seeds. And where seeds were, there was dinner for his brother.

He found them, the pillowy flock of Hens, a-pecking in a little clearing. He blew them up with one roaring tackle: BOOM! And he took their places, his wings laid back, his head down, pecking, pecking, just like a chicken, stuffing seeds and corns and mushroom and fungus and sand into his crop until it swelled, until it bulged from his neck to the size of his bursting love for Russel.

Now Pertelote stood watching him. When he charged back to the Fox, she followed at a distance; and she was not smiling.

But he was. Chauntecleer was grinning like silly victory.

Russel's eyes were glassy and unclosed. His body was limp. Yet the Rooster grinned on him, announcing, "So we've turned the corner, right, brother? Give me a minute. Let my gizzard grind the grain, ho-ho! And then, who needs teeth? Look at me: never had a tooth in my head my whole life through. Ho, ho!" He took to pacing again, back and forth before the Fox, grinning.

But Pertelote caught his eye, and she was not smiling. Her

eyes went down to the still, still Fox. Chauntecleer's eyes
followed. Then she looked again upon her husband, and
gently shook her head. Chauntecleer saw that, and his face
collapsed. His whole expression changed. He glared at Pertelote. With his claw he began to beat his throat at the crop,
slowly at first, and then with greater speed and greater impact;
it should have hurt him. It should have burst that crop. He
glared at Pertelote, scorching her. He hissed, "Don't you say
it. Don't you name it, woman, and don't you judge me with
your eye. I'll go to the end, the *end!*" He struck his crop with
knuckles of his claw. "And why? Because I could not," he
hissed with ruinous emotion: "Because I could not save my
Mundo Cani!"

The poor Rooster raised his head, as though in dignity.

The Hen, however, dropped her eyes and gazed at the
ground. No, she did not say it. Chauntecleer her husband
approached the Fox with infinite gentleness. He crouched
before his brother. He slipped his whole head and his neck,
too, into Russel's mouth, down, down to the root of Russel's
tongue, and there he brought forth the burden of his crop,
meal made moist and wholesome; and there he left the offering. He withdrew, and then began to stroke the Fox's throat
in order to help his swallowing. Again and again, with unspeakable tenderness he stroked Lord Russel, his claw like an
ivory comb, his own eyes shut absolutely tight. Into the night
he stroked.

No, Pertelote did not say it. She watched these ministrations, and finally she wept, but she did not say that Russel the
Fox was dead.

She suspected that Chauntecleer already knew.

Six

Preparations

There went up a cry in the middle of that night, a lingering scream, a calling, and a singular wail of rage. It did not arise to heaven. It went out across the sea, like a lonely boat for battle:

"*WYRM!*"

Lord Chauntecleer the Rooster stood alone on the shore of an endless sea. Behind him lay a dead land, flat and salted by the war that had been fought between the Animals and the Basilisks. Countless bodies had gone down upon those plains. Countless hearts had ruptured there, and throats had bellowed before they were torn. Now there was the wind only, and the pewter light of the moon: cold, shadowed as though in a vision, and still.

A wall of earth humped in the moonlight, the piece of a wall, bent in an arc, the piece of a circle. It was naught but a ruin now, what once had been a round, closed battlement against Wyrm's forces. Once it had protected the Animals, when built by the Rooster's engineering. But it had suffered the monster's destruction. Now the wind took dust from its top, and the moonlight tombed it:

"*WYRM!*"

Chauntecleer was the single figure in all that landscape. He stood on the beach. Seawater hissed at his ankles. His head was up, and his neck was straining, and his eyes were blazing, rabid, as though he could see for miles and miles, and down the curve of the horizon: "*WYRM!*" He was calling as far as he could see; he was roaring with astounding power,

"*WYRM!*" The breakers themselves could not out-thunder him. Chauntecleer shrieked with the freedom of hatred. Hatred was the force in him. And his cry was the lonely defiance of grief against infinities.

"*WYRM!*" across the waters.

"*WYRM!*" and his body doubled with the fury, but he never shut his eye.

"*WYRM!*" to the farthest swell of the sea, the sea named Wyrmesmere since Wyrm had caused it to be, by which he'd changed the face of the earth and weighted the planet—

"*WYRM, I WILL KILL YOU FOR WHAT YOU HAVE DONE TO ME!*"

But the water hissed at his ankles.

And the moon made skull's eyes in the waves.

Russel the Fox was dead.

Sweet Pertelote sang Lauds that morning. Her song was so full of quiet communications that the Animals woke up knowing, and no one needed to ask: a certain night had passed; a certain day had come. The night held death. The day demanded preparations. Poor Russel, poor Russel had finally—

But *Pertelote* sang Lauds!

"Lady Hen," said Wodenstag, his brothers ranged behind him, "where is the Rooster?" Their faces were slack, their hearts racing; they were not far from panic.

"He went to make arrangements," said Pertelote.

"Will he come back again?"

"He only went to get a grave," she said. She smiled at the simpleness of the Mice, and then she saw that she shouldn't have. Their eyes went wounded; they sucked their tiny lips.

"He wasn't *here*," they pointed out, "when we woke up!"

"Aye, that's true," said Pertelote, and she tried to reason their trouble away: "But that's because he couldn't sleep all night."

"Lady Hen, will he come back?"

Pertelote gazed at them. "He's been gone before," she said, evidence of consolation. "He has always come back."

Wodenstag said, "Uncle Russel is dead," and the eyes of all of the Mice agreed to that. "We want to cry for Uncle Russel. But we're scared, and we have to know, and we wish you would say it. Is the Rooster coming back again?"

"Ah, Wodenstag," murmured Pertelote, marveling at the wisdom of the Mice, but all they wanted was simplicity. "Yes, cry. Do cry. Cry and be sad for all of us, and never worry: Lord Chauntecleer is certainly coming back. He hasn't left us. We're still together—"

The Mice withdrew on tiny feet, the mourning filling their eyes.

Pertelote whispered: "So free to be honest, little Tags, you are free to be sad as well."

John Wesley Weasel, on the other hand didn't drop a tear.

He'd had his look at Russel before the dawn, after the Rooster had slipped into the night. He'd had his talk with Russel. He'd had his say, though he couldn't allow as how it had relieved him much, and of course he'd no idea what it did for Russel, on account of Russel was dead.

"John," said John, "he don't understand buggars what can't control theirselves, no." This is how he talked to the Fox, and how the Weasel fashioned a farewell. It sounded mostly angry. "Gets good advices, yump; perfectly clear commandings from the Rooster, yump; has a working brain atwixt his ears, yump, yump; can hear it: saying, Shut up, Foxy, *shut up!* Does he shut up? No!"

John Wesley had a little head upon a long body. The more he talked to Russel's corpse, the louder he got; and the louder he got, the higher went that little head. He was outraged.

"This buggar goes to working his mouth and can't stop. Is killing him, and won't stop. Like as if John, he should bash his own head against stones and never stop, never stop till chunks

of his brains is sticking to his cheeks—and never stop. *Foxy!*"
hissed the Weasel, furious. "Foxy, ain't nobodies to blame for
your dying but your own self! Oh, shame on you! And does
you think John Double-u, he'll give you some tears? Ho, ho,
buggar: not one! No, not a single tear from *John's* eye, no. Not
for stupidities and dumbnesses, on account of, if a Foxy can
kill him own self, well, then a Foxy gots to cry for him own self.
There!"

There.

John Wesley Weasel made an end of his vigil respecting the
Fox. Before the dawn, he marched away from that corpse with
his head so high his forepaws barely reached the ground. He
didn't cry; not with his head up there. He went about looking
down on the world. All day long he lurked at the edge of the
Animals' activity—in the middle of which the Fox lay—looking
down on them.

The Hens and the Mice washed Russel and combed his coat;
they anointed his fur with an oil pressed from the gland at the
base of a Hen's tail; so Russel took on a ruddy gloss, rich, red,
and beautiful, and the sun struck copper from his shoulder.
John Wesley looked down on all that.

Some of the Hens sat aside for the better part of the day,
weaving with their beaks a pure white cloth of the down of
their breasts, carefully, carefully. Others dipped their feathers
in wormwood and brushed the Fox's eyes and his paws with
the ointment. Its bitter odor touched the air, and by the air,
their souls; it loosened their tears till soundlessly they wept.

John Wesley looked down on all that: down, so down that
his neck ached and his forehead hurt from frowning. But he
didn't cry, that Weasel. No, not so much as a tear. And that
was just fine, because the longer he didn't cry, the righter he
was in his blame of the Fox.

There!

Toward evening a great black Beetle felt his way across the
dead land. He climbed the earthwork. In dust he slid down the

seaward side, and he moved on tweezer feet. Chauntecleer, fixed in a brisk wind, still on the shore of Wyrmesmere, watched him come. The Rooster's breast-feathers seemed like a skirt swirling about him, snatched by breezes. His eye was narrow, his jet beak pointed in the direction of his looking. He stood as still as a post, waiting.

The Rooster and the Beetle knew each other from disasters of the past, for the Rooster had seen his three sons dead, and the Beetle had buried them. Black Lazarus was a gravedigger.

Neither stood on ceremony. When Lazarus had struggled into earshot, Chauntecleer threw wide a wing and pointed with a primary feather. "There," he said, indicating a spot as bleak as any other. "That's where the Fox was bitten, sir. There's where we will bury him."

The wind had thrown Wyrmesmere into a high fit of waves.

The Beetle maneuvered himself to assess the spot. He sat still.

Chauntecleer went and X'ed it with a raking claw. "We'll have one hero in this place where we can memorialize him, one good reason for remembering."

"We're near the sea," the Beetle warned. His voice was as dark as his body, and as slow.

"He fought near the sea," snapped Chauntecleer.

"Aye. But the water's a dreary grave, don't you know," said Lazarus. "It'll scour the hole from underneath, could cause a fearful stink o' the bones and maybe send them topside—"

"Then keep the water out."

The Beetle, his whole head hidden in a hood, sat still, considering.

"Well," he said. "Could be a crypt could trick it—"

"Dig one."

"Aye. Dig one. 'Twould have to be in stone—"

"In stone, then. You can dig in stone?"

"Aye. 'Tis my profession and my skill, digging in any sorter substance as presents itself. I can piece it for you. Only—"

Chauntecleer jerked his impatience. "This is a dead land,"

he cried suddenly down the wind. "Damnably crabbed and cold and dead. There can be nothing below *but* stone. Find your stone, Black Lazarus, and dig the Fox his crypt, and keep your 'onlys' for those confused by the thing you do."

Without another glance for the Beetle or for Wyrmesmere, Chauntecleer returned the way that he had come, a figure ignorant of the wind. He crossed the ruins of the earthwork. He passed the place where the coop once stood before the war, and he disappeared into the northern wood.

And here was a shock the Rooster did not notice: the wood was naked. All in a fortnight the trees had lost their leaves to the ripping wind.

Autumn is the killing season.

Seven

Compline and a Private Matins

That night sweet Pertelote experienced a further sorrow and a mystery, both of the soul of her husband.

Chauntecleer returned with the dusk, *like* the dusk, silently and full of meditations, withheld from all the Animals yet compassing them with his spirit. Visibly, the Hens relaxed at his coming, and the Mice went up to touch him. Reassurance. The Weasel, John Wesley, finally allowed his head to lie on the ground, and all were reserved from one another.

Chauntecleer went to the Fox, a pool of shadow in the darkness.

Jasper fussed nearby. She picked at the ground. She smoothed herself in a hundred places. She glanced at the Rooster, but he gave her no recognition, not any invitation for the talk. Finally the anxiety burst from her of its own accord:

"Does it look like him?" she pleaded. "*He!* He, I mean. Does he look like him?"

How often hadn't Pertelote answered the selfsame question?

Chauntecleer looked toward Jasper, a steady gaze that lasted two minutes together, embarrassing the Hen. Then, softly he said, "The very image of him, Jasper." And then to all the Hens: "I'm proud of the thing you've done today. Russel looks at peace. Please go, now, and roost."

They did, gratefully. They ascended the cold branches over Chauntecleer's head, glad to obey, needing now with all their hearts the clean command and obedience. So much else was grim. So much was undefined, unsteady underneath the moon.

"Thank God," thought Pertelote, "for Chauntecleer." She went to his side, who kept by the side of the Fox.

Darkness:

And Chauntecleer, without raising his head, crowed for the Hens a Compline of nearly unbearable tenderness. He was rigid, to be sure—but as a tuning fork is rigid: it sheds music so penetrating that the very core of the pain is stung to sweetness.

Thus Chauntecleer: "Hear my prayer, O Lord," he sang, muscles like tungsten taut in his neck. Pertelote felt the tension.

But the Hens heard the music. They responded in their turn and in their melody, as though the evening stars sang together: "And let our cry come unto you."

"Keep me as the apple of your eye."

Voice, and a chorus of voices; cantor and choir: the Rooster and the Hens, who had no house, no wall, nor roof against the weather, wove a home for themselves by singing Compline, this familiar ritual; and the night was less frightful for it; and order established itself; and one could believe in a peaceful sleep after all—

They answered "Hide me in the shadow of your wings—"

Then, when the Hens had yielded altogether to the safety of the Compline, Chauntecleer changed its traditional word. No warning. He ambushed them, as it were, and accomplished quickly, quietly, a remarkable healing. He lanced their bereavement:

"Keep him," he sang in the same rhythm, "as the apple of your eye."

Hens stumbled on the switch.

Him? Not *me*, but *him!* Who?

Ah! See? The Rooster is gazing at Russel the Fox. Him.

The focus changed; the Hens responded in their turn and in their melody, "Hide *him* in the shadow of your wings." No suppressing it, anymore. Here it comes, and we are caught.

And Chauntecleer: "In righteousness shall he be borne to you."

And the Hens, fervently: "When he awakes, your face shall give him Joy."

Ah, the skill of Chauntecleer! He included even the dead in this common litany of the night; but Russel's death night *became* the night, and death was rendered common, ah! He enfolded the dead even in the hearts of the Hens, and they were permitted, then, to mourn their brother freely. Mourning was given voice, easy words, old, familiar words; Compline *was* that voice; and the impacted pressure of the Hens' souls found release. They wept. From the deeps of them, they wept; from deeper, even, than Russel, and back to the war, they wept. Their sobs in the branches above were enormous, like a wringing of the clouds.

Pertelote's eyes went warm and damp, but she was smiling at the thing that she had seen, the extraordinary priesthood of Chauntecleer. Then she stopped smiling, for she saw that in him was not a scrap of relief. His eye was as dry as glass. Rigid he began, rigid he remained, in precisely the posture he took at dusk.

But his voice was healing, and none could see him but Pertelote. At the right time, as the sobbing changed from desolation to relief and a certain washed luxury, the Rooster raised that voice again, softly, softly singing: "Weeping may endure for a night—"

They heard. They nodded. But for their crying they couldn't answer.

Yet Chauntecleer insisted, as though the Compline, the song and the drama, weren't done until someone could name him a new name, find one final line to transfigure the whole song heretofore: "Weeping may endure the night—"

They knew the answer. They understood it, too, as they never had before. But Chauntecleer wanted to hear it, wanted the mouth to *say* it: it should enter the night by speaking. He urged them: "Weeping may last for the night—"

And then Pertelote, gazing at her husband, answered. In a voice so crystal that Hens were stilled by the listening merely, she sang:

"But joy shall come with the morning."

Chauntecleer shot her a glance and said, "Amen."

Pertelote didn't blink, responded, "Amen."

Then all of the Hens above them, with a heartfelt gratitude, agreed: "Amen. Amen. Amen."

So went the public Compline of this Rooster, Chauntecleer. And so the Hens were persuaded into a deep and holy sleep: a divinity protected them. It was good.

Yet he himself was not persuaded.

Pertelote wanted to talk. But the night would not allow it. *He* might have. Upon that particular night, Chauntecleer might have, in his more overwhelming pain, bowed to the pain and the cure of this Hen's conversation, Pertelote, well skilled in every virtuous plant and healing herb. But it happens that little things of seeming little consequence can shift the course of monstrous events forever thereafter, and a whole history may turn upon one whimper.

The night did not allow their talk.

And the little thing that thwarted it? A Mouse. The youngest brother. Samstag. That, and Pertelote's compassion.

Near midnight there arose from the ground a sobbing, a lonesome wail, like "Hooo" and "Hooo." Pertelote could not ignore the need there, and it did not subside again into sleep. All the world's an empty place when one voice weeps uncomforted.

Finally, then, she moved away from Chauntecleer and Russel's corpse to the Mouse's hole.

"Samstag Mouse," she spoke in low love. The cold air bit her throat. "Is that you?"

"Well, and yes," the smaller voice came up. "It's me."

"Are you awake, then?"

"Yes." Sobbing paused.

"Then you are not dreaming? This isn't a bad dream?"

"No, Lady." Her *this* must have touched the chord in him again: "Hooo. Hooo."

"Is there something I can say to you?" she asked.

"No, Lady," said the Mouse. "Thank you."

"Well." She knew the need: "But I will wait here, if that's okay with you," she said.

"It is a kindness," said the Mouse.

Small sobbing continued a while. Then there was silence, and Pertelote almost tiptoed away. But the wee voice asked, "But will you hold me?"

Pertelote said, "Yes."

So a little Mouse slipped out of his hole with his head low down and stole beneath a Hen's wing and was comforted by soft feathers and the beating of her heart.

"Lady?" Here was another voice from the hole.

"So?" said Pertelote. "Wodenstag. Are you awake, too?"

"Well," said that one, "Samstag is the youngest of us all. Samstag couldn't help crying. But, you see, we are all awake. Yes."

"You are strong enough not to cry," said Pertelote.

Wodenstag said, "Yes."

"But sad enough to be lonely."

Wodenstag said, "Yes."

"Then I have wing enough for all of you," said Lady Pertelote.

One by one the Mice came up, their heads hung low. Body by body she gathered them together under her wings. Then she made her warm breast homely by humming, and soon the Brothers Mice, all seven, were sleeping under feather.

The Hen had her brood for the rest of the night. Everything in the world fell silent. Cold autumn put a skim of ice on standing water, on the edges of the Liverbrook—

And then came the groaning of the darker soul, and the mystery.

Chauntecleer—she could not see him—stirred. He must have thought himself alone, because next he spoke aloud. His own private Matins.

"Wyrm for a day, Wyrm for a season," he groaned. "But who can endure it forever?"

Pertelote felt a tingling in her body. The voice was so familiar. But the words were nearly blasphemous.

"You could have healed him!" she heard. He was talking with God! Was God listening to him? He was involved in a mortal wrestling. She heard the dry leaves grind, and she heard: "Ease me! Ease me! Tell me that I am not, all by myself, responsible for— Ahhh! *Who am I?*"

Oh, Chauntecleer!

Then Pertelote heard her own name, and she shuddered. Her name in her husband's mouth made the eavesdropping seem so guilty.

"She did more than you to save a Fox!" Dear husband, don't challenge God. Please stop at the limits! "But failed," he said with a chilly clarity. "So we are all there is," he accused. "But we are nothing after all. We bear the weakness. I, I bear the memory and the shame. I can't—*ahhh!* I am not able—"

A long pause gapped in the night, and the darkness flowed

into it, and her heart stuttered against the little Mice below, and she desired that he be done. But he wasn't. Not to God did he speak his next sentence, but to the corpse; yet he spoke it feelingly, as though he expected an answer, as though tomorrow depended upon that answer:

"Brother Russel, Brother Russel, what will I do?"

Silence.

Silence, and Chauntecleer became a stone. The emotion left him. He returned to the plainsong of the Compline and sang it in a nasal crow, words ancient and familiar, but words meant for himself alone—and for God, if he supposed that God was listening.

"Weeping," he chanted, "may endure the night. And what shall come with the morning?"

And he answered himself, coldly, "A funeral. A funeral."

This is the way that it was, in those days, with Lord Chauntecleer.

Eight
Scats

Through the woods the Animals filed with their offering. Seven Hens held Russel in a white woven shroud, three to a side, three to a side, and one at the foot. The body was heartbreakingly light. Death had eaten him away. Seven beaks were quite enough.

Children chicks accompanied the Hens, trying to see in Russel the war that had killed him, but which to them was no more than the elders' stories. They hardly knew why they were so sad.

In the back of all was John Wesley Weasel, frowning mightily and walking wayward, as though he had nothing to do with processions, but obeying.

In front of all strode Chauntecleer. The sun through leafless trees made him magnificent: his coral comb a battlement, his feathers proudly golden, his beak black, his nails white, his legs azure, his manner commanding, his manner unapproachable. No Mouse spoke to him on this day. Nobody made a sound. The Animals parted the leaves like a long snake slithering.

A funeral.

Pertelote watched Chauntecleer and kept her own counsel. The Mice moved close beside her.

A funeral. And perhaps they were going to bury the war forever. Perhaps their memories would find rest in Russel's grave, and these tears be their last tears. A creature can cry the worst tears, if she knows they are her last tears—

Ah, but Keepers of the universal evil can never retire to a quiet insignificance. They participate in the universal; the good order of the whole creation looks to them, and what they are gives heaven pause, whether they know it or not. No: never, never did the stars influence the lives of the Keepers; that is a fiction. Rather, the Keepers, when they so much as walk, tip planets. It's a terrible responsibility, but there it is. The sobbing of a Mouse, that tiny privacy, shudders the empyrean; and though he'd never ask such a vast importance upon himself, yet there it is: he keeps evil. He needs to keep it well. So his well-being becomes a matter of cosmic discussion.

A funeral? A small, communal ceremony? Yes, of course, but so much more: it was a quasar, that deep and soundless pulse through space, a signal of the end, and the beginning.

Let no one wonder, then, that Wyrm himself saw fit to attend this funeral. He did. His future was in it.

But neither is it blameable that none of the Animals knew his presence. They were Animals, after all, concerned about their minor, mortal passages and troubled to get the details right, the earthy courtesies; and why not? Russel the Fox had been their friend. They owed him complete devotion. So this is the way that it was:

A funeral for Russel, for Russel alone. But Wyrm sent something of himself—

Black Lazarus the Beetle met their procession south of the wood, just as the Animals broke onto the plains of the dead land, and the ruined earthwork rose before them. His lumpish crouch was premonitory, and his blackness forbad them. Chauntecleer hesitated a moment, then motioned the rest to wait behind. He approached Lazarus. The Beetle labored his body into a turn, then he and the Rooster went forward.

This is what Chauntecleer said:

"There'd better be a reason why you stop us, Beadle Lazarus!" He didn't look anywhere but dead ahead.

"Aye," said Lazarus, as they moved to an obvious hole and a mound beside it. "I've digged you a crypt, sir. I have, sir, digged you a crypt. But—"

"But?"

"Oh, sir. It leaks."

"What does that mean?

The Rooster went at his own pace. The Beetle tweedled behind, his haste a difficulty.

Before they came to the grave, Chauntecleer was hit by an odor so strong that he snatched at his nostril and gagged. "What—?"

By sheer strength of will, he went into the suffocating cloud. He thrust his head out, over the edge of the hole, and looked down. It was stony and well scooped; but at the bottom lay a long black extrusion, a thick ooze curled into a smiling, passive pile.

"Slugs!" gasped Chauntecleer. He'd been holding his breath.

"Oh, no, sir." Lazarus seemed unaffected by the stench.

"The pressure. 'Tis matter and slickery from the bottom of the waters. I feared that the sea—"

"Waters? Waters? The water?" said Chauntecleer. He gazed with a most vile loathing south, to the laughing sea, and he hissed, "Wyrmesmere!"

"Aye. I feared that the sea would want in, and didn't I say it? But the stone is solid, and 'twould have to be a fissure—"

"Wyrm!" hissed Chauntecleer. "You! Wyrm! I will— I will kill—"

The Rooster broke into a fit of trembling. Then he turned back to the Animals watching him, who held the corpse of Russel among them. Then he turned to the sea. And then, suddenly, he leaped into the hole. With his beak he stabbed the thing that lay there. It seemed to wrap itself around him, beak and neck, but he whipped it about with the snapping of his head. He flung it flat to the floor. He scissored it in his beak and thrust it beneath his right wing, where he held it and hid it. Then he was ripping feathers from his breast, covering the stony floor, golding the floor, lining the grave with his own softness: a carpet.

"There will *be* a grave!" he gasped.

He leaped again from the pit. "Now!" he roared, but he checked himself.

Ignoring Lazarus, he marched back to the Animals, his right wing clapped to his side. He took a position again in front of his handful of questioning creatures; and, answering nothing, he led them, stride by stride, to Russel's grave.

There will be a grave.

There was a grave. There was a ritual. Of the most exquisite grief, there was a remembrance of Russel. Seven Hens bowed and lowered the body, anonymous in its shroud, down to a pillow of golden feathers. One by one the Animals dropped the dust upon it, and clots of earth, and all that Lazarus had dug throughout the night. Mice, their bits. John Wesley, his spatter of pebbles and anger. The Hens, the softest sweep-

ings. And when the body was gone, and when the Fox was
hidden in a mound that rose above the plains, Lord Chauntecleer the Rooster stood on top of the hill and craned his head
until his beak was aimed at heaven; and he crowed. Dear God,
he crowed, oblivious of the effect upon the Hens. Slingshot:
he shrieked for grief. Hundreds and hundreds of Animals
were sucked into that crow. A host of spirits flew to God upon
that crow, and all who died in the war, of which poor Russel
was only the final casualty. It smote the Hens, this passion. It
stung sweet Pertelote. And Lazarus, experienced in a thousand buryings—for this was his profession and his skill—astonished himself by weeping.

Then Chauntecleer did not move.

When he was done, he stood precisely where he was. But he
was nowhere among his Animals, for his eye had hardened.

It was up to Pertelote, finally, to usher the Animals away—
glancing at Chauntecleer—and back into the wood, and they
went. And the Beetle, in his turn, left too. Yet Chauntecleer
stood on Russel's grave, with his wing held tightly to his side,
like a cripple; and who knew when he departed?

That night no one came to sing the Compline for the Hens.
No one came to touch his Pertelote. No, the darkness remained an alien depth, and the Animals did not sleep.

Nine
Wyrm

Now, the Serpent was sly. Brutish and powerful he was too,
thick in the bowels of the earth; but brute power thrown
openly at the Keepers had had the effect of making meekness

strong, and love had sacrificed, and Wyrm had caught himself in the silken webbing. Brute power had finally earned him an absolute blindness, since he lost his eye to a single flailing Dog. The light went out. The subterranean darkness became complete. Force had failed him.

Nevertheless, the Serpent was more subtle than any Beast above him. He took what he could from the loss. He studied his mistake, and he contrived. He kept that Dog. Near, near to him was Mundo Cani. He studied that Dog and learned, and he contrived.

Because he hated God with an everlasting hatred.

And he meant to darken the suns of his universe. He meant to destroy the work of his holy hand: chaos, cold, and the illimitable dark! He meant to sink the mighty God into the same deep gloom which now was his own world.

Therefore, he brooded, he brooded and contrived.

His little filth at the funeral—what was that? A hazard. A chance. A sort of trolling in the sphere of the Keepers, patiently, to see what might come of it or who might rise and hook himself. Wyrm could have set a thousand such snares: hatred trained him in an endless perseverance. As it happened, the Rooster reacted marvelously. He sprang the trap. Instantly, Wyrm read vulnerability and the rightness of the times. Instantly, great Wyrm committed himself unto a stratagem both perilous and heinous. And he began.

Contriving and alternatives were at an end. The monster began a thing from which he could never retreat. So rash, so cunning was the thing, so total his commitment and his courage, that, except he meant destruction, the generations might have worshipped him.

Sum Wyrm, sub terra! Ah, nearly a God!

Now he began,

his own self-sacrifice—

On the same day when Chauntecleer stood with Wyrm's corruption underneath his wing a Bird flew over northern territories, a plain brown Bird whose life had always been a lonely one. She was strong, but she was not lovely; and though she could fly remarkable distances, she always flew alone. There never seemed to be a destination for her flight. Merely, she flew—on crepe wings, in solitude, and full of unsatisfied desire.

She yearned for loving and to love. But who would notice if she disappeared, since none in the world had loved her?

Now and again she tipped her head in flight, glancing below at waters and at shores, at tundra and the great shawl of the earth, which is its forests. She had a bill of unusual length, well-rooted in her skull and sharp as any needle at the end of it. It looked like a deformity. When she glanced down with one eye and then the other, this bill would switch the air like a rapier.

It happened, as she flew, that she heard a music rising from the ground. This was curious; no sounds should reach her at this height; nothing but the soughing of the wind. And the north land was forbidding, and the autumn the solemn season. But this sound had the distinct melody of a song, great and sweet and modulated, patient and wise. She lowered her left shoulder and circled wide to listen.

One who sang such a song as this must surely be more ample than the Whale, and ancient. But there were no seas below her. There was the land only, and no Creature visible. But there *was* the song! She descended on wondering circles, while her flesh tightened and her eyes stung to hear the melody. It moved her. And it grew not louder, but sweeter.

It was a love song.

Wordless, it was urging some woman nearer and nearer, calling her to its home, where it had little and nothing to give her but honesty and music and attention. And what did it ask in return? A kiss.

So careful, this song. So enchanting! The Bird drew her circles tighter and descended, because she envied the woman who received this kind of care.

But suddenly the song had language, and *brown* it colored its beloved, and *plain,* and by a score of rhymes it described the Bird herself, and she was shocked and bewildered to be the one—how could she be the one?—whom the singer was wooing. The song repeated its promise of honesty, for, it said, there is not love where there is not honesty, and it did not pretend that she was beautiful, and that was an overwhelming kindness to her.

The Bird limped on the air. It was too difficult to fly any more, and rhythm left her. Toward the melody—toward a narrow valley and a cavern at the bottom of it, a hole she had not seen before—she fluttered, and she landed there, in the valley, and she bowed her head, embarrassed; but she bowed her head like a communicant, and she listened.

"Please," sang the beautiful song, still no louder than when she was three thousand feet up, but piercing her. She twisted with its pain. "Please come in. I will not lie to you; I am too old. But I will love the thing I see."

"This is a mistake," whispered the Bird, and she meant a thousand things by that. She trembled.

"I am too old for mistakes," sang the song, startling her: her private words were heard.

"No, I will go away," said the Bird.

"Where?" sang the song, and the melody showed her a wasteland, and that was her life. "Where?"

The Bird raised her head and pleaded, "But who am I?"

"Someone who can kiss me," sang the song. "Once. Just once. But no one else could kiss me as you can. Please come in, my Bird of plain intelligence."

My Bird!

Ah, what a confusion! *My* Bird? Then did she belong to someone? She panted. She gazed into the cavern, but the darkness did not trouble her, for darkness could enclose her, embrace her as softly as thought. This is what the song said: the song said, *"My* Bird."

Spinster Bird. Brown and plain, poor Spinster Bird, she laid aside discretion; she took hold of her heart; and she entered the cave.

Down and down in darkness she went, like walking the nave of an endless cathedral, and she felt as though she were the first figure of some grand ritual, for the music brought her step by step in honor. She felt beautiful.

"Fine, fine, that you should come," sang the song.

A midnight marriage. Who would have believed it? The brown Bird felt tears on her eyelids, and yet she thought that she might laugh. She was happy, for this is what the song said: the song said, "Mine." And now she was going to meet its singer.

"Ah, so near to me," the low tones of the song. They seemed suddenly to be in the same room together, two of them. "Stop a while. Be still a while and listen." She did. She was; and then there came a passage of such aching memory and pleasure that the poor Bird lay her head upon the stone and sobbed completely. The song revealed to her his history, for which she pitied the singer, an age of long-endured injustices, bitter, undeserved attacks, all borne courageously, for which she gave the singer sympathy and her heart: how well she knew exile and its loneliness! Ah, here was a kinship. The song trembled at its theme. So did she. It was a world harsh on such as they! But then, devoutly, the song proclaimed the virtue that suffering works in the sufferer; and it ended with a magnificent hymn of triumph.

Silence. They shared the silence together. Surely there was a bond here, to be one in memory, in darkness, and in silence.

Then, "Kiss me," said the singer.

"Where?" said the Bird. "I can't see you." But she was willing.

"Here." The sound was focused, now, directly in front of her.

She felt flesh with her cheek—moist and soft, a living, pulsing flesh. This was real.

"There!" said the singer as soon as she touched him. It was a new sound, sharp, demanding. "Now!"

She put the tip of her beak to the flesh.

"What was that?" said the singer.

"A kiss," said the Bird.

"That was no kiss!" There was a driving rhythm in the music now, and urgency. "Press it! Make me know it!"

The Bird put her beak to flesh again. She pressed, but weakly.

"Well?" cried the singer.

"I might hurt you," said the Bird.

"Hurt me! Hurt me!" drummed the music all around her. "I *summoned* you to hurt me!"

All at once the Bird was frightened of the dark.

"What am I kissing?" she whispered.

"Me!" blared the music. "Me!" it declared. "The center of my brain. Drive it home, woman!"

The Bird shriveled. This was more than she could understand. The sound beat faster than she could follow. Yet for the third time her long beak touched flesh because a pressure gathered at the back of her skull, and directed her—then pushed! Her beak plunged into that organ, deep, deep, until her whole face was buried in pulp; blood flooded her mouth; the blood burst all around her, and she fought to be free, for she was drowning, but her thrashing only lacerated more and more of the spongey tissue—

A scream went up, a cry of absolute triumphant agony, and the Bird froze. *"Domine!"* the cry. *"Domine! Domine! Consummatum est!"*

The Bird was stunned, by the hugeness of the sound, by the passion utterly unlimited. She fell. She fell to stone and lay very still, afraid to move. She could not understand.

Blood cooled at the root of her feathers, was sticky on her eyelids when she blinked.

She breathed: "What have I done?"

"Murdered me." The voice was immediate and hoarse. Seduction and music had gone out of it. It said, "Open your mouth."

Before she could move or think, her beak was seized. It was slurred apart, and a caustic liquid ran to the gag of her throat, where it burned; she jerked and tried to cry, but was held fast. When, finally, she coughed, a lump slid from her mouth, and that was her tongue, and nothing was left in her throat but raw pain, and she could not, could not understand.

"You'll never," hissed the voice, "tell a soul what you have done." The voice was old and broken, diminished to a mere rustling of leaves. "Yet, you kissed me," it whispered. "For that I give you your life. Leave me. Get out of here. I am dying—"

But how could she move? She couldn't understand events: their speed, their sounds, their purpose, her part, the blood in her ears, the nearly incidental soreness in her throat—and this, that the greatness of the voice seemed suddenly to have shrunk to something less than her. Or else she had swelled. All the laws were gone! She was bewildered; how could she move? How could she put one claw down, one wing out?

By one word, then, the voice shot understanding to her nerves, if not her brain, and sent her poor wings beating. One word, and the singer revealed as if in floodlight the horror of the intercourse just accomplished, and she leaped from the sight. Or else the word alone was terrifying:

He named himself.

Lowly, he whispered the last word ever he spoke in the flesh.

He said, "Wyrm—"

Then she wasn't thinking at all. Mere instinct tried to fly through black, winding corridors, up and up for sunlight. And her wings were shattered. The hollow bones were splintered. Flight, too, was taken from her, forever.

Ten
The Dun Cow

When Lord Chauntecleer descended from Russel's grave, his iron eye flashing, his manner sharp and martial, there was really only one thought in his mind, one mild intention so childlike that it belied this fierce exterior: it was to wash. He wanted to be clean.

So, he wasn't punishing the Animals by denying them Compline. Nor was he avoiding Pertelote. He didn't even think of these. Nor of Russel, if the truth be told. Nor of the time of day—which had gone to sullen evening before he left the battle plains. He marched through the wood with an intensity that looked like threat, and with a strength to back the threat; but he was not aware of this, nor even of himself. Merely, fiercely, he wanted to wash himself. This was a problem not insoluble.

So his stride angled toward the Liverbrook.

The night arrived ahead of him. He found the stream by listening, hearing the constant rush of water in the distance, baffled by the trees. He felt trembling in the ground and wondered that he'd never noticed that before: the stream and the ground affecting one another.

He came to a stony narrows in the stream, below which were falls. Before him the water was thrown into a white boil, and these together made the roaring. Upstream there spread a flatland and dark water in the moonlight, dark because it was still. Chauntecleer paced upstream, watching the bank on his right. He looked angry, belligerent; but inside of him was such a wordless, painful vulnerability that he *had* to frown—or cry;

and that was his feeling; for conscious thought, there was only this: to wash. He was seeking a likely spot to wash.

Presently, he thought he found that spot.

A thin spit of stone stuck into the stream. Sidestepping, the Rooster slid along it to the end, and his right side hung over the stream *past* the end, and this was on purpose because all day long he'd held within his right wing the ordure he'd scoured from Russel's crypt. He meant to drop it there.

Now, a drastic change came over Chauntecleer. To think, suddenly, of that obscenity beneath his wing, to think of actually *moving* the wing, of opening it to empty it, despite the hours he'd held the offal against himself, was like letting go a wound long held: consciousness occurs, and pain. It sent Chauntecleer into a vile shivering, nearly a fit.

The fixity in his face shattered. All his feelings came rising up: frightening! And he was tired, a fortnight's tired. Few resources, the shields all down, the Rooster began to tremble so violently that his shoulder hitched and would hardly move.

"Oh!" he said. He couldn't loose the wing. It was cramped to his side. "Oh, no!" and he rammed it with his beak.

A rush of helplessness seized him. Something had to happen. He had to *do* something, or he'd lose control altogether. He threw his head to heaven and clawed at the wing, standing one-footed. He raked it as though it were an enemy, breaking skin—

Two things happened, one right after the other.

The wing, by main force, was prized wide enough that the filth therein fell out. But Chauntecleer didn't hear its little plop.

Expressionless, his face still turned toward heaven, but his body convulsing for having to fight against itself, his body not his own, the Rooster himself toppled backward into the stream. That was a splash he heard.

But he was unable to command his movement or to swim. The water carried him downstream, and he watched heaven, and he seemed removed from it all. His muscles fibulated until the frigid water soaked through feathers to the flesh, and then the shock contracted him. The Rooster knotted and began to sink.

"Well, so what?" he thought. He heard ahead the roaring of the narrows. He was floating toward white water, and he thought, "Why not?" It seemed, suddenly, a remarkable way to be cleansed absolutely, to die. He was still watching the velvet heavens.

Louder and louder that water. Surprisingly loud. It began to deafen even the heart. And the bank went fast by him. Then all at once he was snatched crossways—*he* was snatched! He was no longer detached. And the current pitched him round one rock then over another like a rag, and *he* was thrashing now in the steady thunder all around him; but all the universe was a spouting flood, and he was rolling over and over, and he'd lost direction. His skull cracked against stone. This was no longer serene. No! This was a treacherous, painful game, and he was scared. He broke against another stone. The shock went down his spine. Spume gagged him. But he was past the rocks before he could grab one, and then he sailed for the falls.

What should he shriek? Who could hear him? For an instant the stream allowed him to surface. The current was smooth and terribly swift. No sound here. Silent speed and impossible power. Look: there was one more dark obstruction before the water curved into the falls, and Chauntecleer was borne straight for it: one black shadow, and a final collision—

"Ahhh!" he moaned before he struck it. Pure fear and screaming: *"Ahhhhhh!"*

But the bump was a soft one!

Flesh!

And then he did not hold to it, but it took hold of him. A slender rod slipped under him, sought to balance him, lifted him bodily from the stream, swung him, and laid him gently on the shore—and the roaring was suddenly far away, for the falls had nothing to do with him any more. Earth did. His face was buried in the earth.

He breathed. Chauntecleer panted in that doubled position for a while, catching his breath and allowing his mind to catch up. The wounds pulsed on his skull, and he thought, I am so tired. And he thought, I don't care, I just don't care.

For a flash he thought, I should have drowned—

And then, incredibly late, he realized that he hadn't the choice of drowning. He hadn't crawled out of the stream on his own, but someone had saved him. Who—?

Ah, but he knew who.

Chauntecleer the Rooster, his face pressed in the soil, held perfectly still to feel the night around him. And in the night he found her. He was not alone.

Smell her smell, the clean sweet straw and cud. Hear her breathing, soft and nearly soundless, yet gently blocking the roar of the falls. She was there. Feel her warmth. She was very near. Chauntecleer felt a radiation against one side, while the other side was chilled in the wind.

And her eyes. He knew.

It was the Dun Cow that had saved him, her single horn that had found his balance and had placed him on the ground again. She.

He did not move.

He knew. He knew. He remembered the great, melting sympathy of her eyes, in which he had sunk when he was grieving the death of his sons, sunk and rested. He knew that even now, not a foot away, she was gazing at him, at *him*, allowing her heart to be the closure totally of his torment: another self to suffer with him, comfort in the company. She was giving herself: listen! He needn't be alone. He would look and see the welling of tears in those brown eyes, steady, laving tears: God's angel weeping for God's beloved. He could look and lose himself in consolation, and heal the death of Russel, and heal the whole scurvy war, and heal the Dog's—

He didn't look.

His mind shut.

Oh, God, this was cruel! In that moment by a pounding falls, Chauntecleer discovered that he could not raise his face to look at the Dun Cow, not in the eye, not in her eyes.

He wanted to die.

No! He wanted with all his heart to be held and loved by this dear Creature of God. He wanted to be a child in her bosom and to have all things right again. *But he didn't deserve it.* Foul Cock! Foul Chauntecleer!

He felt her move. The quality of the sound around him changed, and he knew that she'd shifted weight. There was a moment of panic when he feared his silence had sent her away. But that wasn't it. She'd brought her great face close to his. Through her nostrils, now, she breathed warm breath on Chauntecleer.

It scorched him. He cried out: "Why did you save me?" It was an accusation.

She breathed on him again, and he felt it as an agony. "Don't," he pleaded.

She did worse. She put her muzzle forward, and she touched him. He shrank from the touch—too real! Her nose, too warm, too loving; he literally shuddered and whined, "Why didn't you let me die?"

Oh, God, this was wicked! This was cruel! It wasn't the Cow he felt in her breath; it was himself, his own shape truly. It wasn't the love of the Cow he felt in the nuzzling; it was his own wretchedness, so long suppressed. What a terrible thing loving is! Chauntecleer kept seeing *himself.* Vividly. By contrast. And the greater the Dun Cow's love, the more hideous he. He simply did not deserve it: there's the pain. No, no, O Lord God!—the pain was worse than that, and how much can a Rooster take in a single night? "What are you doing to me?" The pain was that the less he deserved her love, the more he desired it.

Who can understand these things?

The nearer she came to him, the lonelier he felt! She was too holy.

He curled himself into a hard, defensive ball and whimpered, "Don't you think I know I failed the Fox? Does anyone have to tell me?"

The Dun Cow lowed. In a voice of impossible grandeur, the Dun Cow lowed into Chauntecleer's ear, and he heard her, and his feathers went on end, because he understood her.

She said, *Look at me.*

He was horrified. He couldn't. He simply couldn't. "I can't," he whispered.

Immediately beside him, she said, *Look at me.*

He screamed, "What'll I see? I'll see me. I'll see more than my failure for Russel. I'll see the whole bloody war. I'll see the Dog—" He took air and bellowed straight into the ground: "I know what I am! Do I have to *see* what I am? I can't!"

But she lowed, *Look at me.*

He broke. But he didn't look at her. He said softly, "I know you. You want to forgive me." And then he said, "But don't you know—that your forgiveness is my punishment? So then you are justified, but I am killed. Oh, please," he said, "tell me something I can *do* to deserve—"

She said, *Look at me.*

In despair he repeated, "I can't."

But she was not dissuaded, not by his passion, not by his reasoning. Again, for the fifth time, with the same depth and with the same yearning, the Dun Cow breathed on him and pleaded: *Look at me.*

Then this is what the Rooster did: he said, "Go away."

And this is what the Dun Cow did: she arose to four legs standing. She burned him one final time with her gazing, and she obeyed. She left.

So then the waterfall was like a silence, a roaring, reviling silence.

And Chauntecleer, still without shifting his position, burst into tears. They were childish tears, great, wracking sobs, and a total abandon to his sorrow. The dirt smeared on his beak and face.

Oh, this was an intolerable loneliness! Why had she come at all? Hadn't she known her holiness would torment him? Was it to scourge him with his own character, and then to leave him, exposed to his ugliness, choking on sin? But lo: he was crying because she *had* left him, and he was so lonely. Yet he had told her to go, because he deserved the loneliness—

Who can understand these contradictions? Guilt is a knot, all the cords tangled and yanked together. And then it is a knot, a thick lump in the gut, and a twisting pain. That's what the Rooster received in this unhappy meeting with the Dun Cow—the knowledge of his guilt. It is a tumor worse than grief.

Chauntecleer wept. Soon he stopped thinking and he cried for the pain alone. He rolled to his side. He held his balled claws up to his abdomen, pressing there, and he cried till his head lay down, and his legs relaxed. He cried till the sound of the falls went away. He didn't so much as seek a roost. He tucked his head beneath his wing, and cried till he fell asleep, and even then the sobs shuddered in him.

In the instant before sleeping, the name came to him, bright and sharp like lightning: *Mundo Cani Dog.* Him!

He jerked once, violently.

And then he was dreaming.

Pertelote's heart went out to her husband when she found him. His feathers were ratted and sour from old water. His face was grimed, dirt in his mouth, dirt stuck to his tongue, his temple cut and caked with blood. Lord, what had he done? He slept on his side, as she had never seen him to sleep before, a helpless, impotent position for a Rooster. And he slept at noonday—

He was suffering. He was dreaming, working his claws and his beak, seeming to shout, but saying nothing. Or trying to shout. Who could tell? He was suffering in the hidden places, secretly. What could she do for him?

She tried to wake him. She called his name. But he continued fast in his troubled sleep.

Well, so she sent the Hens down to the bottom of these falls, where there grew a tall hemlock tree. She set them the task of turning that tree into their new dwelling, and why not? For here was Chauntecleer, wasn't he? She asked the Mice to go with them, to dig mouse holes. What she did, she gave the Rooster privacy for his perturbation. What she did, the only thing that she could do, was: she held him. She wrapped her wings around him. She murmured his name over and over again, as though he were a child. She loved him, though something in him was hardening into mystery, and she could not understand the trouble. Yet she loved him. Therefore, while he struggled, she held him and she hurt.

"My dear. My dear. My Chauntecleer."

Here ends the first part of the book called Sorrows.

PART TWO
LACERATIONS

Eleven
Parable

A certain sluggish Sea Turtle goes nearly nowhere, grows fat on the gloomy bed of the sea, seeks no food, allows the food to come to him.

He yawns, as it were, perpetual yawns. His open mouth looks like any other ragged cavern in sea junk, except that his tongue dandles upward and twists precisely like a worm, a curious, loopy, blameless, and tasty worm. So, some earnest Fish, to satisfy his hunger, darts for the worm. So, this Turtle, to satisfy *his* hunger, snaps shut his mouth, and all that's left is a swirl of bubbles. No worm: there never was a worm. No Fish: he's part of the Turtle now. No hunger for either one, thank God. And the cave's become a smile.

Now, here's the point:

Which particular Fish the Turtle shall eat, why, that's a nearly impossible question. The odds against one Miranda's providing a smile for the Turtle are very comforting to Miranda. She needn't live in constant alarm. But that the Turtle shall have his Fish, why, that's no question at all. One shall surely happen by, and one shall act as Fishes act, so one shall die.

The Turtle may eat his Fishes one by one; but his faith is in the species whole. Not because of Miranda, but because of *Fish* shall he live (yet the last he snapped was Miranda's father; so Miranda, though she needn't be alarmed, is very sad). Certain things are certain. Fish will be Fish. So the Turtle has opened his mouth again in the perfect trust that it will be filled, and he hasn't swum an inch.

And here's the point of comparison:

Wyrm in prison has allowed a flue between the surface of the earth and his lair below, a winding, descending corridor. For him there can be no ascending it, not so long as the Keepers keep him: it isn't stone, but their woven spirits which deny him freedom. But the Keepers are free! Therefore, they *may* descend the chimney he cannot ascend.

The Netherworld hath ingress and stairs!

This chimney opens at the deepest corner of a short, sudden canyon, an old limestone cleft which runs from north to south in the colder, more northern region of the earth. The canyon, then, as remote and unremarkable as it is, is Wyrm's narthex, and the small cave in the deep of it, his portal.

But Wyrm has arranged for his portal one detail which a passing Animal might remark after all, and which might draw that Animal's closer attention: a plain brown Bird of shattered wings sits in a bush and in misery, uttering nonsense because she has no tongue, but warning, so she supposes, the good-hearted against going the way that she has gone. She has made it her devotion forever to block this portal, to protect anyone, anyone from the unspeakable evil that bulks below, and from the horrible memory that is hers.

She thinks she is a guard, and would die in the duty.

In fact, she is a tongue dandling upward, the lure of the evil that bulks below; and one day she shall be his token.

Wyrm trusts the Animals, Animals whole: one shall certainly happen by and then shall act as Animals act. There isn't the slightest doubt that his more immediate purpose shall be accomplished, for there are many Animals in the world; and there isn't the slightest interest in who gets used in the act. In this he is like the Sea Turtle. Both can wait, and neither shall ask the name of the one who comes.

In another matter, however, he is unlike the Sea Turtle. That Beast merely swallows and yawns again. But Wyrm has a stratagem, a plan, purpose upon purpose, at the end of which there is no longer the species but an individual, a Creature of very particular character and station. He is by nature and by appointment a leader. And he most certainly has a name.

Wyrm wants Chauntecleer.

Great Wyrm needs Chauntecleer the Rooster.

On the way, he'll take whomever comes, casual in his killings; but finally his freedom depends upon the deliberate soul of *one*. One: and then all!

Finally, Chauntecleer. First, Chauntecleer, and then the whole creation.

But though evil may be careless of the names of those it manipulates, a careful report cannot be. Goodness must find in every Creature his significance and call each one by name.

So, then: who was it that happened upon the canyon and the brown Bird and Wyrm's dismal portal?

The least of all God's Creatures on earth. Ferric Coyote—Him—

Twelve

Ferric

At the edge of the great northern forest, at the foot of steepling pine, low, low down, crouched at his forelegs, up in the rear, grinning, it seems, with all of his teeth—a Coyote is hiding.

He *thinks* he is hiding.

In fact, he's in full view from three sides, with only his butt to the tree trunk; but this is the way he hides: he freezes. Poor Ferric! He's convinced that perfect stillness effects perfect invisibility. And he is not grinning. He's scared. His cheeks go back to his ears when he's scared, and his eyes narrow into two pitiful darts crossing at his snout, and the snout itself seems to sharpen. Ferric! Fear turns him into one long, taut nerve, an arrow fixed mid-flight, or a bowstring which, if it's only touched, would hum at a high pitch: *eeeeeeee!*

Ferric has frozen this way often in his lifetime, since life itself is for him a dangerous proposition. The Coyote is cursed with senses too keen for a fainting heart. His ears are dishes; they hear everything. His paws are raw, and his bones are hollow tubes and his skin tympanic; they feel everything, magnified. His eyes are perpetually frighted; they see every twitch in nature, and any twitch may be malicious, for no twitch that he knows doth love him. Well; none but Rachel. She loves him. But she is inexplicable.

All his life poor Ferric has fallen into freezes. But lately the dangers have multiplied tenfold, and he's begun to ache with hiding. Because of Rachel, whom he loves in return, but who has *no* fears whatsoever—none. Poor Ferric: he yelps, and he hides for two. And suddenly, three weeks ago, his wife took a notion to travel; so they left their little territory of forest, which was at least familiar to them, and set off on a trip which has agonized the Coyote nearly to death: *one,* because they've trotted (no—*she* has trotted; he has skittered and dashed and crept and frozen and dashed again) through alien pine, trespassing; and *two,* because he hasn't the slightest idea where they're going nor when they'll get there.

"Where, Rachel?"

"I'll know it when I see it," she says.

"Why, Rachel?"

A wink. An exasperating, knowing wink! "You'll know it when I tell you," she says.

And he: "For God's sake, Rachel, when?"

"When you're able," she says, and she laughs, and she goes.

And he could never allow her to trot the world undefended; therefore, *zoom!* In a weary panic he has shot ahead of her, to scan the world for danger and to save her life, to freeze for two.

Poor Ferric! His speed has not rewarded him at all. Instead, it has presented him with the most disastrous sight that he has ever seen, and he is now paralyzed in a freeze of spectacular petrification. He simply had never imagined that such scenes could exist; he had almost bolted into it himself, was saved at the last instant from that calamity by instinct, quickness, and a skidding stop.

Ferric Coyote has come to the end of the forest.

Ferric Coyote, with a dreadful eye, is staring at open spaces!

There is nothing on the land before him, nothing, nothing at all. No trees nor tree trunks, hills or valleys, bushes or thickets, or anything to contain his gaping soul. Infinity! Why, one more step and he would have exploded! It is a land without protections, a plains without a single hiding place. The Creature who ventured such a vast immensity would go stark naked. And behold! It has an ending. So when the Creature reached that ending, curved below the sky, what then? Well —he'd fall off, that's what.

Poor Ferric is frozen beyond his known capacity. Yet one part of him keeps moving: his gullet. The Coyote swallows a thousand times at the sight.

Then comes Rachel, and the Beast's heart nearly fails.

For does she acknowledge the diabolical fraud that nature has played on them by coming to an end, and is she impressed? No.

Or does she so much as stop to take account of their terribly altered circumstances? No!

That woman! That red, relaxed, that reckless woman! When she draws beside him, she looks and giggles with delight. She whispers, Lovely!'' and "What an abundant God we have."

He says all he can say in his freeze: *"Tssssssst!"*

She glances at him, smiling, then kisses his wooden jaw and trots straight outward onto the blank.

He huffs. He puffs. He hyperventilates. And through his
grinning teeth he produces the steam of extreme alarm. Ferric
is a petcock:

"*Tssssssssss!*"

Well, Rachel recognizes the intensity of Ferric's speech, if
not the sense of it. She pauses and turns to look on her bleak
husband. Oh, she is so lovely, and so vulnerable! Gently she
comes back to him, all her joints loose and her expression
content; and she nuzzles him—him sharp as a drawn arrow.

"Oh, Ferric, be at peace," she murmurs. "This isn't terrible.
It's exactly what *should* be. Give me six minutes to look—"

"*Tssst!*"

"—and I'll be back, and then I'll tell you the good thing God
is going to do for us."

Then this is what happens:

Rachel with a fine bush tail, as healthy as Ferric is thin;
Rachel trots sixty yards across the faceless landscape, and
disappears.

Ferric blinks. There isn't even a scream in him, but a thousand needles prick his neck. His hair stands up. This horror's
too sudden to have a name. She didn't leave so much as a
shadow behind. She's gone!

"Rachel?"

All at once he's on his feet.

"Rachel!"

The Coyote gathers his strength, his legs on a single spot
of ground, and springs. The arrow is shot. He scorches the
ground:

"*Rachel!*"

Then, as smoothly as she disappeared, she reappears again,
head, breast, and legs above the ground. And what is that?
What *is* that? She's laughing!

Okay. So Ferric stubs his forelegs down. He thrashes out a
turn and takes himself back to the cloaking forest again. He
doesn't turn around. No, she can have his tail, for all he cares
—laughing in the face of his fears.

"Oh, Ferric, Ferric!" she exalts, coming up behind him, "I knew that I would find it, and I have!"

What Ferric had, he had a headache. He had a wife.

She's breathless. So is he. She's laughing, and she tries, with her nose, to tickle him. He puts on a very severe expression. Hmph!

"Did you see me vanish?" she laughs. "I vanished. And do you know why? Because there's a canyon there, invisible from here. Right?"

Hmph, woman. Hmph! You want me to say right. But I say *Hmph.*

"Listen. A stream of water runs through it. Water spouts at the north end, where I was, and runs down the narrow bottom, and isn't that just wonderful? It's exactly what I've been looking for. It's why we came."

"Good," mutters Ferric Coyote. "I have a headache. Let's go back."

"Back? Oh, Ferric."

Rachel comes round to face her husband, nose to nose; then she lays her neck beside his own, and she urges him to lie down, and so does she. They lie quietly a moment. "Ferric," she says into the silence, "no. The whole purpose is, we came to stay."

Stay? Stay in a vast and limitless land? It is at this point that the Coyote begins to groan. Tired after a long, tense trip, he goes to mewing in his nose.

"Shhh. Shhh, good husband. We can't keep wandering any more. We have to stop, on account of the thing that God is going to do for us."

Rachel, *what* is this mysterious thing?

Ferric is sighing, nearly whining.

Rachel whispers, "What I've been looking for, Ferric, is a home. We need a home for all of us, and the canyon is watered, and the canyon is well protected; there isn't a better place for you to hide in—"

Us? Ferric halts on that little word. He says, with a careful courage, and a whole new fear: "*All* of us?"

Then Rachel grins till the tears are standing in her eyes, and she gazes at her husband. "Yes," she whispers. "Ferric. I am going to have our babies."

What Ferric Coyote says then—on the edge of infinity, sky and land and the bewildering future—is, "Tssssssssss—"

Babies? He's found a new reason to freeze.

Thirteen
Dreaming

Chauntecleer's dreaming. It's a nightmare in absolute darkness, and there's nothing he can do about it.

He fell asleep beside the Liverbrook with his head beneath his wing, his nostril close to the oily smell, the sour smell of that ball of filth. By his deep breathing, it invaded his throat and run through the passages of his body, ascending to his brain; and now it has become his dream. The dream is an odor.

He is surrounded by a rank, choking air—cold, and he is shivering; dark, and he is blind; vast, and he finds no walls to touch.

He might be in a vault. His feet—he moves his feet—touch stone.

The mood is morbid, one of unspeakable oppression.

Someone is dead.

Suddenly, at such a distance that he has to cock his head to hear it, a woman wails, and the wailing overwhelms him: one single sound so lonely, long, and hopeless! Chauntecleer gasps at her frail desolation, her calling, calling, her calling with no hope of an answer, but calling in some inarticulate tongue until her voice shakes like a dead leaf in the wind. "Jug, jug," she cries from the rim of the universe. "Jug, jug," and the Rooster's heart is split. "Jug, jug. Jug, jug. Tereu—"

He can't stand it. He sucks breath, swelling his lungs with the carrion stench. He strains his neck and crows like the bugle: "Woman!" And an echo: *Woman.* "What do you want me to do for you?" *You! You! For you.*

The echo is a shock, like a battering in his face. He throws up his wings, and when his voice has died, so has all sound with it, and he listens; with all his might he listens; but the woman is gone, and he is buried in his loneliness.

Oh, God! He frightened her away. Or else he lost the last little notes of her calling in his crow. Always he acts too violently. Always he kills things in his fervor. And now he yearns for even the misery of her voice. She, at least, was someone—

But then begins the second episode of his dream, and this one's worse.

Another voice sounds in the darkness, terribly near, terribly mild and beautiful, and altogether unctious. It runs round him like oil.

Sing, says the voice. And the voice says, *What shall we sing?*

Too calm. Too courtly. Self-assured. Even in this foul place that voice is in command: it can be quiet because it is so mighty. Chauntecleer wants to go home, now. He wants this dream to stop. He's in the presence of pure force—

We'll sing of heroes, says the voice. *We'll remember them gratefully, song by song,* says the voice. And the voice says, *How right and proper to praise the great who went before us.*

Chauntecleer is snapping his head left and right, and he trembles. He knows that voice! And he's impotent within it. He can't see!

"Stop it," he whimpers.

Harmonize, says that voice. And the voice says, *We'll make duets of epitaphs.*

It drives on, like the clouds.

Of whom shall we sing? says the voice. And the voice says, *Of Russel the Fox.*

"No!" yelps Chauntecleer. Power is one thing; but power disturbing his friends is obscene. "Let Russel be!" How puling are his own denials. Foul Cock! Foul Chauntecleer! He can't even defend the name of his friend!

For there rises now a litany, a narrow plainsong filled with the Fox: no rhythm and no rhyme, but a counterpoint so elegant as to seem sacred, and a line made lovely by simplicity. So the Rooster's confused by guilt, because this is, after all, an exquisite memorial, and why should he object to it? Pride?

He bows his head below the chant and hates himself.

Foul Chauntecleer.

In time the plainsong dies away.

Whom next shall we sing? says the voice. And the voice says, *Mundo Cani Dog.*

But that's a name he absolutely cannot hear! Now Chauntecleer breaks and tries to run away. But the stone is endless, and the voice is ever at his ear.

Yes, the Dog deserves our singing, says the voice. And the voice says, *The finest of us all.*

He can't stop it. God, he knew the dream would be cruel! This is the one name that most scourges his soul and beats him with savage remorse. "I said," he shrieks, running, "I said that I can't bear to remember him!"

But the voice drives on, like the clouds.

Who once belonged to the Keepers, says the voice. And the voice responds, *Who now belongs to me.*

"Please!"

A hero in either camp, says the voice. And the voice agrees, *Since I have learned so much from him.*

Then, sing!

Again the chant begins, modulating sweetly on the name of Mundo Cani, his woeful nose and his holy deeds, his humility and the immemorial sacrifice—

And Chauntecleer is shattered.

He collapses in darkness, curling tightly to his pain precisely like the child who knows nothing but the ache, lying on his side. "Wyrm. Wyrm. Will you never let me be?"

That's the voice he recognizes. Wyrm's—

All at once Chauntecleer woke up under Pertelote's wing. He flung her aside and screamed from the tops of his toes, from the top of his lungs:

"WYRM!"

"Chauntecleer!" cried Pertelote.

The waterfall thundered below them.

For a moment his eye was wild, darting all around himself. Almost he screamed the vile name again, but he caught himself and ended staring at the Hen.

"Chauntecleer?" she said.

He drilled her with his eye. Then he demanded, "What are you doing here?" He drove the question into her like a nail: "Why didn't you leave me alone? Why couldn't you just stay home?"

Pertelote was lying like a rag beside the stream, but she answered. "Sir," and she whispered, "we came to be with you. Wherever you are, that *is* our home."

"I'll kill him," he said.

His poor wife tried to find her footing. It was a blazing eye in his head. She had been loving him so gently until he opened it. Therefore, she was hurt the more, and she did not understand.

Fourteen

Freitag First, and Then Chalcedony

So it was that the nomad Hens found new quarters for themselves in the Hemlock by the waterfall, easily roosting in its branches and glad to have cover before the winter began. Its boughs hung down like a thatched roof, mildly silver underneath its needles; its trunk went up like a mast; and it stood at the south face of a stone cliff which broke the cold of the northern wind. Nearby the water plunged over that same cliff, sometimes misting their tree; but the mist had become ice in the morning, roofing them, and the everlasting thunder caused them to roost closer together for the talk. They felt very private and warm inside their tower. They could have lived that way forever—

—except that the Rooster himself had grown as grey and cold as the weather, and there was not a Hen among them who could not be affected by his mood. Nor a Mouse. Nor a Weasel, for that matter.

Chauntecleer brooded. He'd become fiercely introspective since the move, forcing the Hens to wonder whether the Hemlock was wrong after all; and individually they checked their own recent behavior for some offense against him. But Chauntecleer had never been silent about offenses, so they were confused. He did not strut among them these days. He stood apart the day long, staring at the ground. And sometimes he'd fix his eye upon one Chicken, flustering her altogether, until she'd scoot away a step or two and find that he was staring at the place where she had been—not at her. Then she felt peculiar: invisible.

It was a penetrating eye in his head. But it seemed to see nothing. Like a sculpture.

"Lady, he's ailing," said Jasper.

"He is," said Pertelote. "I don't know why."

"Maybe you could slip some medicinal into him?"

"It's not his body, Jasper, not his body. It's his mind."

"Well," mused the lardier Bird, "forgiving me the rudeness," she said: "Maybe a romp in the woods? Just you and him alone—?"

"Jasper."

"I *said* forgiving me—"

"But I said it's his mind—right? He has no eyes for me these days, nor desires either—"

Chauntecleer brooded. As if thinking were a whirlpool, a furious sucking of all his attentions, the Rooster stood apart and lost himself in deep, deep frowning.

In the morning, his Lauds sounded like sleet, waking the Hens with a miserable chilliness unlike the sunny praise that they were used to. So then it was a question which grey was the cause and which the effect: did the iron-grey sky cause that crow? Or did the sullen grey Rooster cause that sky? Nobody asked the question aloud.

Terce and Sext and None were spikes, stabbing the Hens in their labors. They bent to their work and thought, "Why is he so angry with us?" The Canonical Crows had *never* been used for punishment before.

And the Vespers he crowed was a mere "Quit."

And Compline dumped them to sleep—castaways.

This clock of his grew cold and careless until it simply banged them through their days and they simply obeyed. No longer did Chauntecleer interpret their moments and their experiences to them, nor did he recollect the past to weave it into the present, nor did he call them unto a hopeful future; but that's what his canon used to accomplish. He used to, by praising them or fussing at them, assure them of importance; and because he did it with such variety and skill (that Rooster could crow an arabesque! on the other hand, he could crow plain, puritanical proverbs in single syllables) he was the glory in their homely lives. When they were moved to wonder about the value or the worth or the pageantry or the grandeur or the simple logic of their common existence, why, they looked to the Rooster, that golden Cock! More specifically, they heard the message implicit in his regular crows, and their wondering was straightway laid to rest. It didn't even become a question. They were content.

But lately the Canonical Crows had grown empty, so much sounding brass: always at the right time precisely, but always perfunctory, always hollow. How could a Hen *not* be affected by the change?—yea, though not a single duty of his was neglected and none could charge the Rooster with malfeasance in his office. He was so righteous; they felt so confused. He hadn't avoided *any* obligations; yet they felt altogether avoided.

Chauntecleer brooded. And the world indeed turned grey.

But the Brothers Mice loved him, and they believed always in the possibility of healing. Moreover, they had an absolute faith in pats on the back and smiles and nods and tiny salutes —and humor. And where their Rooster was concerned, they'd never felt the least hesitation or fear.

"It's his mind," the dear Lady Pertelote had said.

His mind? Well, then the Brothers Mice determined among themselves to soothe the Rooster's mind, and they chose Freitag, for his obvious talents, to be their point-man, as it were—

Thus it was, one colorless afternoon, that as Chauntecleer paced south along the Liverbrook with his wings back and his head bent down to the ground, he developed a double—a tiny self behind himself. Here came Freitag, hopping like a bird on two legs, his head bent down, his forepaws clasped behind his back, and his little face drawn into the most frightful frown.

The big Cock moved; the little one moved.

"Hum," said Freitag, suffering heavy melancholia. "Hum, hum, hum."

Suddenly six more Mice sprang out of the ground in front of Chauntecleer. They sat themselves into a perfect line and immediately began to clap. The Rooster drew up his head and stopped.

"Look!" they cried, pointing behind him; and he turned and blinked at Freitag. They clapped like the perfect audience. Then they said, "Watch. Sit down and watch." Then they fell silent, smiling.

And Freitag commenced to act.

"Heh," said the Mouse. This was a sigh. He mopped his face with a dainty paw. He rolled his eyes to the skies above, and spoke. "Oh, 'tis a monumental sad thing, to be alive," he sighed. Then he prayed earnestly: "If only a body could walk the world another way—than to be alive. Heh and heh, oh mercy me." Freitag bent beneath the burden and delivered a truly tragic moan. That Mouse moaned for a fully sustained thirty seconds by the end of which there wasn't a scrap of air in his tiny body and he looked like crushed misery.

"Hurrah!" cried six Mice in a line, breaking into applause. "You've *got* him, Brother. Watch, Rooster! Watch! No one can imitate like Freitag!"

Now Freitag sat on his haunches and began to pump his little head up and down. In perfect solemnity he spun both forepaws like propellers. He pinched his mouth.

Wodenstag leaped up and gestured. "A Rooster," he announced, "about to crow!" Then he rushed back to his seat.

Still spinning his paws, still pumping his head, Freitag cried, "Stop, sun!" Amazing! He managed a wattle under his chin. "Halt, moon! Don't none of you clouds go potty now. Listen to me, and I'll tell you the time of day, because how would you know without me?" Imperious was the squeak of that command. "How could you live without me?"

Just then it seemed to the Mice that Chauntecleer had allowed a little grin at the corner of his beak. Well, that's what

they were looking for, and that just shattered their restraint.
They giggled and giggled with helpless delight, because the
Rooster would love it. Chauntecleer would love what Freitag
could do!

Wodenstag cried, "Go!"

And Freitag's neck shot out an inch. And Freitag's eyes
squeezed shut. And the whirling paws pushed down, like
wings; and the whole body rose impossibly on two hind legs;
and Freitag's mouth stretched to prodigious proportions, and
Freitag crowed:

> "KICKY-KEE-DIDDLE-DEE-DEE!
> ME-*I*-MAKE-THE-LAWS-UP-FOR-YE!
> AND-HERE'S-THE-MAIN-ONE
> TO-KICKY-YOUR-BUM:
> *SHUT-UP!* AND-LEAVE-A-ME-*BE!*"

Oh, what a crow! Straight from the good old days!

The poor Brothers simply collapsed, laughing and beating
each other on the back, howling till tears came to their eyes
and they were reduced to the blowing and the beeping of their
noses.

"Oh!" they sobbed. "Oh, dear Rooster, isn't it—?"

But Chauntecleer turned on his heel.

With neither a word nor a grin nor a compliment nor the
ghost of caring, he walked away from them. The laughter was
murdered in their very throats, and the Mice felt sudden embarrassment to be lying all over the ground in such contorted
attitudes.

But Freitag, little Freitag, the second youngest of the Brothers, blessed with a special talent and cursed by it—Freitag
fought with all his might to keep his lower lip from trembling.
Yet, even before the Rooster had paced around the first bend
out of sight, Freitag failed.

Chauntecleer brooded: how could the Animals *not* be troubled?

They were thrown, as it were, upon their own devices;

there's freedom in that, of course; but it could also cause disharmony when one device hinders another. They were permitted the enlargement, each, of her own character; but that also allowed the enlargement of the faults within those characters; and a certain self-centeredness could be justified when the prevailing law is "Every Hen for herself."

Jasper wasn't an evil Hen. Truly. She was just big, which is no wickedness. But bigness causes appetites, and appetites cause carelessness.

Likewise, Chalcedony was not useless among the Hens. Neither was she despised. Truly! She was just crippled. She had a claw that wanted always to ball up, like a spider dying; and therefore, she was slow to scratch seed, late in eating it, and the thinnest Chicken of all.

For most of their lives these two had maintained a workable friendship despite their differences, because the Rooster had a discerning eye and had divided goods according to need, not according to appetite. But the Rooster was brooding, these days, and blind. So what? So natural tendencies went unrestrained. So plain Hennish nature became a problem.

And so what?

So here came Jasper at a charging speed, all health and bulk, wheezing single-mindedly, her eye upon an open seed: Chalcedony's. And there went Chalcedony, spinning sideways from the bump of Jasper's body. And before she could cry out, there went the seed down Jasper's gullet. So fat grew fatter, while thin was forced to fast.

This was a serious affliction for Chalcedony. She grew more anemic than ever before, and her eye seemed larger in her head because of the waste of flesh; and she was tired. Too tired to argue.

"Please don't do that," she'd say to Jasper, and she'd repeat wanly, "Please."

And Jasper would answer with tons of apology, because the Jasper satisfied was altogether different from the Jasper hungry: "So sorry. *So* sorry! Can you ever forgive me? I don't know what's come over me these days. I can't help myself. You want to know the truth? The truth is, I didn't even see you standing by that tidbit. Terribly, terribly sorry, little Chalcedony. Forgive me, okay? I won't do it again—"

But she did it again. The Jasper satisfied always reverted to the Jasper hungry. She did it habitually. She wasn't evil; just big. But big was getting bigger all the time. And thin was getting tired.

So Chalcedony broke a promise she had made to beautiful Pertelote, never to wander away alone. During the daylight hours she wandered farther and farther from the Animals at the Hemlock tree. She pecked a little food wherever she went, eating slowly and carefully, trying to remind herself that she *should* be hungry, and, now that she could, she *must* eat. The conviction itself was dwindling within her. On the other hand, daydreams flourished inside of her, for the more she went alone, the higher her private fancy flew, until it was nearly a rapture. And what did the Hen imagine for herself? Well, she'd be ashamed for any in all the world to know it, but 'twas to be a Lady. A Lady! A fine aristocrat of the most exquisite manners, breeding, dress, and dishes. A Lady, eating delectables. A pampered Lady, feeding on dainty bits—and beautiful. A Lady.

In her dreams she ate very well.

In reality, however, it was the autumn and late in the season; and the trees stood shivering beneath a low, grey sky with not a leaf to cover them; and the Rooster was distracted in his soul; and Sister Jasper troubled her existence, and Chalcedony hardly ate at all.

She fed on the air of her fantasies, and she wasted.

And then one day she wandered numbly into a valley north of the Hemlock, all unconscious of her surrounding until her claw crunched on something and woke her. She looked down. With a start she looked up, and around, and discovered the valley to be crowded with a host of tiny bodies, all of them dead and still and weirdly silent.

"Oh, no!" she whispered.

They were Cicada husks. The ground, the rocks, the bark,

and every rough surface was studded with the dried skins of ten thousand Cicadas, each one split at the back, each one gripping its position with brittle legs and wide, transparent eyes. A valley of bones! thought Chalcedony, and the silence frightened her. All at once she imagined that she stood in the theater of a terrible war, where there had been whirring wings and strafing, hordes of attacking warriors, horrible slaughters, screams and the death rattle—past, now, past and silent, and nothing left but the field, the hollow clutter of the dead, and she to walk among them.

Little Chalcedony swallowed. She made her own noise. "Hello?" she peeped in a tiny voice. "Hoo-ooo," she called. "Is somebody there?"

Nobody answered. None of the skeletons budged. Ten thousand vizards frowned around her, all of them empty.

She said, "Hee-hee." That was a giggle, meant for herself. And since no one challenged her, she scolded herself more loudly: "Ooo, Lady, don't you know?" she said. "They fly, Cicadas. They don't fight. It's in their nature to leave their skins behind. But so many," she whispered, staring. "So many—"

It *was* the seventh year, after all, the traditional date of Cicadic migration, and though she'd never seen the wonder herself, she'd heard stories of the daytime sky gone dark as midnight, filled with the clouds of living bodies, ticking and whirring from one horizon to the other—the year of Jubilee! They'd flown to a farther refuge.

Chalcedony the Hen put forth her beak and pecked one husk. It cracked and fell to the ground, leaving six good limbs behind. Well, that was easy. She plucked one—and as soon as the calcium stuck to her tongue, this is what she did: she ate it.

It crunched. It tasted gamy, salty. It chewed down to a sticky morsel. But it satisfied the gizzard in her. And the thin Hen giggled.

"Well," she said, hardly allowing her next thought to be true. "Well, well!" She ate a second and then a third, and soon that Hen was gobbling husks and laughing at once, stuffing herself—until contentment crept upon her, despite her troubled life, and the next thought proved itself to be true after all: this valley was hers, her own possession; and it was full of ten thousand dinners!

What a day for Chalcedony!

In that moment a marvel occurred for the little Hen: her dream came true. As proud and picky as any Lady ever was, she began to mince among the skeletons. "Too tiny," she declared with a sweep of her tail, rejecting a husk. (Whenever had Chalcedony rejected anything?) "No, sir, you're too tiny for the likes of me. I take the best, thanking you." And "La-de-da!" she scoffed, so hincty. "La-de-da, no, never nothing but the best for Dame Chalcedony."

It was a glorious afternoon in the life of this Hen. Fullness, finally, made her free, and she could almost think herself to be pretty. At the very least, refined. Oh, she sashayed her tailfeathers left and right, and she walked sublimely on her balled claw, making little of the limp. And then, in a whisper as devout as any prayer, in gratitude at the evening of that day, she asked, "Why mayn't Chalcedony eat as well as another?" And she answered herself with a sigh. "Well, she may. She may."

With dusk came the ending. But how could she bear to let it end?

"Snacks," said Chalcedony in her kingdom. "Wouldn't a Lady want snacks at midnight? And wouldn't she deserve them, if and that she had them? Well, think on that a moment." She thought on that, deeply—though she was aware of the danger that Jasper might see and seize any new food around. Yet she had grown bold today. Therefore, "Yes!" she said. "Chalcedony's answer is yes." A delightful answer it was, too; tickling her down to the abdomen. "So then. But how to keep snacks to herself and herself alone? Ah, there's a puzzle, surely."

In darkness little Chalcedony crept back to the Hemlock, arriving just when others were settling on their roosts. There swelled a monstrous bulge below her left wing. There was a dreadful poverty written all over her face: poor, poor Chalcedony. But there were giggles slipping from her beak.

Jasper, dull to variations in the spirits of other Hens, didn't notice.

Neither did Chauntecleer the Rooster notice, that spectral Lord whose passing was a chilly thing.

Pertelote alone came near Chalcedony, asking in private, "Is something the matter?"

"No, ma'am," she said. Then shrewdly she bethought herself and cried, "Yes! Yes, ma'am. That is—no more nor usual. Life."

"But you're limping worse than yesterday," said Pertelote.

"Oh, that is such a true statement you made." Chalcedony frowned as solemnly as she could. "Hee-hee!"

Pertelote cocked a suspicious eye at her. "And you're making strange noises in your nostril," she said.

"Burps, my Lady," said Chalcedony so sadly. "Burps."

Fifteen
Home, and the First Watch of the Night

In Ferric's mind, the prospect of babies and the panoramic emptiness before him were equally foreboding: either would confuse the rules of life as he understood them; both threatened experiences totally foreign to him, since he knew near nothing of either one; both would strip him bare-naked, one in the daylight down to his pitiful bones, the other, by harsh responsibilities, down to his pitiful, no-account, worthless, craven and unable self. Both, therefore, caused the poor Coyote to blink, merely to blink, and to lay his chin flat on the ground.

Well, he would have turned tail and retreated from either one, except that he hadn't the slightest idea how somebody retreated from the onset of babies; and so far as the wasteland in front of him was concerned, Rachel kept walking into it!

He had to watch over Rachel in her rashness. She was his wife.

Through baleful eyes, therefore, he watched Rachel.

But he did not follow.

That woman, casting constant glances of delight in Ferric's direction, none of which he acknowledged; that woman, humming to herself some silly music in her nose, as though she were actually happy or content or something; that woman went forth and trotted the plains with an easy, bicycling rhythm, flipping her paws all fearlessly, while on Ferric the only thing that moved was his eyeballs. She took the measure of the hidden canyon, pacing it from its northern to its southern ends; half a mile she went, while Ferric's eyeballs rolled a half an inch, and his nostrils blew a sigh.

She kept looking down, tipping toward deeper spaces. She'd take a cautious step, then scramble back again. And always she'd glance toward Ferric, but never did he show a bit of tooth: not a smile nor the least encouragement from Ferric. Neither would he show anxiety, oh, no! This was her choice altogether; she knew where he stood on the matter. He sighed; he wondered to himself: if he screamed *"Fire!"* would that woman answer, "Just a minute"? Ferric sighed with the force of a blast. But only his eyeballs moved.

Then Rachel nodded, as though making a decision. She turned and came the sixty yards toward him, bringing her happiness and so forth, her smiles and her humming and so forth.

And did he respond? *Hmph.*

On the other hand, did his clear disgruntlement fret her

any? No! Not a whit! Not a cloud in her sunshine. *Hmph!* What Rachel did, she lay down beside him, smiling. She stroked his frosty snout with her muzzle. And then the next thing was that she kissed him.

And did he respond? No, he had more convictions than that.

But did she fret? No! In the sweetest, most ingenuous of voices, she said, "Excuse me," and she asked, "Are you busy?"

Ferric blinked twice. But Ferric, grim-fixed, did not respond.

She began to pluck at his whiskers. "Just tell me if you're busy, Ferric," she said with a downcast, soft humility. "I really don't mean to bother you if you are."

His eyeballs slid back and forth. He lifted his lip a minimal degree and hissed, "Yesss," between his teeth.

Poor fellow: he'd responded.

"See? That's exactly what I thought," said Rachel brightly. She stood up, taking her warmth away from him. "Well, you stay here and finish your business. We both have jobs. Probably yours is more important. But I have to find a way down into the canyon, though I haven't seen one yet. Tell you what: I'll go and look alone, okay? Because you're busy, I mean. And I'll test whatever I find. And if I fall, I'll call you, okay?" She began to trot away, briskly, business and efficiency. "I'll probably scream," she said.

Scream?

Ferric's eyes popped wide open, and his ears sprang up. Scream! Then he narrowed his eyelids down to concentrated darts and troubled himself to think very hard: surely she wouldn't—of course the woman would not—no one would—Rachel had more sense than to—

Yet there went that healthy bush of tail gadly across an alien plain, and he knew, Ferric just knew, that the front end of that woman still was grinning!

Hmmmmph!

In the end, it was Ferric who found their home for them, yes; and they denned in the canyon after all.

But it wasn't altogether Rachel's coyness that persuaded her husband onto the naked plains nor any romantic foolery that sent him headlong down a gorge; that sort of recklessness simply was not in Ferric's character, because he really believed in the dangers. He really was a frightened Coyote, and could not be tricked from his fears. No, in Ferric's case, it was only perfect fear that cast out fear, one with a greater torment than the other—and on that particular day, one Wolf in the forest was a more convincing argument than Rachel's grin, and a more certain torment than all the strangeness of the plains.

Ferric knew what a Wolf could do.

Before Rachel had trotted twenty yards, Ferric felt shocks that couldn't have come of her light body. Shocks: the ground pulsed. A drumming shuddered at his paws, a rhythm from eastward directions. Now, Ferric's fears had sharpened his senses to a nearly caustic point, and he knew what he felt, precisely as though he had *seen* it:

Wolfspaw, padding the earth. Shocks: Wolfsprowl!

Next he caught a scent on the breezes, and Ferric could even name the name. There was coming a Wolf in slow lope through the forest, white-faced, white eyes, a winter, winter Wolf with shoulders rolling and as strong as timber, yellow teeth, a low nose, and a name of the north: Boreas!

Zoom!

Ferric was shooting across the plain in serious alarm. He passed Rachel, hissing, *"Fire!"*

"What?" she said.

Good God, the woman said, *What!*

He described a huge circle on the plain, returned to her and hissed, "It's Boreas in the forest! For God's sake, run!" and on he streaked toward this canyon.

She was right: the gorge was there. He met it at its northern end. Without a pause he hurtled the cliff and descended. This wasn't suicidal. Ferric's eyes, so quickened by fear, saw in an instant a fall of stones like stairsteps going thirty feet down, and his paws brushed those stones. To his right, the water burst out of rock. To his left it flowed away between high walls. He hit bottom and spun around, all in a single motion. Next to the stone staircase, set low in the cliff, was a small cavern, a little cave. "Refuge!" he thought. He bolted up the stairs again.

"Rachel!" he cried.

She was trotting, smiling.

"Aw, Rachel!" he pleaded. Her pace seemed never to vary —nor her mood either. Woman!

Down he dropped again, praying Rachel behind him. Around he whipped on the canyon floor, and, like the Swallow into her chimney, he popped in the cavern and froze.

So then, here came Rachel, picking her woman's way down these giant-steps, congratulating him on his sharp eyes, though, she said, she knew that he could find the way once he put his mind to it: chattering. And when at the bottom she saw the little cave, plugged with Coyote-butt, she broke into yips of pure delight.

"*Tsst!*" warned Ferric. "*Tssst!*"

"You found it!" Rachel could not contain her gratitude. "Oh, Ferric, I love you. No one could ask for a better home for the children. No one could have a kinder husband than you—"

That's how they came to den in the canyon.

But then, in the following weeks, the weather changed. And Rachel, too, who had never changed before, changed. And Ferric had a whole new riddle set before him in the person of his wife. For her change seemed to have nothing whatever to do with the weather's, and he was confounded.

Winter commenced. Two days after they had gone about scenting a little territory for their own, the winter began with weird, inexplicable shifts, a sort of colliding of the elements, so that Ferric Coyote grew wary; he paced constantly; he started at little noises; he rolled his eyes restlessly.

And he felt silly, since Rachel did none of these things.

But he couldn't help himself. Look: through several days together the winter sky would oppress them with humidity and a steady drizzle, would so laden the air that a Beast could see his own breath, yet he would sweat in the closeness. And pace.

But then in any given night the cold would hit like a fist: sudden, absolute and numbing; and the moisture froze so fast, 'twould seem as with a click; and the north wind might scream across the land, or else the wind would kill by the cold alone, lazily touching all things to ice. Nobody hung his tail outside the Den on such nights, and by morning the muddy world was transfigured. Ferric climbed the stones to find the plains pure sheets of ice, slippery under his paws, the sun blinding him by slanting from its surface, the air crisping his whiskers and stabbing zero to his lungs. He'd gulp, and suffocate. And the great pine trees he found cased in ice, sparkling, tinkling lightly, and yet splitting the limbs by its weight, causing tremendous crashes in the forest. Little Ferric gazed, then, on a cold *Eisreisenwelt,* so lovely and so sepulchral.

Who wouldn't pace nervously at such a spell?

Who wouldn't feel tiny between the seasons?

Yet tomorrow—or three days later, when a Coyote had begun to adjust to killing temperatures—a thunderstorm might come stumbling up from the south, yellow, ireful skies, a stupid and lumbering thunder, totally out of its time and place, yet bellowing round and spouting as though offended by some indignity—by ice? Certainly, ice was abolished under this gigantic, untimely displeasure and spit; and then the mud was back.

This was no winter like any Ferric remembered. The spheres themselves seemed hateful of one another, battling for dominion. And the Coyote reacted in kind, skittering up and down the stones, batted back and forth by the cold and the clamor and the irrational lightning.

But Rachel? Why, Rachel seemed oblivious of convulsions in the heavens, detached from the world itself, from reality!

So that next to her, Ferric's jumpiness seemed merely neurotic. Look: there could be the crack of thunder, the rattle and the boom of thunder right above them—and Rachel might sink suddenly inside herself in spite of it. That red Coyote might melt into internal meditations, allowing a smile to curl at her lip, and distance to glaze her eye—and she would hum. *Hum!* No tune, simply a sort of purr at the end of every breath, and contentment. But the first drops of the storm would be splotting her skull!

"Rachel!" Ferric would try to waken her.

He truly worried over her lapse. Strange days, but a stranger wife!

Because look: sometimes the woman would rise up laughing, a laughter so hearty that the tears would run from her eyes, damping the fur of her cheeks. And Ferric would stare about to find the joke, and, finding nothing funny in all this wintry world, would desperately try to comfort her, to console her hilarity. Well, it seemed manic. Then what did he get for his efforts? Nuzzlings! Kissings and affections in unreasonable quantities.

Or else—again, for no reason that the poor Coyote could discern—she would suddenly sob. It didn't matter where they were. They might be walking the creek of their canyon—that one water which never froze—when all at once she'd bow her narrow head and pause and weep as though her heart would break. Poor Ferric! Now *he* would nuzzle *her,* and he would mutter how that everything was all right (though he was convinced it was all wrong), and he'd *There-there* her, and he'd *Why-are-you-crying* her, neither expecting nor receiving an answer. He would feel a clumsy, ignorant fool beside the woman, a perfect stranger, because why *was* she crying anyway? Did she hurt? Had he done something wrong? Who was this Rachel anyway, these days?

Skinny Ferric felt a constant turmoil in his stomach, which is the way that he worried; and he showed his teeth in stretching his cheeks: the weather and the woman at once, but neither one the cause of the other's distress! And Ferric was caught between.

Didn't they have a Den, now? He liked the Den. Didn't she? Couldn't they brave the winter together? Or what? Or what—

One evening, after another such perplexing rain of her tears, Ferric screwed up his courage and faced his wife and fixed her with a probing eye in order to imply how serious his question was about to be, and he said, "Um." That's how he began. Conversations, too, could be a danger. "Um," said Ferric Coyote, gazing at Rachel, the two of them standing belly-deep in running water between cliff walls. And then, with much more force: "Um! Rachel!" And he nearly shouted at her: "Wanna-talk-about-it?"

"About what?" she smiled. She was back to smiling so quickly!

"I don't know," shouted poor Ferric. "Something. Something's—in you," he roared. He tried a grin. It didn't work. He abandoned grinning.

She, on the other hand, brightened into the sunniest of smiles. "Why, Ferric!" she giggled. Behold how she'd swung from weeping to laughter in no more than two minutes' time. "Ferric, there *is* something in me!" she giggled. And then her face grew thoughtful. "And I *have* talked about it," she said. Her slant eyes slid from his countenance to deeps he didn't recognize.

"I've a friend," she said. "I've found a friend, at the far end of the canyon. I've spoken with her, and she listens, though she has never spoken to me. There's a tragedy in her eye; and her wings are too crippled ever to fly; and she has no tongue, Ferric. No tongue in her beak. A plain brown Bird whose name I do not know, because she cannot tell me. *Jug,* she says. *Jug,* so sadly, and *Tereu.* Well." Rachel drew her sight back to Ferric's face, Ferric Coyote's wounded face; and she smiled. "Well, I visit her, and I talk, and I feel so much better, now."

She kissed him. "Thank you," she said, and she trotted down-stream, leaving him alone—alone, forsaken even, his narrow mouth hung open.

His wife had a friend he didn't know about?

She has a private life?

Someone else comforts Rachel? Worse: she gives her sym-pathies to someone else? Is this why Ferric couldn't account for all her changes? Ah!

Yes: he abandoned grinning. He went straight to the frown, did Ferric Coyote—but not for anger. Rather for resignation. He watched her tail snake the water, southward to her friend, and he knew the truth. He was the least of all God's Creatures on the earth, ever and ever afraid. It was right for his wife to seek her consolations elsewhere. It felt sad to him; but it was both right and to be expected.

No, Ferric wouldn't stand in her way. He lowered his head and waded slowly back to the Den, dumbstruck at how quickly a whole life might turn around, and all he'd wanted to do was to comfort her, and here he was, wondering if he should hang around for tomorrow.

I've found a friend: it rapped in the poor Coyote's mind like a verdict. But why shouldn't she? He himself couldn't make friends; but that was his way, after all, his fault, his weakness —not hers. He'd never, never thought before that his weak-ness might be hindering her. So, who was it that made her cry these days? Who else? It was her nature to be a happy Coyote. Smiling, and so forth. Humming. Of course she should have friends.

So, thought Ferric, sticking his snout into their Den; maybe he should go away.

Because, what did he have to recommend himself to her? He kept forgetting, in her presence, that he had nothing at all.

Yes, thought Ferric; he would go away.

And that's the reason why he curled round and round him-self in the Den, making a donut of his tail, his nose in the

middle of it. He sighed; he closed his eyes and fell asleep.
Tomorrow.

"Ferric!"

In the middle of that same night, now whistling with the wind, Rachel woke him, hissing, "Ferric, Ferric, come here and touch me!"

Blinking, instantly tense, he crept to her side in the darkness.

"Here," she whispered below the weather, and she drew his cheek down to her belly, pressing him against the soft nipples there, bare flesh.

A hundred feelings rushed through the poor Coyote all at once:

He was so embarrassed by nipples!

He choked with pity for Rachel, whose midnight actions were more irrational than ever. Why would she mash his face into her belly?

He felt pain, true pain, thinking he had no right to this intimacy, on account of, it was all his fault anyway, and he was about to repair the damage by leaving tomorrow, but here she was, being so familiar that how *could* he leave?

And then, there was this:

Her belly rared back and punched him in the ear.

Straightway one Coyote was freezing in the doorway of the Den, glaring at the tummy of the other—while the other was trying with all her might not to laugh.

"Rachel!" Ferric stuttered. "Company! You got company in there!"

Well, that was a pure hilarity to her way of thinking, and she lost control. Rachel collapsed and laughed like a glorious fountain, kicked and rolled and called his name. His ears shot up in bewilderment, and his poor heart was utterly helpless to understand proceedings any more.

"Ferric! Ferric!" she sang at the top of her laughter, louder than the wind. "You don't know how much I love you, Ferric!"

She came forward. She took his jowl between her teeth and drew him to herself and coaxed his head down again, down upon her soft and swelling nipples, down upon the finest fur, the smoothest skin; and she stroked the stiffness in him.

"It was your child, Ferric," she said. "O my Ferric, who takes such good care of me. It was my gift to you that you felt; and I'll give it to you yet, sooner than you know. I'll lay them here before you, and I'll name them one by one, and you won't be afraid of them then, for they shall be beautiful. Ferric, I have just one wish for you." Whistles the wind. Whistles the winter wind, but Ferric only had ears for the sweet absolution of his wife. "O my solemn husband," she whispered. "I wish that one day you will learn to laugh."

Well, that was a good night after all. He was still the scared Coyote, small below tumultuous elements; but before the morning he admitted that nipples were nice for lying on. And homes were not bad to have. And wives may not be strangers, even if they can't be understood. And once in a while it is possible for a pitiful, no-account, worthless, rust Coyote to cease his agonizing, to lie down and to feel safe.

He didn't leave in the morning after all.

Sixteen
The Second Watch—Dreaming

The wind from the north, that shrieking wind, goes bitterly over the earth, striking ice to all the lands: winter, and a very dry cold—

Chauntecleer is dreaming in spite of himself, the same dream again.

Well, he has tucked his head beneath his wing, where the breathing moistened an old filth; the moisture loosened an odor which the Rooster sucked in through his nostril and the odor fumed into his brains—and thick and helplessly, Chauntecleer is dreaming.

He stands on stone, abjectly. He knows what's about to happen, and it does.

Far in the darkness the woman wails as she has wailed before, no nearer to him, no less aggrieved, no different; and yet the Rooster is sickened all over again by her sorrow and his sin. "Jug, jug!" They are the only two in an endless desolation. If one is sad, then one should help. "Jug! Jug!" But he cannot even find her, the wretched Cock! And if he could, what would he do? He can only rock his body back and forth, listening to her loneliness, unable even to tell her that someone is listening, that someone else is lonely, too. "Jug, jug," she weeps, a solitary woman. All the world is a wandering, solitary woman! "Jug, jug," unspeakable sorrow. And finally, as distant as death: "Tereu."

She's gone.

The blackness is vast and empty, and Chauntecleer is allowed an interlude to suffer his guilt. Like a tumor in his gut is the feeling that he is responsible for that woman, and the uglier premonition that if one night they met, she would despise him.

Chauntecleer hates this dream.

But the dream will play itself unto the end—

Suddenly: *Sing,* says the voice, like coldness all around him. But then the second voice is the sharper shock, and he snaps erect. It sounds exactly like his own. A cocks-crow asks, *What shall we sing?*

A new twist in the same old words, a more insinuating torment. Why can't he see?

Of those we remember, says the voice. And the cocks-crow answers, *So! Our happiness is in their histories.*

And who's the finest of us all? says the voice. And the cocks-crow asks, *Of you and us together?*

Aye, your savior and my guide, says the voice. And the cocks-crow responds, *Why, Mundo Cani Dog.*

"That's not me! That's not me!" Chauntecleer cries. "I didn't say that name!" His blind eyes rolling, his whole body trembling—

But his negative is nothing in this dream. A chant goes up, echoing as though in marble arches, down stone hallways—a passionless plainsong, dipped in wax.

O God, the Rooster groans, folding himself into a ball; how often will he have to suffer the punishment of his fault? Two times? Ten? Forever?

The chant dies away, and there follows a universal silence. Chauntecleer shivers painfully and waits to wake. He has been accused. This is when the dream will usually release him stunned into the world again—

But he doesn't wake. This silence is premonitory and unfinished.

There is, says the voice, *there is one other to commemorate,* says the voice. And the cocks-crow whispers, *Who?*

Chauntecleer holds very still. Water's dripping somewhere. Who?

Him who listens, says the voice. But the cocks-crow whispers, *Who?*

The voice says, *Chauntecleer.*

A sound like wind, like the shrieking wind starts in the Rooster's ears.

And the cocks-crow whispers, *But he hasn't passed—yet.*

Passing, says the voice. *Passing.*

The shrieking sound, thin and weird, rises a pitch; it pierces Chauntecleer's skull and cuts his throat. It's him. It's his own beak open, his own tongue thrust out, and his own voice, whining. He's trying to say no. He's trying to deny the whole ungodly ritual. But all that he can produce is a mute and lingering scream.

Not my name.

When a Lord lays down his lordship, says the voice, *what is that?* says the voice. And the cocks-crow whispers, dreadful of the truth, *A passing.*

Not my name! Not me. My God, I want to die!

When strong hearts weaken, says the voice, *what do you see?* says the voice. And the cocks-crow whispers, *A dying.*

Even so our brother Chauntecleer, says the voice. And the cocks-crow whispers, *Who will believe us when we sing?*

Any who see the bones, the bones, says the voice. *The bones shall condemn a Cock. And bones shall vindicate our singing,* says the voice.

Chauntecleer has never hurt so much in all his life. He can neither shape nor stop his screaming.

Sing, says the voice: *Dirges!*

Then descends a chant so cold and hard that it falls like the flat of a hammer against his temple. Now! Now! Now!

And he wakes.

And it is in fact the north wind shrieking through the top of the Hemlock. Gleefully.

Seventeen

The Third Watch—Wakings

"Don't! Chauntecleer, please don't go. You've *got* to sleep."

The Rooster stood stretched on a Hemlock branch, prepared to fly. Wind, though it caught only at the top, made the whole tree tremble; and Pertelote was pleading, "Don't."

Chauntecleer began a vicious sentence, "You—" He bit it off. He lowered himself and gazed at her as though discovering something. "Are you still awake?" he said.

"Always," said Pertelote. "Always when you leave I am awake."

"You know, then."

"I know. This I know, that you leave me. You wander abroad the whole night long. I know. It's what I don't know worries me—"

"I get restless."

"You are tired."

"I can't sleep."

"You don't want to sleep."

"I don't sleep well—"

"No! You hate to sleep!"

"A few nights, Pertelote—"

"A few? A few? Shall I count the *weeks,* dear Chauntecleer, since you've allowed yourself one good night's sleep? Tell me, when did the winter begin? Better yet, tell me: why don't you sleep?"

"I've got to go."

"Don't!" she cried. Softer: "Don't. Stay with me."

"Oh, Pertelote. What good would that do?"

The Hen bent her head in the darkness, then, and whispered, "You might touch me tonight. You might not pull away from me tomorrow morning. Some good."

For a long moment Chauntecleer sat utterly still upon this lowest branch of the Hemlock. Hens slept all above them, and above the Hens, wild, scudding clouds and a bright moon and the ceaseless wind. The night was frigid, the moon an absolute zero.

The waterfall thundered less these days since the water sheeted down a sluice of ice; and the shores of the Liverbrook, winter-bitten, were snaggled with a thinner ice; and Lord Chauntecleer was cold, simply cold. Cold was the thing that made him shiver.

"I've got to go," he said.

Pertelote cried, "Why?"

But he leaped and left her behind. He glided twenty yards and landed and stood still in greylight, and looked, and saw his dim moonshadow lying down beside him.

"Because I am so cold," he whispered. Why else?

But the shadow, which could be seen only from the side of the eye, seemed unsatisfied with that. Why?

"Well," said Chauntecleer. He shrugged. He glanced around the frozen night, and the wind blew. "Well, to see the Animals," he said. And he said, "This is a very good reason: to see my Animals."

Afterthoughts may turn into very good motives and opportunities in their own right. Lord Chauntecleer went to see to his Animals. Twenty yards back, by Rooster struts.

Ah, how long had it been since he'd smelled the smell of the Mouse's hole? Such a warm, consoling odor, like bread-dough, close and yeasty, altogether homely. The dear Mice! Why, Chauntecleer wondered as he breathed their sleep-smells in; why had he denied himself this kindness? His shoulders were pressed against their entrance, his head and beak sunk to the hollow of their quarters. He felt a sob thump in his chest. His breath, when he drew it deeply, sounded like a sigh.

Immediately, a tiny voice spoke.

"I'm sorry, Rooster," it said.

"Freitag?" Chauntecleer was startled by life. "Is that you?"

"Well, but I wish it wasn't. But it is, dear Rooster," said the Mouse Freitag. "It's me."

"You're still awake?"

"Well, but I don't have the right to sleep."

"Freitag. You sound so tired."

There was silence in the Mouse's hole. Then a tiny rustling. Then a different voice spoke. "He is very tired, Rooster; you are right. But I think that maybe what you're hearing mostly is that Freitag is very sad."

"Wodenstag?" said Chauntecleer. "Are you awake, too?"

"Oh, well, yes," said Wodenstag.

"Rooster?" A third voice, the youngest of them all.

"Samstag! What is it?"

"You see, we are all awake."

"Why? It's the middle of the night."

"Well, we haven't slept for a long time, now."

"Shhh, Samstag," whispered several of the Brothers. "You shouldn't mention such things to the Rooster. He doesn't need to worry over us."

But Chauntecleer was right there, listening. He wasn't far away. "In God's name, tell me," he said, feeling like a stranger. "Why don't you sleep?"

Samstag whispered, still as though he were not there, "I think that I will tell him, Wodenstag, on account of, he asked." And to Chauntecleer: "We stay awake with Freitag, to keep him company."

Chauntecleer said, "Freitag—" But the mere speaking of the Mouse's name unmanned that Mouse. He began to cry: "Hoo-hoo. Hoo-hoo," such a pitiful snuffling and so polite that Chauntecleer felt gross and clumsy. He truly didn't understand Freitag's trouble, though all the Brothers seemed to. How long had this been going on? How much had he missed? And why should tiny Mice protect their Lord—?

The Rooster, by willing it, restrained his own confusion; he gathered all his care and all his sensitivity into a gentle voice and spoke for the Mice alone.

"Do you remember?" he asked slowly, "how I took you from the river long ago, when you were nips about to drown?"

"Yes," said Wodenstag and Donnerstag and Sonntag. "Yes. Yes," all of them full of solemnity.

"Do *you* remember, Freitag?"

Freitag said, "Hoo-hoo, yes, hoo-hoo."

"You were so brave, to climb from the river onto my back. Remember? And you trusted me, and that's why I could save you then. Remember, Freitag?"

"Hoo-hoo."

"Do you trust me now, enough to lay your trouble on me? So that I could help you now? I still help, little Tag. I don't hurt Mice. Do you believe that?"

"Oh truly, truly—hoo-hoo."

"Then tell me, why don't you sleep? Why do you cry?"

Freitag fairly wailed, "Because the Rooster *is* so good. That is the trouble." Then, deep in a wee gloom: "Because I am so wicked. That is the trouble."

Chauntecleer's face burned hot—a rush of shame at this innocent division of good and evil—and he couldn't speak. Freitag could.

Freitag said, "A wicked Creature doesn't have the right to sleep."

"You are *not* a wicked Creature!" Chauntecleer struggled to keep his voice from sounding angry.

"Oh, yes, I am very wicked," sighed the Mouse. "Because—" And then the words tumbled from him: "I made fun of you, Rooster. I mocked you, yes, yes. I walked like you walk, and I crowed like you crowed, and all my Brothers laughed at it, and you would never hurt me, but I hurt you, dear Rooster, because you didn't smile at what I did, but you were kind, you didn't scold me either. You . . . you just . . . you just walked away from me. Oh, Rooster! Hoo-hoo-hoo."

Chauntecleer snatched his head from the Mouses' hole and raised his face to the dark tree-forms beneath the stars, and he wanted to cry. *You just walked away from me.* The wind shrieked a manic winter in the woods. The moon accused him. The Rooster felt naked. Walking away: that was *his* sin, not Freitag's! Yet that little Mouse accepted the fault without a second thought, because that little Mouse—and here was the worst pain—that little Freitag loved him.

He put his head into their hole again. With fierce restraint, he counted his words like coins. "You think you sinned against me?" he asked.

"It is the way that I am," said Freitag. A bleak answer, a bleak Mouse.

"If you sinned against me," said Chauntecleer, "then it's my right to punish you, isn't it?"

"Yes."

"But not your right at all. You have to accept my will."

"Yes."

"Freitag?"

"What?"

"My will is not to punish you. So you can't punish yourself any more with not sleeping. Freitag?"

"What?"

"My will is to forgive you. I forgive you. There is no sin any more. It's gone. Do you hear me? Forgiveness makes a sin gone, and you are good again. Good Creatures have every right to sleep. Go to sleep, Freitag. Go to sleep, now. Can you go to sleep?"

Freitag took a long time to answer. Oh, God, why couldn't all the world smell as kind and woolen and comforting as a Mouse's hole on a winter's night?

Finally the honest Mouse answered, "I don't know."

Chauntecleer said, "How if I told you one thing else?"

"What?" said Freitag.

"That I love you with all my heart, little Tag."

"Yes," sighed Freitag, infinitely relieved. "Yes, that makes a difference."

Wodenstag asked, "Then we can all go back to sleep?"

"Do I love you any less?" said Chauntecleer.

"No?" said Wodenstag.

"Then, good night. Good all of your nights. Sleep, Tags. Sleep please."

"Good night, Rooster. Rooster?"

"What?"

"And we love you."

Ack!

Chauntecleer pulled himself into the winter wind again, sucking huge breaths of air. Ack! *Ack!* That was exactly what he could not hear, this loving him. Freitag could hear it. All the Mice could hear it, because they were truly, truly innocent, and their hearts were so good, so worthy of the love. But Chauntecleer the Rooster was a curse. The more that *he* was loved, the more he deceived, and the farther he was from the truth and from all who *would* love him! This loving, *ack!* This loving was a scourging.

Almost he buried himself in the shrieking wind. Almost he flung himself deeper into the night. But suddenly the wind died for an instant, and in the pause he heard a small sound, a nearly inaudible crunching to his left, behind a thicket at the base of the stone cliff. Somebody else was wakeful—O poor Chauntecleer! Somebody else had secrets he knew nothing about—O incompetent Lord of the Animals!

The crunching softened to a chewing, and the chewing ended with the smack of a narrow beak. As a criminal drawn to his own crime, almost seeking the pain he deserved, Chauntecleer stole toward the thicket. The wind resumed its whistling insanity, covering his approach; and he peeped to the wall; and he saw the white shadow of a Hen, alone, bending away from him and pecking something.

"Chalcedony!" he wailed.

Instantly the skinny Hen whipped around, recognized him, fluttered for a moment, then covered her something with her butt. She plopped down, embarrassed.

Chauntecleer cried, "Does nobody sleep any more? What are you doing?"

He sounded so angry that he shocked the truth from her. "Snacks, sir," she said.

"Snacks? Snacks? What are snacks!"

Chauntecleer's cry meant to encompass the universe. But Chalcedony took all things personally and in particular. Miserably she stood up and stepped aside, admitting to the nest of insect limbs beneath her. Her secret? Crushed skeletons and dead skins.

"Snacks," she said.

Chauntecleer stared at the junk, astonished. He looked closely into Chalcedony's face and saw, to his enormous grief, a Cicada leg hanging at the corner. She fed on garbage!

"Well. Well—" the Hen hastened to explain. "Well, Jasper doesn't never leave me eat, no blame on her. So I keep me some little snacks where she can't see nor gobble them afore I do, you see. And come the night, I'll steal from my roost—but I'm sorry now that I do—and maybe snack a bit, then steal back, thinking to myself that, Who's the wiser? Who's the worser for my little habits? Thinking, No one. No one. So I've slept the better these nights. But maybe I should of shared, sir? That's what you're thinking, by your silence, sir, that how come Chalcedony's so selfish? And why didn't she share? Sir—?"

The Rooster only gazed at her, long and intensely.

"—and you're right," she whispered, blushing, answering for him. "Why mayn't Chalcedony share a treasure, if and that she has one—"

She ran out of words. His unwavering gaze shamed and baffled her, the Lord of the land, raking her with silent judgment. So what could the poor Hen do? She began to curtsy, and then she couldn't quit. Up and down, up and down, grinning silly, she curtsied, and her lame claw ached.

It was a hoarse whisper, when finally the Rooster spoke. "What have I missed?" he said.

"That I eat, sir," she chattered excuses for him. "Nothing else. It's what I do."

"No—*you,* Chalcedony," he whispered. "How could I have missed seeing *you?*"

"Oh, you never, sir," she said. "I'm right here, was always right here, never did no planning to be somewheres else— save here—"

She curtsied furiously.

"Chalcedony," the grave whisper, a rasping: "Look at you."

"At me?" Oh, 'twas a terrible thing, to be the object of this conversation.

"And this garbage!" he said, more scornfully. Suddenly he reached his beak to the corner of hers, and she flinched, because either he was going to strike her or to kiss her. He did neither. He picked the insect's leg, then spat it to the wind, and then she was flustered, truly.

"Snacks," she mumbled, "sir." How ugly she must look.

"Look at you!" he cried. "One Hen as skinny as pinch—but I never saw it before. Oh, Chalcedony, can you forgive me?"

That was a frightening switch. No, Chalcedony didn't know about forgiving. She knew about weeping. Now she just wanted to weep and to disappear.

"Are you angry?" she whispered.

"You shouldn't be so skinny," cried the Rooster.

"I'm working on a cure," she whispered.

"You?" he barked. "You?" roared Chauntecleer. His voice battered her, and the sobs rose up of their own accord, so then she was crying after all. "No, *not* you," thundered Chauntecleer. "Me! I'm the one responsible! I should feed you. I should make you fat. Dear God in Heaven, one of my Hens is eating garbage."

Chalcedony couldn't think up excuses any more. She plain cried to be so wrong, wrong to have brought her snacks back home, wrong to be so selfish—

It was at this precise moment that John Wesley Weasel came running from the south, bellowing news in the night.

Chauntecleer groaned, *"Nobody* sleeps any more."

Chalcedony just lay down, trying to make a privacy of her tears.

"Is troubles southward," shouted the Weasel, bounding through dead leaves and fetching up in the Rooster's face. "Troubles, you bet, and might-be the Rooster, he doesn't wait till daybreakings to do somethings about it." The one-eared Weasel was grinning. He positively delighted in bearing bad news, because crises put him at the center of excitement, and centers were fine places in which to strut. "By-cause, if furry buggars sees this, might-be they passes out, what not, at the frightfulnesses. Hello, Chicky," he grinned at Chalcedony, and she shrank.

"Don't you sleep?" hissed Chauntecleer.

"Rooster, he roams about; John, *he* roams about," John said proudly. "Each to each and same as t'other."

Chauntecleer closed his eyes, then opened them again, preparing for still another word of his criminal neglect. "What, John," he whispered, "is the trouble in the south?"

"Fox-face," announced the Weasel. He winked at Chalcedony, verifying terror. Chauntecleer stiffened. "Ooo, Fox-face ghouling on the plain," hooted John Wesley.

Chauntecleer was suffering. "I do not," he whispered, "understand you, John. *What* is the trouble?"

"Why, is Fox-face. Is Russel-bones come back again," said John. "Grave couldn't keep a Fox down when the ice pops— and whoops! Threw him bones back up again—"

All at once it seemed as though Lord Chauntecleer doubled in size. His feathers stood from his body, and a vicious hissing erupted his beak. He threw out his wings and leapt into the air. He beat them savagely, rising to the shrieking wind, and then himself tore south in the streaming and gone.

"Chicky," said the Weasel to Chalcedony, "gots to go, John does. A Rooster needs a good somebody by him side. Because who's not ascared to look at death? Why, John!"

One Creature was cheerful in that winter's night: just look at the effect he had on Chauntecleer. Grand! One ran south excited.

The other lay alone, waiting until she was truly alone. Then she arose and pushed her insect parts together in a tidy pile. Chalcedony was ever neat. She scratched a little hole in the earth and swept the whole pile into it.

"No more snacks for my Lady, no," she whispered. "She's got her whimsies, doesn't she? Why mayn't my Lady say no when she wants to—and still remain a Lady?"

But she hung her head at the roost and said, "No Lady never ate garbage, no. Chalcedony's no Lady."

Eighteen

The Night's Fourth Watch— Confession

John Wesley was a totally different Weasel when he rushed back to the Hemlock just short of an hour later. He'd lost cheer. His brains were all full of the thing he had seen, and it took him a while to focus on Pertelote, yet he'd come to warn her, to get her, something. He kept yanking at his single ear.

"Lady Hen?"

"John Wesley, is that you?"

"Lady Hen?"

"John! Speak up—I can't hear you in the wind!"

"Miss Pertelote?"

Pertelote sank from her branch and found the Weasel somehow stalled at a distance from the tree. He stood watching her come, his head tipped sideways as though they were both troubled by the same question, though she didn't know the question. He looked with a certain hunger into her eyes, yet she had the odd sensation of sightlessness in *his* eyes. He was gazing inward at a memory.

"John," she said. "What's the matter?"

"Lady Hen?"

"Yes. It's me." The wind howled around them, so she put her head quite close to his.

Finally his eyes came to focus, and then concern spread all over his face. "Is a Rooster!" he confided to her. "Rooster's crazy, John thinks. Lady! Rooster's brains is buggared!"

"Chauntecleer?"

"Him. The Rooster."

"You've seen him."

"But he didn't see John, no. John, he's a ghost to the Rooster, oh."

Pertelote's heart bulked inside of her. "Please, John: where is he? What's he doing?"

"To the Fox's grave, Lady—"

"Why?"

"By-cause John, he sent him—"

"Why, John?"

"By-cause him Fox-bones come up on the ground, and John, he seen—"

"John! Why is Chauntecleer there? What is he doing, that troubles you? John! Look at me! What's wrong with Chauntecleer?"

"Oh, well. Oh, well. Rooster—he's pecking on corpses, now. What should somebodies think? John, he don't know: Rooster's fighting the Fox-bones now."

Pertelote put her claw on the Weasel's shoulders, startling him. Straight into his eye she said, "You'll stay with the Hens, then, won't you, John."

"Lady Hen, she goes to the Rooster?"

"Yes."

"Good!"

In an instant, each trusted the other's capacity—"Good!"— so that a little assurance entered this blithering night, and they parted, John Wesley Protector, the yearning Pertelote the Healer.

A high wind is hard to fly in. Darkness makes it worse. Worst of all, the woman was distracted, her mind repeating a foolish refrain: "He didn't say dead, he didn't say dead," and her stomach clutching at the fear of what her husband might be, if not dead—but "dead" was the greatest horror, and he didn't say dead! John didn't say—

She flew into a grove of trees. Her wings hit twigs. Spider-webs lashed her eyes. A splintered limb gouged flesh from her earlobe, stunned her, and she tumbled into the ground. When she shook her head, the blood whipped forward to her face, and she tasted it. She did not fly again. She stood. She found her balance. And with her head thrust forward, her wingtips low to skim the ground, she ran.

There were patches of fog on the battle-plains, so that she saw the sea and then saw nothing at all—the sea in starlight, then a damp, chill, personal gloom. West she ran, a little lost: how far to Russel's grave?

WWWHUMP! went the breakers from Wyrmesmere, rolling toward her on the left, standing and bowing, collapsing a dreadful weight, then retreating with a hiss down the shingle. The streaking wind had raised up Wyrmesmere. The sea was awake: WWWHUMP!

Suddenly she heard ahead of her a sound like a siren, this in spite of the constant wind and the sea still pounding periods. The sound was urgent and distant, both; it was high and hateful, was dragged out infinitely long, and must have crossed the sea to its horizon. It might have been the wind, resolved into a living voice: *"Weir-weir-weir-weir—"*

Winter ice sank into Pertelote's soul. She shuddered with the cold and with recognition, and she went forward. It was not the wind. It was Chauntecleer, calling with all his might. It was the solitary Rooster, calling across the sea, *"Wyrm!"*

Not dead. He didn't say dead. But then what was he, if not dead? She ran forward.

The fog dissolved in front of her and a figure appeared on the plain, dark, bent, struggling. Pertelote opened her mouth to call, but she did not. Forms took shape in the starlight. She saw, and a horror silenced her.

The Rooster had clamped Russel's carcass at the neck, had locked his beak behind the skull, and by sudden jerks was yanking his brother seaward. The corpse did not complain. Black shadows sat in Russel's eyes, and in his mouth was a bottomless shadow; and Russel had a grin. His tail slid like a rope. His four legs turned under like straps. He was ghastly skinny. He was bones, Russel. Russel was bones.

WWWHUMP!

Nor did Chauntecleer stop at the sea. He took the slamming waves upon his back. Pertelote gasped. But the Rooster went into the icy waters and drew the Fox's body after him. These two rose in the foam. But the breakers overpowered them, swallowed and spat them like lumps of mucous.

"Oh, Chauntecleer," Pertelote breathed, afraid for him. "Chauntecleer!"

The bodies went under a sweeping water. Five beats of her heart, and miraculously they surfaced again, beyond the breakers. Pertelote's heart rose up. Chauntecleer had a driving will. Behold: he butted Russel before a steady swimming, and Russel rolled over and over, like a log. Two intrusions on the sea. They were two details on a wide immensity, star-flecked. Pertelote hardly knew what her husband was doing—but he was not crazy.

There came, finally, a mighty thrust from Chauntecleer and a separation: the Fox went nosing toward the deep. A Rooster stayed behind. But a voice went up from the waters: "I will remember you, Lord Russel!"

Pertelote's wing was at her mouth. All at once her heart broke for the lonely memorial in her husband's voice, all by himself giving honor unto the dead. He did the thing alone. He didn't know that someone was watching—

"The water's your grave, my brother!" he cried seaward, but Pertelote heard. "Your journey, endless; but that is the way it should be." But then he wailed such a lamentation that tears burst at Pertelote's eyes.

"How many have I loved like you, Lord Russel the Fox—"

Then he lost strength in the water, and the will went out of him. Rooster's can't swim! Roosters weren't made for swimming. He splashed in desultory fashion generally toward the shore, then the waves grabbed him like a rag and twisted the poor Cock over and under; they lifted him, pitched him into the shallows and overran him with a traveling spume—and he didn't fight them. Pertelote ran to the beach. She waded as far as she could. Then his body rode forward on a surge, and before it sucked him back again, she seized his tailfeathers in her claw and rooted herself to the earth. Then it was Pertelote who dragged him again to dry ground. His head lolled to the left.

"Oh, Chauntecleer," she whispered. "Oh, please, *Chauntecleer!*"

He didn't say dead. He didn't say dead, O Lord!

The Rooster groaned, out of a mortal exhaustion. She felt a rush of gratitude so deep that it felt like laughter. He sighed, "I had to do one thing right," and then he lay still, pasted thin with wet feathers.

WWWHUMP!

Pertelote made towels of her wings and chafed the poor Cock's body to make the blood run. "It's me," she whispered. "It's me, Chauntecleer. I'm with you now." Whether it was the cold, or the weariness, or her presence, she did not know; he began to shiver violently, and she cried for him. "Oh, Chauntecleer! Oh, my suffering Chauntecleer," she wept. And then she could do nothing but hold him, tight, tight to her breast, fighting the shivers for him. "Chauntecleer—"

She rocked her husband. He hadn't fought the sea; he didn't fight her either. He was a chick beneath her wings. The wind: now, finally, the wind relaxed and coiled in the wood north of them, sighing merely; and the sky lightened to a cold, cold grey; and she closed her eyes, in order to see nothing.

She rocked the victim till her back ached. And deep in her throat she sang a husky lullaby:

> "—the summer's summer, long gone by,
> The evening when my Lord and I
>   Were young:

> He took my tears on faith, and I
> Would stroke his neck, and I would sigh
>   This song—"

"Pertelote," said Chauntecleer, a baby's voice beneath her.

"What?" she said.

He paused, then he whispered, terribly tired, terribly wretched, "Go away."

Pertelote's first reaction was panic. She stopped rocking and singing together. But her second reaction was so swift that it was done before she thought of it. She said absolutely, "No." And she held him the tighter.

"Please," he whined. "Oh, Pertelote, you're killing me."

The Hen put her head up with stiff dignity, though she kept her eyes closed and she released him not a whit. "No, I am loving you," she said.

He sagged. "You are loving me," he said. "It is your love that hurts so much, so much, so much, sweet Pertelote."

"I don't," she said. Oh, he was a mere bruise in her embrace. And he was such a mystery, surrounded by his private phantoms. She hated his phantoms. "I do not understand this," she said.

"Tonight the poor Tags loved me, and I could hardly stand it," he whispered slowly, "because I don't deserve their loving. It's a lie. And now, you. God help me, Pertelote, I don't deserve—"

She broke in with singing. Her head held high, her mind in flat denial of his talk, she sang the lullaby with rather more brass than before, a verse that damned this weakness with strength from the past. She sang:

> "He peeled a straw, a summer's thistle,
> Blew on it, and made it whistle
>   Dreams.
> And who was I to say he couldn't
> Build a world secure with wooden
>   Beams?—"

"Pertelote, don't!" the Rooster wailed, his shivering uncontrollable.

She looked at him. In the dirty light his face showed agony. "You are special among us, Chauntecleer," she declared. "You have always been. We look to you—"

"*Ahhh!*" he choked. His own eyes remained closed, compressed in pain. "Don't praise me. Don't love me. Don't remember the past, oh, Pertelote! I am not worthy of it now—"

"Not love you?" keened Pertelote. "I cannot love you? Chauntecleer, what are you doing to *me?*"

He thrashed his head from the left to the right. "Chalcedony!" he wailed. "That Hen is a miserable stick, suffering my own neglect. I know my sin. Who's fault is it if Chalcedony dies?"

"She won't die!" said Pertelote.

"No thanks to me."

"Chauntecleer! Do life and death depend on you?"

"They do. They do."

"Oh, Chauntecleer, what kind of a pride is this?" Pertelote was fighting for her own possessions. "These are unreasonable burdens, impossible to bear—life and death."

"I couldn't save Russel," he cried.

"So?"

"I lost him. And then I couldn't even honor him with a decent burial—"

"So?" she cried louder than he. "We *all* tried to save him. We, none of us, have to carry the guilt. Russel talked. What could we do about his talk? It was in his character to talk—"

WWWHUMP! went the sea.

"Shut up!" screamed Pertelote at the sea.

And Chauntecleer shrieked as he tore himself away from her, "It's Mundo Cani Dog!" He stood shivering on his own claws, glaring at her in the filthy dawn. "It's Mundo Cani that condemns me, Mundo Cani I can't clean from my mind, not from my memory, not from my soul— Stop it, Pertelote! Don't touch me any more!" She had reached for him. *"I know what I am!"* he wailed.

Pertelote felt as though the ground moved beneath them, a quake beyond her comprehension. She saw the dark earthwork behind him, a huge hump and a dead memory; she noted that the wind was gone; all in one electric instant, never thereafter forgotten, she saw the sea, the wood, and Chauntecleer between—his eye a bright red rivet.

"Wyrm had split the earth," hissed Chauntecleer, "and we looked down, and there we saw him, and I was Lord of this land, but what did I say?"

"Chaun—"

"I said, 'Why not?' I said, 'Why not'! I stood transfixed before that horror—Pertelote, don't lie! I stood still before the monster, and I said, 'Why not?' I gave up. I surrendered my soul and all the souls of the Animals to death with apostasy and the pitiful whimper, 'Why not?' There was a hole in the earth?" Chauntecleer drove his beak into his gut, and he cried: *"There was a hole in me!"* His eye rolled. "Then who came? Mundo Cani came. Mundo Cani bounded to the chasm. Mundo Cani taunted Wyrm. He turned Wyrm's eye—and here is the vile truth: all the while I hated him! Pertelote, do you hear this? Can you believe it? This is the truth—I despised the Dog. But *he* is the one who leaped headlong into the pit, down and down where I refused to go, down to the eye of the Serpent. And *he* is the one that stabbed it, *he* that spurted eye-jelly over himself, *he* that roused the monster to such violence that Wyrm smashed rock and closed them both inside, both inside, both— He sold himself, that Dog! He saved the Animals alive. And me. He saved my life." The Rooster threw back his head and cried like a siren: *"I loathe the life he saved—"*

The sea toppled a mountainous wave: WWWHUMP-AH!

And Chauntecleer cut his cry in half and struggled to be still.

Pertelote withdrew into a little ball, watching the Rooster

through a screen of grief. Now she knew the cause. And the name. And who consumed him within.

Chauntecleer dropped his eye like a flag descending. It was morning.

He whispered, his throat thick: "Mundo Cani's fall was my wrong and my responsibility." He whispered like little leaves scratching stone: "I wish I could . . . do something. *Do* something. Go down to hell and say to the Dog, 'I'm sorry,' and bring him home again. Some recompense," rasped Chauntecleer. "Oh, I would die to purge myself. Dead, I could receive your love." There was a dreary grin, then the frown of an honest proposition: "Or if the Dog were here—Lord, I could be loved again. Pertelote," he pleaded. "Do you know how much I want to be worthy of your love?"

WWWHUMP! The sea beat its forehead on the shore.

Pertelote nodded. She shook her head.

All at once he put his face near the side of hers and brushed her earlobe with primary feathers. "Blood?" he asked gently.

She nodded.

"You cut yourself coming here."

She nodded.

"See?" he whispered. "Do you see what I do? I hurt Creatures." He gazed at her. "Pertelote, you are God's kindest thought. He put wings on the meditation he didn't want to lose, and a bright red marker at her throat, and he called her Pertelote. Why ever should such loveliness love me?"

Somehow, these last words were for Pertelote more terrible than any others; now, finally, she began to cry. She bent her head to hide it. But her shoulders shook with the sobbing. He could love so well—but she couldn't? Ah, mighty God! What had they come to?

"See? See? See?" he murmured. "Tears. Well," he sighed, resigned. "Well," as though something had been relieved after all, and something accepted: "I don't have to lay my whole lordship aside. There are two things I can do. I can crow Lauds. I can feed Chalcedony." Bleak, the future. "I'll do those—" he said. And then she did not see, but she felt, that he departed.

Enormous weariness takes up space and can be felt—here, and gone. He had fought the sea itself that night, and he thought such defiance—such love for a carrion Fox—worth nothing at all! She felt that weariness. He had wrestled his phantoms until the breaking of the day, and though he may not have prevailed against them, yet he had named their names, a monstrous accomplishment. Pertelote felt that weariness. So she felt it also when he gathered them together and bore them away, leaving her to emptiness.

Oh, heaven, go with Chauntecleer!

Pertelote lifted her eyes and looked into the emptiness. She saw the wall, the earthwork. Once the golden Rooster had engineered that bulwark to protect a thousand Animals against the Enemy. When it was round, so long ago, the Coop had stood in the center of it; and they had slept inside the Coop. Pertelote remembered those good nights inside the Coop—long, long ago. And now she sang:

> "—made love to me so slow and sweetly,
> Sighing names, he came discreetly
>   Home;
> And I to him gave children after;
> I it was had cried through laughter,
>   'Come'—"

The sea snagged at the shore. It raised a wave, like the hood and tooth of a cobra, and struck: WWW-*WHUMP*-AHHHHHH!

Pertelote had never felt so lonely.

Here ends the second part of the book that chronicles descents.

PART THREE
WHATEVER THING DEATH
BE—

Nineteen
Hello, Benoni

Rachel Coyote stood at the door of the Den on a small plateau. She lifted her head; she drew a smile around her narrow snout; and she listened.

Rachel could hear with her heart. With her heart she heard her husband skitter across the plains above, and with her heart she heard him sneak into the forest. Ah, Ferric. He might be quiet as a cloud upon his paws, but his nerves made a crackling static, and his fears fairly shrieked. Daily he went to the forest, now; and though he never told her why, she understood the secrecy: he was protecting her from the world. Dear, dear Ferric.

One day he would laugh.

Dainty Rachel, red Coyote, she lowered her head and stepped into the south-running stream. Purposefully she waded down the canyon, turning where the canyon turned. She had her daily secret, too.

A dry shelf ran along the water to her left. If she were fussy she could walk it, but she was near term, now, and rather liked to float her swollen belly in the water, cooling the sensitized nipples.

Icicles hung from the sheer canyon walls on either side of her, the water that leeched down through the rock and had frozen drip by drip. These icicles grinned, like rows of teeth, fangs; elsewhere they drooped like tightly grizzled beards; farther down the gorge they stood columnar, from the foot to the rim of the cliff. Ice, ice from the world above. Well, it was winter. No one expected respite from winter in this northern climate. The days were little and cold and grey; but Rachel didn't complain because here was a blessing: a canyon stream that kept forever the same temperature, breathing steam into the wintry atmosphere.

Rachel proceeded through a cathedral-grandeur, ice pillars rising on the left and on the right of her, her step made slow by the kindly water, which sometimes she paused to lap. Holy clouds surrounded her. Soon she fell into a contemplative mood. She held her head all to one side and smiled and seemed a sacred thing.

The babies were moving.

This was one reason for her secrecy these days and for her regular walks away from Ferric. The babies moved often, now, and often with surprising pain. In Ferric's presence she bore the trouble silently, since any hurt in her distressed the poor Coyote past sense. There was no good in Ferric's knowing that infants trouble the womb. On the other hand, Rachel had a thrilling need to declare that pain, to consider as best she could, to feel, to *know* every last detail of this exquisite experience, this carrying life, this bearing of babies. Such knowing meant dropping into sudden silences—without a husband's asking why; or weeping, without that husband's falling into a panic. Moreover, such knowing sometimes urged sweet Rachel truly to cry out, to give voice to the pain, to *hear* it in her own ears, straightway to laugh and say, "That's it! I understand!" How could Ferric handle that kind of behavior?

Or how could he ever comprehend that Rachel took pleasure in the hurt, in the hurt itself; that these tears were dear to her?

Or this, the wonderful thing now dawning on the woman: that suffering is a holy work and graceful indeed?

Let Ferric protect her, dashing bravely through the dangerous world; in her way she protected him from knowledge too wonderful for minds of the matters of fact. Even so did she love her husband and her children at once, though the loves were different one from the other.

The babies were moving, and they were very big. Ahhh!

But how can one keep secret forever her marvelous revelations? Finally she needs to tell them, doesn't she? To share them, explain them in the ears of an other—to validate them, for heaven's sake! To hear one other soul agree: "That's it! I understand it, too!" And then to smile together because "It is so good!" It is so valuable. It makes a life worthwhile—

Well, that was the second reason for Rachel's regular trip downstream: such a someone else awaited her at the deep end of the canyon. A plain brown Bird with an extraordinary length of bill and damaged wings had accepted Rachel's friendship and had given friendship in return. Unto this Bird she told her revelations. And what did the Bird do then? She hopped to the coat of the Coyote. She picked parasites from the roots of the fur and rubbed oils to the surface and glossed it; by strong claws she combed the coat of the woman: she groomed dear Rachel unto a shining beauty. She did this patiently and well, who was herself no pretty thing. But this was the way that she talked. This is how she said of motherhood, *I understand it,* and *It is very good.* For she had no tongue in her head and all her words besides were "Jug, jug" and "Tereu."

She did communicate, that plain brown Bird, both eloquently and selflessly; and Rachel tingled all over her flesh with the message. They had become fast friends. Two women bound together, each by a wound in her body, though one's was peculiar to her and one's was the genius of her gender: suffering may be—aye, suffering could possibly be—a holy work, and graceful.

So the babies were moving. So the mother floated down to her companion, this day too, to take the benediction of a friendly presence.

And so it was that she barked a raw bark while gazing at the plain brown Bird. The Bird was still in her bush, still perched in the wiry tangle that hid Wyrm's portal, the flue that went down to the Netherworld, the hole that blew one everlasting note as through an organ pipe. The Bird had just lifted a crippled wing in greeting when Rachel surprised herself with a bark she'd not expected. She woofed. Her eyes looked fleetingly shocked. Then suddenly she hunched her spine, threw up her head, and howled, long and painfully—

What Ferric hadn't told Rachel was that the White Wolf Boreas roamed the forest. And what Ferric was doing, daily, was watching the Wolf.

He had no notion ever to fight Boreas, huge at the shoulder. His notion, in fact, had been to flee. Oh, he'd have surrendered a hundred square miles at a pinch and gladly—if Rachel had not found her "home." But she had, and he loved her. So his alternatives were reduced to one, a canny, nerve-wracking observation of the enemy. It was some small advantage, to know and not to be known.

But it took all the courage that a poor, skulking Coyote could muster just to approach the Wolf and to watch him.

Boreas moved with a slope-shouldered power, his nose near the ground, his white eyes shifting, his muscles taut to the hip, his paw so monstrous that four of Ferric's could collect into a single print. Boreas moved in casual possession of the whole world round, whereas Ferric was the alien, anywhere he was. Boreas slung his tail low: contempt! Ferric stiffened his tail straight out behind him: tense. Boreas ambled. Ferric Coyote darted thither and yon, ever to keep downwind of the Wolf and upcountry if he could. This is what one knew and the other did not know; but he who didn't, didn't care; and he who did, died with perpetual fright.

So went the vigil—until this particular day, when Ferric's anxieties doubled with a new discovery. Oh, it was a miserable advantage after all, to know and not to be known.

Ferric saw his Wolf in the dead center of a clearing, while he himself lay low between roots. The Wolf stood still, listening, twisting his ears in various directions. He was a stark white Creature, unhurried and majestic. Slowly he lifted his massive head and woofed twice, twice tightening his stomach. He listened again, and then both of them heard a snarling answer: a smug, malevolent voice.

The White Wolf waited. The Coyote shrank between his roots.

First in black flashes amid the pine, and then whole from his nose to his tail, a second Wolf appeared, coal-black, a blood-red eye, lesser in size than Boreas, but longer in the tooth and the teeth were yellow.

This one presented himself in the clearing before Boreas and grinned. "Notos," growled the White Wolf, and they met.

The Wolves were gathering!

Ferric's mind spun with the implications: expect a pack! When food was scarce, Wolves drew into packs. This stingy winter encased every edible thing in ice so that no one could scratch a decent meal. Expect a pack! And then whose den would they be seeking, and whose wife was too fat to run, and who couldn't fight to save her anyway? Oh, yes—expect the marauding pack! The White Wolf and the black one met, and Ferric saw nothing but a gruesome future in front of him—and a pack!

His loins contracted. He nearly urinated—

And then it was that not his ears, but his heart heard a horror. *What, Rachel, what?* he cried silently. *Why are you howling?* The world was too full of trouble.

Wait! he cried in his soul. *I will be with you!*

And Ferric, like a twitching shadow, was gone from the forest.

Down the stones flew Ferric, hardly touching them. At bottom he cut left, scrambling the turn—and he dived into the Den.

Rachel was there. Oh, yes; oh, yes, the woman had been howling. Oh, yes, poor Rachel was in pain. Ferric fixed an instant in the doorway, his mouth both open and wordless. She lay on her side, her four legs thrust out as stiff as death, her toes splayed, her fur soiled from writhing around the floor, her fur damp, her lungs pumping, all of her teeth laid bare and grinding, her eyes compressed.

This was Rachel, the woman of contentments! What?—

This was his gentle wife twisted on the floor. How?—

"Rachel!" he barked, as hoarse as a bullfrog. "Rachel?" At the sound of his own voice he took to dancing, did Ferric, nervously from foot to foot.

And Rachel herself? At the sound of Ferric's voice she expelled a long stream of sour breath. She relaxed her legs and allowed her eyes to open. They rolled until they found him; and then she smiled; and then she began to laugh. Gentle laughter, like a little brook down pebbles. A gurgling, really; a happy succession of chuckles; but laughter nonetheless, over which she closed her eyes again.

Ferric was angry. *"Tsst!"* he said as some sort of warning. He felt compelled to make a warning. This wasn't right.

Rachel only laughed more helplessly.

He said, "You're laughing!" It was an accusation.

She nodded. He spoke the truth.

He said, "But you're hurting, Rachel!"

She nodded.

"Well!" squeaked Ferric, suffering for her, furious with her, both at once: "Well! No! You shouldn't be laughing when you hurt. You can't laugh!" Against the rules.

But she could. She did. Until warm tears washed her eyelids, Rachel laughed.

Ferric nearly exploded. "What's the matter?" he pleaded of her.

She shook her head. There was a sigh and a lull in her laughing, but no words.

Into her more sober attitude Ferric spoke a sincere opinion: "Rachel," he said, "I think you have gone crazy—"

To which she opened her mouth. Ferric expected a yowl out of it; but a little string broke in her breast, and a brighter, more wonderful laughter than ever poured out.

Then Ferric was beside himself, stomping the ground with

both forepaws together. "Stop it! Stop it!" the poor Coyote wailed, so confused. "I think," he decided. "I think," he tried to explain this conundrum. "I think that you are laughing at me, Rachel!"

Well, he really did, finally, think that—since he surely didn't understand her condition, but she seemed to, and therefore he was the dummy.

That was the cry that arrested the woman. She fell into an honest silence. She gazed at Ferric from lying sideways on the ground. All of her, every limb of her, went limp with weariness. She whispered, "Ferric, I'm happy. And I love you. So I share my happiness with you. You called my name, and there you were, and all my happiness ran out to meet you. Ferric, that's how my happiness comes out: I laugh."

"Oh," said Ferric—fool. She wasn't crazy now, no. So he was just a fool. Because she must be right, but he still didn't understand. "Rachel," he whispered.

"What?" as soft as ashes.

"You stink, Rachel, like sickness."

She nodded, and he was empowered to go on.

"You're a mess, and I smell blood in here, and I can feel your hurting, Rachel, all the way down my back, and I can hear your hurting, Rachel, in all of the air around us, like ticking, like terrible time, but you say you're happy, and I believe you, but I just don't understand. How can you be happy? What's the matter?"

Ferric was trying to be so reasonable.

Rachel looked at him with a nearly unutterable love. "Nothing at all is the matter," she whispered. "I'm having the babies, now—"

Ferric's ears shot up; his brow, and his eyelids, and his lip all lifted.

"—which is hard work and hurtful work, but some of the happiest work in the world. See?"

He shook his head. He nodded, expressionless, his snout a cucumber.

Babies! His heart began to bang all over in his chest. Babies.

He said, "That's fine, Rachel." Formal Ferric Coyote.

She smiled. "It truly is," she said. "Now, don't feel bad, Ferric, and please don't think that I don't like you," she whispered. "But you should go away, now. I'll do what I have to do alone. You'd feel worse to stay here."

He nodded total agreement with her assessment. But he stayed put, staring down at her: babies.

Rachel's breath came more rapidly, now. Her great belly began to heave. But she kept her voice a gentle whisper: "Ferric, go. Please. Run to the end of the canyon; that's something you can do for me. Tell my friend my happiness. Go. Now. Please."

He nodded. He didn't move. Babies!

Suddenly Rachel sucked a tremendous lot of air, snapped her jaw shut on it, ground her teeth and began to force the air out again through a tight, exquisite pain: *"Eeeeeeeeee!"* Her tail hooked up behind her. Her body doubled round, focusing all its strength upon the vortex deep within her abdomen—

But Ferric was gone on the first point of that scream, as though it had jabbed him in the rear.

Zoom! Coyote-blur between the canyon walls! Earnest Coyote, desperate to do some job! He ran with inspiring skill the narrow ledge that banked the stream, his nose straight forward, his tail straight back, leaning into the turns but never missing a footfall, gone, gone, good Ferric Coyote!

As he closed on the southern end of the canyon, where the walls widened into a gloomy yard, nervous thrashings began in a bush, there. A Bird. Long bill, broken wings; Rachel's friend. Okay. He aimed himself toward that bush and that Bird.

His coming seemed to madden the Bird. She switched the air with her bill, crying, "Jug!" a negative. Ferric slowed his step. "Jug, jug!" she chattered at him. He didn't understand. He was a most confused Coyote.

But his run took him straight to that bush; to that bush he went. And though the brown Bird leaped down to his withers, from which she stabbed him in the back of the skull, causing stars of bright pain; and though she yanked backward on his ears, as if to rein him to a stop, that Coyote roared to her at the top of his lungs: "RACHEL IS VERY HAPPY RIGHT NOW!" And: "She told me to tell you that."

Ferric lay before a wiry bush with a Bird on top of his head. Waiting. At the right time he was going to go back to Rachel.

For the moment, he simply could not sort the crowd that populated his brains. Wolves prowling the winter and the territory near their den, Boreas of perfect power, Notos of a sidewinding malice, the white eyes and the red together—and this was only today that he'd glimpsed the gathering.

And Rachel tells him that she's doing a good and happy thing, but it stinks exactly like battle-guts and running blood, and he's a fool, she's smiling.

And when he goes to give good news to a friend, she tries to peck his little intellect to death—then suddenly settles down to nest between his ears: all is forgiven. *What* is forgiven? What did he do?

Wolves: potential attack.

Rachel: attacked, but happily. But even now he felt her writhing.

This Bird, presently picking parasites from his earholes: *did* attack. But she was the only one named as a friend.

Poor Ferric. So small in the universe, so skinny and incapable, confused almost to tears, surrounded by countless dangers—

And having babies.

Having babies seemed to blow his little scrap of life into a thousand fragments. Having babies seemed a terrifying multiplication. Ferric wasn't sure how he'd survive the crisis.

And why was a Bird on his head?

The Bird, for her part, was trying with all her might to apologize. She truly, truly wanted to guard the hole to hell and to protect any other living Creature from the ruinous evil that had engulfed her there. When this bullet of a Coyote came racing toward her, therefore, she could think of nothing but stopping him by any means. So she rode him like a mount and punctured his skullcap, almost drilled him to the brain, which for her would have been unendurable, to sin the same sin twice. She'd forgotten—as the obsessed most often do forget —that one's obsession isn't everyone's. This Coyote didn't even know of the dire portal behind her. He had other reasons for coming, kindly ones, despite his furious aspect.

When he bellowed greetings from her friend, then, she was overwhelmed by her error, and she fell to wiping all the little hurts from off his head. She dearly wished that she had a tongue, to explain. But she hadn't. Oh, like a maiden aunty, then, she fussed all over his scalp, stroking, picking, combing, scratching, curling his hairs, and killing his fleas. And he lay down and allowed it, and she took that for a sign of forgiveness and was glad. She did: she nested between his ears and finally counted this a glorious day, because she had *two* friends.

In its own good time it came to an end.

Gloom rose early in the canyon bottoms, and the evening cold came down like fog. Only a strip of sullen sky could be seen above, and those below quickly became ghosts to one another. The Coyote sat up. The Bird took her leave, hopping again to her habitual bush.

"Jug," she said.

"I think so," said the Coyote. And he said, "Goodbye."

And she: "Tereu."

Oh, it was a rare gift, to have two friends. She watched the skinny, bemused Coyote creep nervously to his destiny. She wanted to comfort him, saying, *It's a good thing, having babies.* But she had no tongue.

Ferric lifted his paw and scratched the stone outside their Den.

There was motion inside, and a very weak voice said, "Come in, Ferric."

He swallowed. And he went in.

Rachel barely visible, Rachel nickered at his entrance in. She was lying on her side, so holy that he drew back, guilty of dust and sin and all the foolery he had performed before. Did he have the right to be here? But quick-eyed Rachel, seeing him grow slack, said, "Ferric, sit."

He sat.

All was still. What a consecrated room their Den had become! He put his forepaws together and was uncomfortable.

Rachel chuckled. He saw the white teeth flash. And then she nudged a damp bunch of something in his direction, using her snout like a spoon. She was so tired.

The thing said, "Pweeeee."

She whispered, "Benoni."

And Ferric, squinting downward, said, "Oh," without the least idea what a Benoni was.

"This is your son, Ferric," she whispered.

"Oh?" he said. A sort of panting began at his stomach, traveling upward.

"Your son," she said. "Benoni, the oldest Coyote."

Then the knowledge flooded him, his throat and his mind together: No, but this is your son! Ferric wailed, *"Oh!"* He stared at the wriggling lump, absolutely struck dumb to be presented with such a thing as a Benoni.

The thing said, "Pweeeee!" And Ferric Coyote burst into tears.

Well, Benoni! You have a face! And a snarling little snout in it! And tiny legs with tiny paws, and pads and nails and all! Oh, Benoni, Benoni!

Ferric lowered his head and licked the Critter with an instant, ineffable love, blubbering all the while exactly like the fool he wasn't going to be again.

Rachel laughed in a tired, pure delight. One after the other, she pushed daughters toward him. Twill was the name of one, and of the other, Hopsacking.

He licked them, all three, tasting Rachel but gazing steadfastly at the wonders underneath his chin. How do you make life, Rachel? How do you do that?

It was a holy room, a holy night, a remarkable woman beside him.

Hoarsely he whispered, "Can they think, do you suppose?"

Rachel chuckled at the question.

"But they're a helpless mess of pottage, Rachel, and there are Wolves—" He bit his lip. He felt the frigid world behind, saw babies before, felt suddenly weak between—and choked. "I mean—" he said.

"Ferric, who do they have for a teacher?" said Rachel.

Well, there was a problem.

"And have you forgotten," she whispered, "how much God loves the little? Besides," she stretched herself out, revealing her belly, "these pups of yours are very shrewd."

She made a clicking sound in her mouth—and then it was that Rachel was granted her dearest wish, that Ferric Coyote should laugh.

For as soon as she clicked, the puppies scuttled toward her. Now, it had taken Ferric the better portion of his life to figure out what nipples were for; but these three knew instantly: they popped those things into their mouths and settled to sucking with loud smacks and flips of their tails.

Ferric's ears shot up.

"Oh, ho-ho, canny!" he roared. At the end of this tumultuous day, the father plain lost his reserve. He switched from tears to laughter at the perfect instincts of his children. He laughed. He laughed while Rachel sighed. And he bellowed, "Canny, canny Coyotes three!" Because, who had smarter pups than he?

With wonderful speed Benoni and Twill and Hopsacking grew.

They sprouted a bright red hair, flecked with rust. They developed pugnacious snouts and little teeth, milk white and needle-sharp. They fought and tumbled and teased and giggled and chained the heart of their father; and they ate.

Weaned, they were brought to the Bird in her bush, who blessed them with "Jug, jug," and then "Tereu."

But weaned they needed a heavier food, and Ferric wasn't finding it, and that worried him more than he could say. It was a snowless winter, a dreary, ungenerous winter; the ice denied him even the bark of the trees, so that he dulled his teeth trying to strip it. But he was a father now, and the children trusted him, *him!* How could he be worthy of that trust if his daily trips grew miserable, his foraging more and more futile?

He himself could cease to eat, to be sure. But not the children. No, not the children; or else, what kind of father would he be?

Twenty

Curious Cobb

"Two things I can do," said Chauntecleer: "I can crow the Crows. I can feed Chalcedony. I'll do those—"

Pertinax Cobb the Ground Squirrel hadn't minded when Hens and some Mice and a certain Weasel of immoderate length had collected at the Hemlock tree across the Liverbrook—and Chicks of a noxious peep. He stood erect at the porch of his own tunnels, and watched the bustle, and he didn't mind.

Neither did Pertinax mind frightfully when it became evident that they meant to *stay* in the neighborhood, troubling the morning with a babel of clucks (and he stood erect to watch them), busifying the day by perpetual peckings at the ground, scratchings, wanderings abroad (and he scrambled down his side of the stream, then stood up to watch them), disturbing the early night with gossip. So sure was he of his not-minding, in fact, that he freely, nay, fearlessly put the question to his wife:

Pertinax ran down his tunnels to the master chamber where another Ground Squirrel like himself was weaving matting for the winter.

"Mrs. Cobb," said Pertinax, keeping his voice as innocent as a baby's. "Mrs. Cobb, you decide: Am I complaining?"

"No, Mr. Cobb, you're not complaining," said Mrs. Cobb.

"Right!" he said, and straightway he ran to resume his position, perfectly upright at his porch, confident, now, that he was indeed not minding, and putting a rather more severe twitch, therefore, to his whiskers.

Pertinax Cobb hadn't minded the golden Rooster either, nor the metronomic regularity of his crowing, because the Bird was beautiful, of a beautiful song, and Cobb fancied himself something of an artist; besides, he valued schedules and self-discipline. He hadn't minded the jolting crow in the early mornings. He hadn't minded the midnight broodings (which necessitated that the Ground Squirrel pop up in moonlight, erect, to watch). He hadn't even minded (though this cost him much patience, not to mind it) that the Rooster never once took a neighborly glance across the stream, in neighborly fashion to greet the neighbor standing there, waiting—

What Pertinax Cobb *did* mind, however, was that at the cold beginning of the winter—when he had expected some relief, since Animals generally retired into a winter's seclusion, allowing other Animals their peace—the whole community began to act as if it were the spring! Boisterous noise! Furious activity! A royal racing about, and a totally untimely scavenging for food. Craziness! The neighborhood was in an uproar, and Pertinax was displeased.

"Mrs. Cobb! What are they *doing* over there?"

"I'm sure I don't know, Mr. Cobb."

"They're piling food! They're digging bins and storing food!"

"Do you think they are hungry?"

"Why," cried Cobb, "they're not eating a bite of it—" Up to the surface he shot. Closely he watched the Hennish rushing, scrutinizing every move, chattering the idiocy of their contratemps. And down he went again. "Nope! Not a bite," he declared.

"Well then," said Mrs. Cobb, "they mustn't be hungry."

"Do you hear that?" said Cobb, cocking an ear. "Do you hear him? He's the one, you know. He's gulled them poor Chickens into delusions. Why, it makes a body nervous to be living so close to such nonsense. Him and his crowing! Mrs. Cobb, tell me straight: do I have the right to complain."

"Well, it ain't natural," she said.

"And who can sleep?" he said.

"Mr. Cobb, you've every right to complain," she said.

"Right!" he said, and he took himself straight to the top of his burrow, where he complained in a mighty and chittering pet.

But nobody noticed—saving Mrs. Cobb, who loved him.

"Chalcedony!" crowed that golden Lord of the Hemlock— quite pointlessly, to Cobb's way of thinking. "Chalcedony will never go wanting again!"

But then an extraordinary thing happened in the environment, followed by a more extraordinary thing in Pertinax's nature, and the Ground Squirrel wasn't the same thereafter.

The Liverbrook froze solid, removing a natural barrier between the neighbors.

Upon finding that there was a hard path between the Rooster and himself, Cobb ceased chattering and grew intensely silent, wondering whether he'd made a nuisance of himself before, and was he remembered.

"Mrs. Cobb," he whispered, "I didn't complain too much, did I?"

"No, Mr. Cobb," she said. "You're the soul of discretion."

"Well, but did I complain at all?"

"No more than was righteous, Mr. Cobb."

"Some?" he asked in fear.

"None," she said with finality.

"Right."

That night he did not stand up on his porch, little Pertinax. He sat in a wad of fur meant to be innocuous, one tiny eye peeping over his own butt, still to watch, being a Squirrel of insatiable curiosities, but now as a lump, a tussock, a natural piece of terrain.

The Rooster, to his horror, did cross the bridge, too stealthy in the darkness to allow a Squirrel's escape, and stood three yards from him. Then the breathless Pertinax listened. First he heard the breathing of the large Bird. Next he heard the song of the midnight broodings—as soft as always, the Rooster sang; but this time Pertinax could understand the words. He listened with less belligerent ears. He listened in humility, being suddenly unprotected and feeling very small. He listened when the Rooster thought no one heard, so the soul was in his song. He listened, and this is what happened: Pertinax Cobb was moved.

It was an eerie flute the Rooster produced.

"Often I open my heart and speak my cares," sang the Rooster, "but there is none to hear them. When I name my memories, they rise before me like visions. My friends are there. But when I reach to touch the ones I love, they fade away, and one by one they pass into darkness, and I am left alone. Why shouldn't I be full of woe?"

Strange! Pertinax felt the night to be peopled, Animals coming and going on the strength of the Rooster's melody.

Even stranger: Pertinax felt sad.

"Why shouldn't I weep for the world?" the song went on so gently. But by some spell it didn't seem the Rooster's voice any more. In the black night another soul intruded, a mournful roll of music, a solitary wanderer with no community at all:

"Who lives as long as he should? Or if he does live long, who isn't haunted by the memories of those he lost? Death, death suffered either way. Alas, for the Pins, the children of my Lady. Alas, for the Widow, the mother of seven, and for the orphans she left behind—"

Pertinax knew nothing of these names. But they were real. They came of a grievous history ghosting the night, and he mourned them, knowing they were dead.

The voice of the singer darkened. He almost thought a great mammal lay beside him.

"Alas, for my Lord!" the song went on. "Where is he now, when I yearn some word from him? Oh, that he would smile once more. If only he would come and curse me one more time, come love me with his scoldings."

The voice faltered.

The Ground Squirrel had altogether forgotten himself. He listened. Deeply, hoarsely the lamentation swelled:

Oh, that he would crow one crow for me in sunlight! But he is gone from me, and who can find me in the darkness? Who can call me from the Netherworld? Not one. No one can come near me any more—

Marooned!

Pertinax gasped at the sorrow in that word.

And then a mystery, a drama occurred in the pitch-black night; for it seemed that two voices arose in dialogue, each an impossible distance from the other, but both of the same source and both calling out of the painful incompletion of their love:

Maroooooooned! Have you forgotten me?

"Forget you? How could I forget you, O my heart?"

Maroooooooned!

"Rest. Please rest, perturbed Spirit. Don't mourn so hopelessly!"

Maroooooooned!

"I can't stand it any more."

When will you come to take me home?

"When God! When God gives me the strength and the wisdom, Mundo Cani! When the mighty God will finally speak to me again. Oh, Mundo Cani. Oh! Oh!"

Then, silence. An interminable silence.

"Do you believe me?"

But, silence.

It was that silence, and the terrible desire of the Rooster left unanswered, that wrung poor Pertinax—and he made a noise. He sobbed.

Immediately the silence changed. It was merely the frozen night again. The Rooster took a quiet step in the Squirrel's direction, so that he was suddenly, keenly aware of himself, and he swallowed his sobbing.

But the Rooster said, "Hello."

Oh boy! Discovered! Look out now—Rooster-blows are next!

But the Rooster said, "You look sickly, little fellow. You shouldn't be sickly. No one should be. You would do me a great kindness," said the Rooster, as gentle as fleece and sincere, "if you'd come take some food with us tomorrow."

"Mrs. Cobb!" said Pertinax Cobb, "wake up!"

"What? What? Oh," said Mrs. Cobb. "Did you sleep well?"

"It's the night," he said. "Go back to sleep."

"Thank you. I will," she said.

"Mrs. Cobb," said Pertinax, "that Rooster is a saint! A blessed, generous, sensitive saint!"

"Do you think so?" she said.

"Mrs. Cobb, I do."

"Well then, he is a saint indeed," she said.

Twenty-one

Incidentally, Refuge

"Wake!" crowed Chauntecleer the Rooster.

An encounter in the night had expanded his vision violently. He'd forgotten how many of the meek there were in the world, and how many might starve in a winter of such scarcity. He meant, now, to feed them all.

"Wake! Wake!" the stentorian crow, made universal by a certain desperation: no, not a single Creature should starve. "Wake!" he blared beyond the scope of his little community. He stood in the top of the Hemlock like a snapping flag, like a flag that strains at the mast. He rang his command to the whole world round. This was urgent: he would suffer no malingering. Oh, how could he forget his duties to the farther multitudes, Squirrels as stunted as Chalcedony, their eyes glazed over with what? With want!

"Wake up wherever you are, and work!"

And the first to come on that first day, crossing the solid Liverbrook with happy conviction, were a Ground Squirrel and his wife, both as neat as Sunday morning in pin-striped coats. They sat up chittering, and then they went to work.

"Wake!" crowed the Rooster in the mornings thereafter. The alarm pealed abroad incessantly: "There's work to be done!"

And Creatures to do it, too.

They came.

Some of them remembered the Rooster's leadership during the summer's war. Some of them had only heard of it in stories now yellowed to legend. Some of them had always acknowledged his lordship, wondering in these latter months what had become of him, but instantly grateful to be obedient again, instantly forgiving him his recent lassitude. Some of them were simply roused by the power of his naked mandate: "Wake!"

They woke. And they came.

Chauntecleer is dreaming.

Is he ever not dreaming?

He dreams the lonely woman and her meaningless "Tereu." He dreams the chants of those invisible voices, stony, cold, and passionless as always in his dreams. And still he loathes them.

But now he dreams, too, a conversation in which he takes part, willfully and personally.

He says aloud, "I hate this dream."

The chanting, the music, and all of the sound ceases as though the director had frowned, or God withheld his breath.

Chauntecleer is at the still center of the universe, where nothing turns.

Then there speaks a voice of infinite consolation: "It is distressing, to be sure." And the voice asks, "Why? But perhaps you'll tell me why?"

"Monstrous!" cries the Cock. "You see me, Wyrm! Wyrm! I don't see you!"

"Oh, Galle, Galle, is that the problem?" The voice smiles at problems easily solved. "Then be at peace. We're on even ground after all. You see," the voice enjoys its own joke, "I can't see you either. No, I can't see you at all. In fact, there are precisely three reasons why I cannot see you. Do you wish to know them?"

For the moment Chauntecleer is reduced to pure hissing by the nearness of this sardonic voice.

"Of course you do," it persists. "First, there is no light, and who can see anything in absolute darkness? But second, even if there were, it would do me no good. No, not a bit of it. And why? I am blind. Utterly blind," laughs the voice as though this were a delightful turn of events. "Why, Galle, you yourself witnessed the wound that took my sight away. My last picture in all the world is of a Rooster gazing down on me, most brotherly, while that remarkable Dog drops like a bolt straight for my

*eye. Ha, ha! The Dog put out my light! But you were the last I looked
at. And I think I saw some sympathy in your face. Am I right?"*

Chauntecleer shrieks at the picture, not looking down on Wyrm any
more, but up to himself—shrieks as though lashed.

"I'm sorry," says the voice. "Is something wrong?"

"Where?" screams the savage Cock. "Where is Mundo Cani?"

The voice says, "Here."

Chauntecleer is caught short by the ease and the simplicity of the
answer. He staggers.

"What?"

"Here," says the voice. "He is with me. I thought you knew that."

With an unearthly intensity Lord Chauntecleer crowed
"Come" beneath the slate-grey skies. He thrust his will into
the winter slowth; and the Animals came.

Sparrows of jerky efficiency, bunted against the cold, were
whipped to work by that crowing, and Chickadees all over the
fields. Swallows swooped the sky.

The Jay of a nasty mouth, complaining and bullying,
couldn't avoid the mouth of that Rooster. He came.

Fat Partridges; the Red Squirrel, lean, leaping and self-
proclaiming, who had thought he'd stored enough for the
winter; Raccoons of the delicate hands; slow Moles with
mighty shovels on either side of their heads—all these Chauntecleer called to the mark, and all of them went to work. All
up and down the Liverbrook the land came alive. This Rooster
had authority and a crow like a lariat: leadership!

The Hens were no longer alone. The Brothers Mice positively laughed to be surrounded by such company. And the
bald winter seemed, in those days, to have become a holiday
after all.

They gathered food. They piled food. They made twelve
hills of food at least. It was a harvest, at the Cock's request—
though out of season as everyone knew; but Chauntecleer
defined his own seasons! They harvested food, and then they
hoarded it.

Seeds, wheat-seeds, weed-seeds, barleycorns and grain; berries both frozen aground and dried on the vine; beans podded and stripped; fruits softened by the beginning rot, the blasted crabapple, the woody pear, the vinegar pulp of fallen apples; hickory nuts, chestnuts, beechnuts, walnuts, acorns, gumballs spiky and unsavory, and the poor kernel of the syca-more; cabbage hearts, sour-dock, meat from collapsing gourds, the rinds of squashes, roots, bulbs, tubers, turnips, beets, herbs, the sweet fiber of young saplings—*food* in sur-prising variety. Who'd have thought so many things could be food? But why not? As many kinds as breeds to eat it! *Food* in abundance, mounded in fields, heaped against the Hemlock cliff, cast up along the Liverbrook and waiting the trench that would bury it. Food: and then they hoarded it.

Chauntecleer, who had inspired this general scavenging, each according to his own kind, now organized them all into a single kind: he administered a unity of purpose and a fine, effective division of labor. This food was for storage. This food was to be stocked for the future, not given to gluttony now. Therefore the Rooster took himself anywhere they might larder their harvest, and he oversaw the preparations person-ally. Open seams in the cliff face were acceptable, so long as they could be ventilated against rot. And some things ought best to be frozen. And some to be buried deep in the ground—

"Pertinax Cobb, here. I know holes!"

The digging Animals digged holes. Cobb had contempt for the journeyman work of the Mice. He tunneled great under-ground bins for storing foodstuffs in, rooms of a nearly echo-ing enormity, well-shored, and floored with pebbles and sticks to keep the food from the moister earth, to allow a healthy draft beneath: marvels of subterranean engineering.

"Pertinax Cobb, here. I know holes."

And his wife said, "Isn't he wonderful?"

But the Bluejay screeched at the hatch of the bin, "Move it or lose it!" And down came the rumble of food. Then up

popped Pertinax Cobb, chattering of the day when someone
would have taken time to admire a job well done; and besides,
Mrs. Cobb had a bruise on her nose.

The Jay flipped his tail and flew away for more food.

The Rooster crowed. The Rooster put order to their disord-
ers.

And the Animals wove themselves after all into a successful
labor force: what a good thing, to have purpose in this slack,
stupid winter! To have provisions for the scarcest of seasons.
To have done it selflessly and together. To have a Lord to lead
them in the endeavor! Did someone say that Chauntecleer
defined the seasons? No—Chauntecleer *was* the seasons. Winter wasn't even a flaw when Chauntecleer warmed and directed them, so well secured them against calamity. Chauntecleer, that golden Rooster: he was the summer's sun.

"Wake! And work!"

We have! We will! Ah, Chauntecleer, crow and crow and
crow forever.

"Ho, Rooster!" cried John Wesley Weasel.

Maybe no one was gladder these days than John Wesley
Weasel. Surely no one loved pageantry more than he, nor
laughed louder, nor beat paws together more vigorously than
John in the middle of bright busynesses. "Do and do and do!"
he shouted, slipping here and there between varmints straining at loads of food. It was John alone who had rallied the
Animal forces against the Basilisks, who had lost his ear to the
Cockatrice and taken a five-inch wound in his side—John of
the boundless energy.

"Haw, haw, haw! Hee, hee!" he roared his delight. "Ho,
Rooster!" he cried to the top of the ridge, where that golden
Lord was strutting, yea, at the very edge. He sat up and made
punching motions with his forepaws, winking furiously as if
there were some private pact between them two alone.

Well, this was the joy of the Weasel, to see that Rooster in
his glory once again. When Chauntecleer ruled as he should,

why then, the world was *right*. Chauntecleer had taught him
manners, once upon a time, and he, John Wesley, had learned.
Chauntecleer had been the single Creature tougher, scrap-
pier, louder, more boisterous than him; so he had learned.
And he was beholden to the one that had civilized him, by-
cause lesser should always take its place below the greater.
Loyalty! Weasels don't questions loyalty.

But when greater collapses into miserable little puddles,
then the whole world is confused, and lesser begins even to
question himself! Lesser gets lost.

There had been a period of turmoil for the Weasel, then,
when he suspected the sanity of Chauntecleer, for he himself
was spinning loose in the universe. "Gloominesses," he was
convinced, "blocks the brains. Thinkings makes gloominesses"—two afflictions John manifestly did not suffer—"and
them what thinks is them what doesn't do." He had feared the
Rooster's melancholy since Russel's death, and even now mistrusted the midnight morbidities of the Cock. Ah, but he forgave them both when the day dawned and his bold Rooster
loosed a brazen crow across the land, scuttling a hundred
sleeps and scattering Critters abroad in lively obedience.
Golden, lordly, unequivocal was Chauntecleer, and loud
again, and ruling as he should do.

"Ho! Ho! Rooooooooster!" cried John Wesley Weasel:
"Why-come suddenly the buggars is busy again? Hey?"

But the Rooster kept pacing at the edge of the cliff, back and
forth.

Perhaps the tumult of Animals had drowned John Wesley's
question.

Yet John Wesley truly wanted to know. The last time such
organization had been imposed on the Coop, they were preparing for war, fine reasons for fine excitement. They'd built
a wall, then, and provisioned its interior; and what a wonderful summer had ensued! Fightings and foinings to make a
Weasel delirious. So what was coming now?

"Roo-hoo-hooster!"

A pumpkin passed him on the left. Mole-dirt moved him from the right. How could the Rooster see him in traffic? Well, then, go to a Rooster!

John Wesley scrambled a wide way around, west till he gained the hill by a leap; then he raced upward, going to see his buddy Rooster.

"Rooster," he called to the figure in front of him; they both were at the edge of the cliff, only the crown of the Hemlock rising higher; and they were alone. "Why-come the Critters, they has to squirrely them dinners away?" Blunt question.

But when Chauntecleer turned, John Wesley hesitated, suddenly uncertain. The eyes. Rooster's eyes were still pinched from thinking. They kept sliding sideward. His eyes, they seemed to see unreal things, and was he looking at a Weasel? "Rooster?" But he was so beautiful! "Rooster?"

"Because," said Chauntecleer, "it's something we can do."

"What?" said the Weasel. He frowned doubtfuller still: A nothing answer, and the Cock's eyes went sliding away again. "Can do?" said the Weasel. "Can *do?*"

What good's a *do* without a reason? Well, John had reasons: "Is enemies coming," he declared.

"No," said Chauntecleer. Flat no.

"Enemies! Sieges, attackings," cried John, not only because he loved these things, but also to put *something* in his Rooster's head. "Blockadings and a bloody bite or two—is coming!"

But the Rooster said, "No, John." And John popped. Such a magnificent comb his Rooster had! So royal a stride. And power. But thinkings is buggaring his—

"Somebody doesn't drill three hundred Critters for 'Some-things we can do,' oh no! What's John, a dummy? Somebody, he doesn't move heaven and earth for plain nothings, no. 'Less somebody's crazy. 'Less somebody, he is crazy." John drove the thought home by glowering, his own eyes most steady, and he demanded, "So, why-come?"

The Rooster focused. And there *was* a fire, there! John saw intensity. Good!

But the Rooster's reason was, "For Chalcedony." The Rooster said, "I want to feed Chalcedony. She's been hungry far too long."

"What?" cried John. "Her what's a runty Hen?"

Suddenly a little fire poured forth flame: "*My* Hen, John!" Oh, Chauntecleer was a furnace. "My poor anemic Hen! My own, my own, my *own* Chalcedony—who shall never be hungry again!"

Confusing. The Weasel glanced down at the mountains of food that banked the Liverbrook, then back at Chauntecleer, who had decreed them. "Nope," he muttered. "Chicky, she won't leave hungry after this some-other meal, nope."

And to himself the cool assessment: "Thinkings buggars the brains."

Then he considered how to save Chauntecleer from madness. He thought: *Do*—which is action. And he thought: Give Rooster *reasons* for doing, cause for consequence, mouths for all this food! He thought: "Get Critters for Rooster to rule and he'll be a ruler for sure! Oh, John can jam this place with Critters! John owes him that. John'll get reasons for so much food—"

Loyalties. Weasels don't question loyalties. Nor this: that Lords should be Lords.

John Wesley had made up his mind. Immediately he slipped backward, hardly noticed, then lowered his head and ran north.

Chauntecleer is dreaming.

When ever is he not dreaming?

"With you?" he demands in his dream. "Mundo Cani is with you?"

"Aye, with me. And didn't I say so?" asks the unctuous voice. "He entered my world. He joined himself to me, that where I am, there is he also. I thought you knew that, Galle. It was the exchange that kept your Animals alive. You said it yourself, that he was the ransom."

"Find you, find you," cries the Cock, greedy at the connection, "and I find Mundo Cani!"

"And didn't I say so?" says the voice. "I love him now as much as you before he became your thorn. Galle, he has taught me a wisdom I wouldn't otherwise have known. Why, he's given me my means for freedom—"

"I'm coming!" blurts the Cock. He strikes a claw into the darkness. "I am coming!" he cries.

"What?" says the voice, perplexed.

"I am coming to take him from you, Wyrm! Look out for me!"

"Of course you are." The voice has a questioning quality, as though this conversation just took an unnecessary turn. "I'd be disappointed if you didn't. We've one battle left between us. But why?—"

The Rooster is past control. With wild delight he shrieks, "I'm going to kill you, Wyrm!"

This is the threat. Since Russel's death, this is the obsession that has consumed Chauntecleer, and lo! It has been delivered to Wyrm himself. He stands poised for any impact—

Instead, there follows that hollow, exasperating silence. Wyrm can be silent. Ah, God! Wyrm can withdraw into occlusion and air. Oh, let the hammer fall! But Chauntecleer has the feeling that he's being measured. Infinitesimal cock!

Finally, the voice: "You haven't asked the third reason why I cannot see you. It is the most significant."

Silence—and what? Is he supposed to ask? He doesn't.

The voice, this time utterly indifferent: "So. The Cock doesn't know as much as we thought he knew. He's a pest after all. BEHOLD!"

The voice, magnified, thunders down the halls of gloom: BEHOLD! I AM DOING A NEW THING. EVEN NOW IT SPRINGS FORTH, AND DO YOU NOT PERCEIVE IT?

The Rooster cries, "I'm going to ki—"

But the dream has been canceled.

Chauntecleer sits in the Hemlock, shivering.

"—so grateful that you've turned your attention to the Animals again," said Pertelote, "that you're raising so beneficial a harvest. Oh, Chauntecleer, you have their hearts and you handle them so well." She observed the distance he wished and did not touch him. But she roosted near enough to feel the body heat. He was breathing through his nostrils, wakeful. Neither had she been to sleep. The night was bitterly cold.

He whispered, "It isn't enough."

"No?" she said. "Why, I think you've salted several tons of food away. You've accomplished a heroic project—"

"It isn't enough!" he hissed angrily.

She gazed at his form, a shivering, haunted husband—but of such remarkable parts. Pertelote breathed a prayer for his peace of mind.

And then she argued for it: "The Tags," she whispered, "laughed today. Is it nothing that you've given someone the security to laugh? And Animals were singing while they worked. Chauntecleer, they enjoyed the day. They were not afraid. Is that nothing?"

"The world is still infected."

"The world—is always troubled, Chauntecleer. That's why good order and friendship are such sweet blessings after all. They make a refuge, don't they? And the worser the world, the better the refuge? The more needful a place and faith against confusion, no?"

"The apple has a grub in it, the earth a tapeworm."

"But we are *here* on the earth. And you are here. And *here* you've made a refuge in spite of the troubles, and that is something extraordinary, Chauntecleer, something quite enough—because what do you call this thing? Why, you call it a home. A home. We are home. Can't you be content with that—and can't you sleep then?"

"When I have the right to sleep."

"Oh, Chauntecleer! Chauntecleer," she groaned. "I am so tired."

Immediately she was sorry she said that, because he had stiffened.

"I'll go," he offered, "and let you sleep."

"No! No," she said. "I can't sleep until you sleep, too."

"Does everything depend on me?"

"Not everything. Me."

"Pertelote, *why?*"

"Because I love you."

The Rooster sat still within that dilemma so long that Pertelote could have counted one to five hundred. She had given up hearing another word from him that night when, barely audible, there rose the sigh on the night:

"Unfinished. Fraudulent, fraudulent. No—it is not enough—"

Twenty-two
Fimbul Winter

Evil is not privation. It is not nothing. Evil is a something, has a source.

This winter was like none that had ever gone before. The cold was not merely cold, but vindictive: it *meant* the bite, and ice was a vengeance, and the wind was a willful thing.

There was a Deer, a Doe devoutly gentle, who went looking for food, still to suckle her Fawn. She did not nibble at the shoots that were enclosed in ice, because she'd learned already that this ice was iron-hard and wouldn't melt. Twice she'd touched her tongue to it, and twice she'd ripped her flesh away simply to free herself, because her tongue had frozen against it. Rather, she looked for tree trunks whose eastern sides didn't shine. She meant, finally, to strip bark and eat it. This was all that was left to her.

When she found a tree with dry bark, she stretched her neck, curled back her lips, and bit. Something cracked; pain stabbed her jawbone, and despair sank into her heart, because she had broken her teeth. Even the dry bark was as hard as stone. And this was her despair, that without sound teeth she would not eat at all. She knew in the instant that she had begun to die, and what would become of her child?

What she did not know was that the trees themselves had petrified, that the cold was not merely the absence of heat, but that this cold had its source deep in the earth. This cold was a something; it radiated from a winding element through rock and soil to the roots of trees and thence through the trees themselves like a creeping paralysis, like numb death, till the tree stood as a granite monument unto itself, hard and dead. Because death itself is not a nothing. It is not the mere lack of life. It is life's enemy and as a *something* takes life's place. Death hates life.

But the sky strained to stay warm in this winter, as though it fought against the cold, and it seemed to weep. But the warring was no blessing for the Animals who crawled between the heaven and the earth, because when heaven dropped a gentle rain, the wind would snatch it and race away, shrieking with laughter; and the earth, when the water gullied on it, transformed it straightway into ribs of ice. Ice! A vengeful ice that denied them nourishment.

Heaven and earth were battling, and *that* was the winter.

The Animals looked up at the sullen sky. They moaned, and they named the season. "Fimbul Winter," they said.

The Wolves sucked their stomachs upward even to their spines, and they growled, "The Fimbul Winter."

Goats dulled their horns on the metallic ground. Antelopes cracked their hooves in the midst of bounding. Countless eyes went dull, and the children fell ill, and a Stag stood by the body of his wife, his Fawn behind him, and he whispered so that the child should not hear: "The Fimbul Winter."

Coldness of *the* Cold. Darkness of the Dark. And dying of Death Itself. Wyrm was doing a new thing. Yet even this saturnine famine was not the gravest thrust of his stratagem for freedom. He was wiser than he'd been before. He knew, if no one else did, that even cold the Creatures could love one another, that killing them might only strengthen their love, and that calamity could tighten the bonds between them. Those bonds—those were the bonds of his bondage! They held him fast. And even now, on account of the winter, a Weasel was running abroad, talking and talking and knitting the Keepers together—and they were hearing him, again, on account of the winter, on account of their suffering.

No: as vicious as it was, the Fimbul Winter was not his finest subtlety. Not frontally against their skulls would Evil invade them, but rather by entering at the heart—

Wyrm was doing a new thing. Even now it was springing forth.

But the worst was yet undreamed of, yet to come.

Twenty-three
Bondings, Bondage

A Hare appeared at the Hemlock. He popped up one morning and sat at attention and refused to explain himself to any but Lord Chauntecleer.

Pertelote greeted him and tried to put him at ease.

"Nope. Nope," said the Hare, as though ease were not a virtue.

His eyes were perpetually startled, looking left and right at once. His ears fairly shouted, like exclamation points, *Bang! Bang!* that he was nervous.

"Said I should go straight to the top," he said. "Said I shouldn't fuss with other Buggars. Said, talk to Him-What's-Lord-and-General-of-All. Said, Rooster."

"Ah," Pertelote smiled. "You mean Chauntecleer."

"Nope. Nope. Yep."

"He's down the Liverbrook," said Pertelote. She paused. She liked the poor fellow precisely because *he* thought he had little to recommend himself, but he'd dared the audience nonetheless. Therefore, the coward was brave. "I'll take you to him," she said.

"Will wait," he said, "here."

She nodded and went for Chauntecleer.

"I think," she confided to the Rooster as they returned, "that he's been talking to John Wesley."

"Well. News," said Chauntecleer. "The Weasel lives."

"No, I don't think this Hare is much for news," said Pertelote, and then she stood back.

"I," said Chauntecleer—and Pertelote heard the weariness in the word, "am Chauntecleer."

"You?" The Hare's eyes gazed north and south while one stood east of him.

"Me."

"Him-What's-Lord-and-General-of-All?"

"The same. Who told you that?"

"Said's name was Double-u. Said I could call him Bloody Warrior. Showed me scars. Courageous sort. I came."

"You came indeed," said the Rooster, not smiling at the scene just painted before him. "What do you want?"

"Said you had enough. Said, more than enough."

"Generous John Wesley," the Rooster sighed. "Enough what?"

"Well. Well." Here, on the point of the request, the Hare grew stiffer than ever, flashing glances at the curious Animal-eyes surrounding him, and he muttered, "Food."

"You're hungry."

"Nope. Nope. Yep."

"It's all right to be hungry, fellow," said Chauntecleer, and he turned to the Mice lined up behind him, watching. "Tags. Roots and stalks, I think. Would you get them?"

While the Mice were gone, Pertelote noticed a moisture in the northern eye of the Hare. Tears—and her heart was stirred. How famished were the Creatures of other territories? She was glad that the Hare had come.

The Mice laid the food before him, and still this fixture did not budge.

"Well?" said Chauntecleer.

The Hare gave a small cough, and all at once seven others just like him came bounding from the wood, snuck to the food, and ate.

The Hare, still at attention, explained: "Kin."

A second load of food produced a second run of shock-eared Hares; and a third another third, until the ground around the Hemlock had exploded in fur and wall-eyed faces. They ate. And after they ate, they nestled, for they were every one exhausted. And when they had nestled, they began straightway to doze. All save the first Hare, who continued erect. When finally he bent down to nibble, Pertelote took it as a sign that all the kin were accounted for and the trick was done.

"What is your name?" she asked.

"String Jack."

"String Jack, sir, why didn't you all come openly, together?"

He nibbled painfully, as though stealing the food. "So many. Relatives. Unwelcome," he said. "Pack and be gone tomorrow."

"Where?" said Pertelote.

He nibbled. He didn't answer that. Nowhere.

"Sleep here tonight, String Jack," said Pertelote, "and tomorrow this will be your home."

The Brothers Mice gave a cheer: "Huzzah!"

Chauntecleer groaned.

Goats appeared at the Hemlock. Some were wire-haired and bony, some shaggy in the coat, all of them with black slots in their eyeballs and bearded.

Nobody had to invite them to talk. Pertelote didn't have to invite them to stay. And Chauntecleer's frown grew darker.

This breed bawled for food the instant they arrived, lifting their lips to reveal great yellow blocks for teeth.

String Jack and his kin had eaten with fastidious manners, a thousand chews to a mouthful. These ripped, chomped, smacked the food; dribbled and dropped the food; swallowed the food with gruntings, and afterward burped up all the food to chew it down again. Then the Goats flopped down and slept. Snored, burped, muttered, and smelled like sour compost.

String Jack, it developed, had come from the wilderness west of Chauntecleer's land. The Goats, who declared that they were of the tribes of Hophni and Phinehas, had traveled from the mountains and the foothills east.

John Wesley was busy.

A Hawk came whistling down from the sky, stooping at a dazzling hundred miles per hour and striking the fear of God into every little Creature who loved his liver and wished to keep it for himself. Mice and the Ground Squirrel found holes with remarkable speed. Hares went up to attention. Moles thought the first part of a thought. Chickens dithered, Partridges circled on the ground supposing that they went somewhere, Goats burped.

But, as it turned out when his talons gripped nothing but the ground, the royal Bird had merely been "sent."

There was, wasn't there, a Rooster here who flew more skillfully than Hawks and the Swift, who fed marvelously anyone that asked for victuals?

Chauntecleer muttered, his frown coal black.

"I beg your pardon?" said the Hawk.

"I swore," said Chauntecleer. "I said, *Weasel.*"

"To be sure," said the Hawk.

Chauntecleer repeated what was fast becoming a litany: "What is your name? What do you want?"

"Sharpshin," announced the Hawk. "Victuals, if you please."

Chauntecleer, still jangled by Sharpshin's manner of arrival, snapped, "Tags!"

A very busy Weasel, indeed!

And Sheep appeared at the Hemlock, too shy to state their business, but hungry nonetheless.

And Pronghorn appeared at the Hemlock. Disappeared when Chauntecleer loosed a swear-word. Reappeared when Pertelote called to them. They leaped like springs. They ate nothing but the grasses, which they wound around their tongues with deep gratitude; and soon they were loving a Rooster as if he were their father.

Cats appeared at the Hemlock, moons waning in their eyes, a high-born arrogance in their hearts, but a hunger in their guts so terrible it overcame their pride.

Animals, Animals, humble and huffy and craven and crass, embarrassed, demanding, or willing to work, and hungry—all of them hungry—appeared at the Hemlock.

Chauntecleer turned none of them away. But he looked down from the cliff on a thousand bodies and was vexed, because he said, "Who am I to care for so many?"

Busy John Wesley Weasel was racing a long way round the lower apron of a barren moor, exulting in his energy, when one wild sound rang down the mountain and transfixed him.

Lonely, long, and full of anguish was the cry, a bugling that thrilled the Weasel to his loins.

But this was a bitterly empty fastness. This was the haunt of northern winds. Who?—

The bugling rose up again. Oh, voices in the wilderness! John Wesley peered to the top of the moor, and there saw a singular Stag with his head thrust toward the sky, his antlers embracing his withers—bugling.

Look at that! One black Stag on the mountainside, declaring himself against the universe!

"Hoopla!" breathed John Wesley at the sight. And he cried out, "Hey!" Here was courage he couldn't help but respect. Who stands alone against the sky to challenge it? "Hey! Hey! Hey!" the Weasel shouted, darting across the moor and climbing with happy speed. "Hello, you somebody!" John has to meet the one he honors, and that right now. A Weasel of compulsions. But that is a Stag of the aristocracy! One, maybe two, in all the world. *"Hey!"*

The Stag saw him coming, dropped his head and didn't move.

"Is okay!" cried the Weasel. "John, he's no troubles. He's a scrapper too, is John."

Fourteen points, those antlers. Deep-chested, the Creature, and thick in the neck: marvelous. But his eyes were low and suspicious—and he did not move.

John Wesley was seldom in his life caught off guard. But he was taken by the great black Stag and didn't see the lesser body leap from heath beside him. He was bumped and slithered forward. Up again in two twists, he tightened himself into a defensive posture and hissed, ready to rip a body apart.

"De La Coeur!" shouted the Stag.

A Fawn, a child wide-eyed and terrified, stamped pitiful hooves in front of the Weasel, presenting her forehead as though it had horns.

This was the enemy?

"De La Coeur!"

Now John was perplexed. He could drop the Fawn with one cut at the fetlock, and he told her so: "Lucky punch! Lucky punch!" he warned her. And he said, "Baby!" But she ignored the warning. In spite of her terror she charged him, and he had to scramble backward.

"Don't hurt Papa!" she cried.

"De La Coeur!" bellowed the Stag.

"Baby!" squealed John Wesley, in the humiliating situation

of running from a child, "John just come to say Hello!"

"Don't hurt Papa!"

"Papas can fend for them own selves!"

"Leave us be!"

"De La Coeur! Lie down!" This was the Stag with final authority, papa and parent, imperious. The Fawn collapsed, so helpless after all. The Stag said, "He could kill you."

"Right!" said John Wesley Weasel. "Is stupidnesses to chase John Double-u." And he sat down as well, to sort things out. "Why-come a baby, she's fighting for her—"

He looked at the Stag, who still had not moved—and he understood. "Oh, Papa!" he said. And then he said, "Oh, Baby! What courageousness in you!"

This magnificent Buck stood four hooves frozen in a low lake of ice, immobilized and faint from his imprisonment. He couldn't have defended himself. This dappled daughter of his had meant to protect him, with her life if she had to.

"Oh, Baby!" John Wesley's heart nearly burst to see such heroism in an infant. The greymoor, peopled with two souls only, was a stage for the drama of defiance; and the Weasel was filled with awe. "John," he said, "John wouldn't hurt such fine somebodies, no." But then, with the next thing he said— which he intended as nothing more than a homely and reassuring compliment—he hurt her anyway. He said, "Your Mama brung you up wondersomely brave."

The Fawn drew a sudden breath, then turned her head aside and burst into tears.

John Wesley himself was smitten. He could murder Basilisks. But he couldn't bear to make a baby cry.

"Well. Well. Not brave?" he stuttered. "Not brung up? Not?—" So strong one minute, so weak the next. Can Weasels ever think up soft words to dry tears? No.

"Her mother," whispered the Stag, and his head was low to the ground, "died. She lost her teeth and couldn't eat. And died."

"Oh," said John Wesley. "Nobodies told me—"

And there matters stood for a long while, till the Fawn's weeping subsided into quieter sadness.

Well: John should have something for sad Buggars. Sadness wants some action to perk it up. "Well!" said John. "Then here's the reasons why John came. Yump! To set a fine somebody free."

He etched the ice around the Stag's hoof, picked a groove there, gnawed the groove, cracked the ice and released that hoof.

"See? Does John want to hurt somebody's Papa? Nope."

The Fawn had raised her head to watch him.

He did the same for the second hoof. The great Stag sighed. Gladly, the Weasel attended to the third hoof, too; but while he made his rapid scratches, he felt a warm sensation on his back. He looked up and was immediately discombobulated. The Fawn had crept near and was licking him.

He coughed.

John Wesley Weasel, so skilled in war-craft and belligerence, had never learned how to handle affection. Therefore, he made a savage face and snapped, "Bite your tongue, Baby!" But he who couldn't convince her that he was good, now could not convince her he was bad. She dribbled all over him in gratitude, her eyes both moist and close and huge. He swore, but it made no difference. Thundering, rough-cut oaths, but she kept licking him. He fairly attacked the third and fourth hooves, damning the ice, intimidating the ice to speedy water, and the Stag stood free.

But then that great body could not support itself. The Stag toppled and fell—and John Wesley was saved, because De La Coeur ran to the neck of her father and left him alone.

"Babies!" he said with a whole new meaning.

But the couple looked weak indeed, and he could not leave them merely to feed on one another.

John Wesley took a deep breath and hazarded again the dangers.

Warily he said, "Is Deers, might-be, hungry?"

They gazed at him. They were starving.

"Now. Now," he warned, "no thankings John, mind you. No slobberings on a Double-u, who's a bloody warrior, fightings, brawlings, and so forth—" He couldn't stand another attack of sweetness out of the Baby. Nevertheless, he described the Lord-and-General-of-All, praising that Rooster extravagantly as foresighted and full of glory, and he directed both father and daughter south to the food bins and to health. And then he shut up.

The great stag whispered, "Black-Pale-on-a-Silver-Field."

"What?" said the Weasel.

"It is my name," said the Stag. "I give it to you whole, as a gift. We will go and find your Rooster."

"Well."

"Bloody warrior?" asked the Fawn De La Coeur, from her father's neck.

John Wesley frowned like battle-axes. "What?"

"Thank you."

"Spit to thanks."

So he said. But she kissed him anyway, and the Weasel was gone across the moor like a shot, running on three legs, trying mightily with the fourth to wipe the sweetness from his face.

Chauntecleer crowed the crows.

Animals who had never known of Vespers or Compline before lay down in gratitude and wondered that they felt so comforted. Eating was one thing. It satisfied the yearning of their bellies. But these regular signals of the times ordained in goodness, these cries in a kindred voice, were something else. They enclosed the Animals against the void. They argued that here, at least, existence was not a chancey thing but protected by a destiny—and the destiny loved them, for it came in the song of a Rooster: one alive! They mercied them and satisfied the longing of their souls. If winter hadn't silenced this Priest, then what could winter do to them?

Chauntecleer crowed.
And the Animals slept.

Deer appeared at the Hemlock, aristocratic both in their stride and in the cast of their heads, handsome, self-contained. They carried long, ancestral names and a knowledge of their heritage. "Gold-Fess-on-a-Red-Field," one announced himself; and another, "Four-Red-Pallets," and another, "Blue-Bend-Sinister."

One Stag came coated in midnight, with white markings at his muzzle and his breast. His daughter wandered lop-legged behind him, and both were silent, because both were cruelly weakened. But this Fawn, dappled like the autumn, was blameless altogether.

Chalcedony, the crippled Hen, noticed the Fawn above all others and felt in herself a motherhood so strong that it took her breath away. Yet she held back. She didn't say anything, though she gazed at the child through wintry trees and the desire to love her cramped like pain in her abdomen. She limped ever at a distance, because she thought: what right have I to bother one so lovely?

The Deer are noble Creatures. And fawns grow up to be Ladies.

Thus the population multiplied all up and down the Liverbrook, back to the fields and through the deep wood. In fifties and hundreds they camped, each tribe according to its lair and custom, and Chauntecleer appointed leaders over families— sometimes with no more than a thrust of his jet beak—in order to administer the feeding of so many. An organization developed. Even the children and the aged sped well, and parents took confidence again, and Beasts looked with kindness on their neighbors.

But the Rooster said, "I can't *do* this any more!"

Wolves appeared at the Hemlock. That was a complication.

The Wolves arrived in a secretive pack, rolling their shoulders, slinging low their heads, prowling balefully through the camp, sliding their eyes to the left and the right. They were a scornful breed, and they caused wherever they went a flurry of distress: meek Animals believe the scorn. Small Animals notice fangs.

One of the Wolves was white with eyes like ice chips; one black with a flaming glance; one was named, so the Animals rumored it, "Favonius," and another "Eurus"—these four gathered from four corners of the utter distances. A fifth was grey but for deep blue eyes: "Chinook," a Wolf well collared in thick fur, great in her chest and thigh, slow-pumping at the heart, possessed of an everlasting endurance. Who could run from Chinook forever?

In troubled whispers the Animals spoke of the Wolves; and when the pack slid by, even whispers ceased. They truly feared these Creatures who roamed the reaches of the earth, who could survive at extremes of the compass and of want. What laws does the *Randgänger* love? Any? None?

Therefore shivers attended the Wolves, and small ripples of panic behind them.

And therefore Chauntecleer charged his crowing with sterner authority and a universal sting. It wasn't only comfort he crowed, but the exaction of order as well, so that the maverick might be contained and the meek feel safe. But that kind of Compline saps the spirit of the singer: it wants so *much* of him! Embrace ten thousand? Prohibit their sins and praise their good works? Bulk greater than the bad, yet descend to the humiliated? And keep them generally *all* from harm?

My God! My God!

Chauntecleer murmured at midnight, "I can't *do* this any more."

Pertelote heard him. She said, "You do it so well, my Lord."

"I am tired, I am tired, Pertelote. I'm tired, and in the end I'll prove unable after all."

"Why? Because once before you ended poorly?"

"Yes! I know what I am."

"You say this, even though the war was not lost, and we didn't die? You say this even though we sit here alive? You say this, Chauntecleer, about our victory?"

"*I say it!*" he shouted. He paused and softened his voice. "I suffer the future," he said. "I truly don't want a one of these Creatures to hurt, Pertelote, not one. But I know the dry rot at the base of things."

"Chauntecleer?"

"What?"

"Can I touch you now?"

"No."

They were nearly enclosed in the Hemlock, since the boughs hung down like drapes, heavy under ice; and the night was dark. There was a privacy here.

Pertelote said, "Is it nothing that I love you?"

He sighed, and it was apparent that even such a question as this sharpened his guilt the more. Nay, it damned him now, right now, as neglectful, terse, and hurting the one he most would not have hurt.

"Not nothing, Pertelote; please don't say that. How could I live at all if I thought that you didn't love me? I would know whose fault that was, and I would die very soon, because that knowledge would kill me. This is the truth. I am not lying."

Pertelote paused a long time after that confession. A great many thoughts passed her mind, and emotions sputtered in her like fireworks, but none of this showed in her face nor her aspect.

Finally, she chose a topic for him and not for herself. "It would be nice if the Dog were here, wouldn't it?" she said.

He said, "Yes." She knew how to ease him.

"The war could be forgotten then for sure," she said. "His old, mournful woe would make us feel at home again. Mundo Cani—he could run like the wind, couldn't he, Chauntecleer? And he loved the Hens no less than you do. And you. The Dog loved you." The Rooster's head bent. Pertelote said, "And I would hold my husband again—"

He said, "It would be nice."
She whispered, "Can't I touch you, Chauntecleer?"
He said, "No."
"When?" she pleaded.
"Oh, Pertelote," wailed the Rooster, "when I am worthy!"
And she turned her head away and wept.

It was in the following night that a Coyote appeared at the Hemlock.

Twenty-four
Rachel's Tale

Benoni the oldest Coyote began his life in play.

Sisters were for biting. Sisters were for cuffing. Mothers were for innocent faces when the sisters tattled. Then sisters were for yanks on the tail when a mother had punished the troublemaker anyway. It was a glad way to be, and sleep was easy, and mornings were right, and the world was good and happy.

But very soon Benoni's attention became fixed upon his father, Ferric; and life took a serious turn.

Ferric was clearly haggard when he brought them foodstuffs in the evening. Twill and Hopsacking would nuzzle his chin. This was the way they persuaded him to reverse his swallow and to present them with lumps of sweetmeats, which they then fell upon, cracking and chewing mindlessly. But Benoni would hold back. He saw the worry in his father's eye, and he knew himself to be the oldest—an important station in life. Trouble matured the child faster than the months: there was less to eat, so he ate less, even as his father Ferric ate nothing at all. And he smiled less.

Rachel watched her son. She saw him to be thinking more than he ought to be, a Pup borne down by burdens. And she noticed that he woke up when his father woke in the morning. And she understood that he hated the shortness of his legs.

While Ferric stood high on the rim of the canyon, staring eastward with obvious tension, Benoni whined at the lowest stone, too small to climb one step. Every fiber in him stretched, and his tail went down with the effort—but when his father launched and left, Benoni stood still on hind legs and cocked his ears and listened.

What could he hear? What did he think?

"I'm going to lose him soon," thought Rachel. "Too soon."

She tried to keep things gay for all her children, playing with them herself and prodding them to speak whatever came into their heads. But Benoni spoke less than his sisters, now. He watched the rim of the canyon.

She led them daily down the stream, splashing in the water that held its warmth and singing thoughtless rhymes. Daily they visited the Bird in her bush, whom the children called Aunt, and who would pick through their soft fur like a clicking scissors. She loved them absolutely. Their laughter sent her hopping all over the bush—

But Benoni began to lag behind when the women set off southward on a morning. And he seemed to recognize a difference between himself and them.

And finally he chose not to go at all.

"Do you think your aunt is silly, now?" Rachel asked when she returned to find her son sitting at the bottom step.

"No'm," said Benoni.

"Are you bothered by your sisters? Are they too foolish for you?"

"No'm."

"But you would rather be here than with us?"

"Yes'm," said Benoni, uncomfortable.

"Why?"

"Oh," said Benoni, "I'm older, now. I'll—I will watch out for the Den. I can be alone, sometimes."

"Yes, you can," said Rachel quietly. She gazed at his soft, earnest face. "What do you do when you are alone?"

"Think."

"Ah. It's a grown-up business, to think," she said aloud. But to herself she said, "Soon. Too soon," and her eyes went sad.

She prayed for this son. And she truly didn't know how quickly the world would snatch him from her.

One afternoon when the mother and her daughters came splashing back to the Den, Benoni was gone.

The mother's manner changed. No. This *was* too soon!

With two sharp barks she ordered Twill and Hopsacking into the lair, where they were to lie perfectly still until her return, then she dashed up the stairs and raced the plains, the thought of her baby by her heart:

"Noni! Benoni!"

The ice world was both grand and deadly. The pine were silent. She trotted into their dark interior, but then she did not know where to go.

"Benoni!"

Echoes laughed. Ice cracked. A load of crystal crashed to the ground, and Rachel ran headlong: *"Benoni!"*

The baby's legs had grown to match his yearning, and he could climb the stones, now. But his wisdom did not match this world. Why hadn't she demanded that he stay with them, even if he didn't like it? It didn't matter what he liked. What mattered was his safety—but the Pine were mighty and blind and careless of a mother's child, *"Benoni!"*

Niii! Niii!

"Where are you?"

You! You!

"Benoni, tell me where you are!"

She heard a faint wail to her left. She froze. Again: it sounded so vulnerable. It was Benoni. Rachel sobbed, then broke in that direction. Extraordinary leaps she took over hillocks and across the ditches. Quick, efficient arcs she described around the pine. And she ran.

And when little Benoni saw her coming, he cried, "Mama!" and darted toward her, a red pellet with serious eyes, so that they collided, and the pup pushed himself hard into his mother's chest, deep and deeper, he wouldn't quit pushing.

She held him, gazing upward. She said, "Where were you?"

He shook his head.

She said, "Were you lost?"

She felt him nod once, and then he burst into tears: "Whoo. Whoooooo."

Oh, how Rachel gathered her son so tightly under her chin! How dearly she pressed him in.

"I was so afraid for you," she said.

Ice slid from the treetops, smashed on the ground, and the baby jumped. Bones and glass rained down around them. His sobbing went straight to her soul, and she swore he would never cry again, and she knew it was a lie.

She whispered, "Were you running away from us?"

He shook his head.

"Oh, Benoni, didn't you know that this is a hurtful world?" she asked.

He nodded against her chest. "Yes'm, I knew," he said. And gravely he explained, "It's why I came."

"What?" Rachel backed away from her son, to look at him. "What?" she said. He averted his eyes. His fur stood out from his cheeks like soft sunburst; his tail was no more than a trigger cocked; but he was a deep little Coyote. "What?" she said. "To be hurt?"

"No'm," he muttered. "But to help Papa."

"Whisht! Your Papa needs help?"

Benoni bowed his head, embarrassed. He nodded.

"Why? Is he so weak?"

"No! Not weak," cried Benoni, gazing at his mother to be

sure that she knew he didn't think his Papa weak. Then he said, "He's—afraid."

Rachel could say nothing to this. *Soon,* she thought behind her glittering eyes. *Too soon.*

"I came to help him fight the enemy," Benoni said. "But I didn't find the enemy. I didn't find Papa. I turned around this time and that time. I turned around too many times," said Benoni, his lip beginning to quiver. "I got lost." And at that announcement, he cried again, "Whooo. Whoooooooo." He crept back to his Mama and curled himself beneath her neck.

She stroked him, his fine, red fur, and wished that the need would never, never end.

"Benoni, Benoni," she whispered. "Who is the enemy?"

But at that moment and in that place, the pup had run out of words. He could say no more than his Mama had said. He, too, said, "Who." And he sobbed, "Whooooooooo."

Ferric—far away from his family, but gone on account of them, to find food—was trying to eat a pine cone.

He had a sour expression on his face. The thing stuck out from his jaw like the abdomen of an enormous insect, its scales scraping his tongue, and he was grinding it soft at the middle. Tasteless and mean, the pine cone! A bitter dinner for anyone.

But what else was there in this deep-frozen world?

Like finger-parings it broke into his gullet. Fibers jammed between his teeth. His eyes watered up. He was miserable, forever conscious of the nasty food he brought his children, and always afraid that this would be the last.

Suddenly the floor of the forest trembled.

And the Coyote froze—the pine cone like a dead wing at his cheek.

Who was this? It was no Wolfsprowl that he felt. The Wolves had left. Besides, whoever was coming took no care to be quiet. Boisterous! Careless! Tramping the earth as though he owned it. *Happy!*

Someone mighty ignorant, thought Ferric in his freeze—

And then a long, brown Animal bounded into view, jaunty on four short legs, smug at his snout, flashing a black eye. He had but one ear, the size of a nickel, but so much energy that the Coyote cringed and wished that he had run.

"Ha!" cried the traveler, and he stopped. "What is here? A wooden Critter, what? Does you move, wooden Critter?"

He walked straight up to Ferric—who hid the harder—and yanked his tail. He punched his stomach, saying, "Hum. Hum." He tickled the bony ribs, and Ferric's eyes flowed water. But he kept his freeze.

"Well, well, John Double-u has seen him some curiosities in his adventuring; but wooden Critters is somethings new, you bet. Hello! Hello!" he shouted into Ferric's face, as though raising his voice would help. "HELLO! HELLO, WOODEN CRITTER. DOES YOU TALK?"

All at once this "Double-u" sat back in astonishment and poked his head up high and hung his paws at his breast, the better to consider. "Look-ee here," he whistled. "Doesn't move. Doesn't talk, tsk-tsk. But what? By Gaw, it cries. Little tears raining down. Wooden Critter is sad. JOHN IS SORRY FOR YOU, TOO! Might-be, teeth gots stuck on a piney-cone, and can't eat no more, makes him skinny and scared. HUNGRY? IS SOMEBODY MIGHT-BE HUNGRY IN THERE?"

For a long moment the one-eared bellower stared at Ferric, tipping his head left and right, waiting for an answer. The Coyote nearly cracked, to be stared at so directly. How could it be that one single Animal could turn this lonely forest into a party?

"Okay. Hungry," said the traveler, satisfied that he had hit upon the problem. He took a deep breath. "LOOK-EE," he roared—and with much gesticulation he explained where food was. He praised the golden Cock in charge of it, and rattled on about the great company of Animals already gathered there beneath the jurisdiction of the Cock, how content they were, so to be fed, so to be ruled.

Ferric, imagining so many Creatures like this one to be all in one place, hissed a little:

"Tssssst."

"NOPE!" shouted the traveler. "IS NO THANKINGS FOR JOHN, NO SIR! JOHN, HE DOES HIS BUSINESS. AND THEN JOHN, HE GOES. BLOODY WARRIORS IS ALWAYS ON THE MOVE."

Then, true to his word, the traveler left as wonderfully as he had come, muttering, "Doesn't talk. Wonders if wooden Critters knows how to listens. Wooden legs, wooden brains—"

Ferric ached.

Society itself had come and gone in the person of a long Animal. The forest fell darker, now, and quieter, in his absence; and Ferric sat down, still sucking the pine cone.

So, there was food to the south. Food for the feeding of his children and his Rachel. Oh, but what a terrifying way to get it, dodging the eyes of a thousand Beasts, daring the dangers, the dangers—

Ferric swallowed his pine cone.

He looked up at the trees for another.

It was deep in the night when this father descended the canyon stone to home; it was through darkness that he heard his son's voice saying: "Papa can't fight the enemy alone." And it was with a certain guilty stillness that he paused to hear the rest. *Fight the enemy, Benoni?*

"So says the Cub?" asked Rachel in the Den. "So says the soft-paw?"

"Don't make me little, Mama," said Benoni.

"You are little, Benoni."

"I'm older than I was."

"Whisht, my son, not old enough."

"But me and Papa are two. I should go with him. He can't fight alone. Papa is scared."

There. That paralyzed Ferric on his own doorstep—*scared,*

Benoni?—too shamed to go in, too much in love with his son just to go. *Benoni?* Instead he stopped where he was and listened.

"Scared," said Rachel with much greater ease. "Of what?"

Benoni whispered seriously, "The enemy."

Rachel lowered her voice. "Benoni," she said, "who *is* the enemy?"

"I don't know." He lowered his voice, too. "I never seen. I only watch Papa's eyes, staring at something I never seen, something so bad that Papa's afraid of it. I feel so sorry for Papa—"

Ferric Coyote sat down in darkness and hung his head. He heard a long pause pass, and the rustle of Rachel's settling herself.

"Noni?" she said.

"I am here, Mama."

"Will you come lie by me?" There was smaller rustling in the Den. Then, softly, "Noni?"

"What, Mama?"

"I don't think you need to be sorry for your Papa," she said. "Perhaps you don't understand why not, nor what a special Coyote your father is. Benoni," she said in a very terrible whisper.

"What?" he said.

"I will tell you who the enemy is. Listen. The enemy is the Witch with No Stomach."

Silence. Benoni squirmed at the horror of this news.

"She wraps herself," said Rachel, "in robes of air and goes through the forest bending the trees as she passes by. Sometimes her robes are as white as the mist. Sometimes she goes softly, and no one is afraid. Sometimes she screams through the branches and breaks them and hurls them down to the ground. Then no one can sleep, because the Witch is angry. And what do you think she is looking for?"

"What?" said Benoni.

And Rachel said, "Why, children."

"Oh," said Benoni.

"Children who have left their Mamas and their Papas and wandered off alone. Children with no one to protect them. Children who thought that they were older."

"Oh," said little Benoni.

"There was a Bear Cub, once, who thought that he was older. He went into the forest and got lost. When the night came, so did the Witch, whipping her foggy gown from tree to tree until she saw him. She shrieked, Benoni. She opened her robes, and what do you think the Bear Cub saw?"

"What," whispered the Coyote Cub, "did he see?"

"Nothing. He saw nothing at all. That's why they call her the Witch with No Stomach. In the middle of her is the place where Nothing is, a frightening sight to see. All of the Nothing of the world comes from her middle. Well. Then she circled her sleeves around the lonely Bear Cub; and this is what the Witch did then: she ate him up."

"Ate him up," said Benoni.

"Up, down, and gone. And nobody saw him after that because, of course, she had no stomach, and little Cubs, when they are swallowed down inside of her, go Nowhere."

"Nowhere," said Benoni.

"Nowhere at all. Nothing is in Nowhere. Nowhere is where Nothing is. And Nowhere is the Stomach of the Witch. The little Bear was Nowhere. But Nothing in a Nowhere can't be very filling, can it?"

"Oh, no," said Benoni.

"Of course not," said his mother. "Therefore the Witch was never full. So next it was a youngling Hawk she ate, and after that a Badger, and pretty soon all of the children of the forest, whishty! were gone."

Rachel fell silent. The silence lasted long, since Rachel was a patient mother. But Benoni was not a patient son.

"Is that the end?" he asked.

"Well," said Rachel. "Well, it might have been the end. Except for one mighty Coyote."

"Oh, yes!" sang Benoni. "A mighty Coyote."

"Listen. All the mothers of the cubs came together, and they wept and wailed for their children, and the whole forest shuddered with their sorrow. 'What will we do?' they asked. 'Oh, what will we do,' they answered themselves. A great Bear came forward and stomped the ground. 'I am strong,' he roared. 'I will beat up the Witch with No Stomach until the children come home again.' But the mothers were wiser. 'How can you beat her up,' they asked, 'if you can't take hold of her?' The Bear put down his head and shuffled away. No One could take hold of the Witch with No Stomach.

"A Hawk came forward. 'I am swift,' he announced. 'I can fly as fast as the Witch when she blows through the forest.' But the mothers were wiser. 'Can you be everywhere and nowhere at once?' they asked. 'For the Witch shakes all the trees and all the branches at once.' No, the Hawk could not be everywhere and nowhere at once. No One. No One could be nowhere.

"And No One could talk to the Witch. And No One could find her. Animal after Animal failed to be the right one to save the children, since all of the Animals were Some One. So what were the mothers to do? Who could help them?"

"Someone?" said Benoni.

"No," said Rachel sadly. "Not Some One."

Poor Benoni felt sad, too. "No One?" he asked.

"Right!" cried Rachel with surprising praise. "Right! No One! No One was the *only* one who could beat a Witch, or else be everywhere at once, or talk with a Witch, or find her. No One. No One alone! Oh, Benoni, you are so wise.

"And here's the beautiful part of my story," said Rachel. "Within the forest there lived a humble Coyote. So humble and scared was he, that whenever they asked his name, he mumbled, 'No One. I am No-One-At-All.' And when they asked him if he was good at anything, he said, 'Nothing.' And when they asked him where he lived, the lowly Coyote said, 'Nowhere.'

"Isn't that wonderful? All of the mothers cried, 'No One, you're the *only* one! None of the Some Ones around can save our children, because they know nothing about Nothings, but you do. Please find the Witch with No Stomach. Oh, let No One go!'

"Well. In no time at all, No One went Nowhere: he went to utter humiliation, which is the Witch's stomach. And there, most bravely, he did Nothing At All, which to him was as natural as loving children: No One never tried to do that. He took hold of a Bear Cub's paw, and a youngling Hawk, a Badger, and child after child, he raised them from the Witch's stomach, back to their mothers—"

"And the mothers were happy?" cried Benoni.

"So happy," said Rachel. "So happy."

Ferric heard that they were hugging in the Den, because his son laughed aloud at the story and grunted with the hug. Ferric sat with his snout between his forelegs.

"Mama?" asked Benoni the oldest Coyote, much less sad.

"Benoni?" said Rachel.

"Is that a true story?"

"Well," she said, "one way it's just a story, and I made it up. But if you think that the Witch with No Stomach is the wind —or maybe she's the winter that's eating us now—then I suppose that it is true after all; and then I've shown you the enemy that frightens fathers, haven't I?"

The cub fell silent a while. Then, "Mama?"

"Benoni?"

"Well—is Papa a mighty Coyote?"

"Your father?" said Rachel in the dark Den, hidden. "Your father, Noni? Whisht, he has a great heart, child, full of the love for you. And he is your father. This is the truth: Ferric is mighty among all of the Creatures on earth."

In the morning Rachel found five balls of food at the door of the Den, pine cones once before their swallowing. She understood their number on sight: one for her, three for the children, and one for the Bird in her bush.

None for Ferric himself.

He had gone.

Twenty-five
Dawning

At midnight Chauntecleer the Rooster wanted to be alone. Night after night he escaped the overwhelming duties of the day not by sleeping but by walking down the hard ice of the Liverbrook alone. He muttered to himself. He stopped and puzzled and came to no answers. He shouted at God, throwing out his wings. He carried the thousand spirits of the Animals in his breast. And he asked nothing at midnight so much as to be left alone.

The Animals who had gathered realized his need, though they didn't understand it. After Compline they nestled to their sleep, and they left him alone.

Nobody troubled the troubled Rooster.

Therefore, Lord Chauntecleer was not pleased to see a shadow cross the stream in front of him. It went from the right to the left and broke his broodings. In a moment it went from the left to the right, a quick wrinkle in the night. Then all was darkness again. But his solitude was gone and his attention was stuck downstream and the frown was stuck on his face.

While he walked, while he watched, that shadow shot five more times across the stream. He counted the times, growing more and more irritated: some busy Creature! Some idiotic shuttlecock!

The seventh time the shadow passed, Chauntecleer fixed

his eye on the wood where it went and rushed to the spot with a great flurry of feathers.

Between two trees, in dim light, he found a frozen little Beast thin as a tweezers and stiffer than toothpicks. He put his Rooster-eye to the Creature's slant-eye and snapped, "Good night."

It was as gentle a command as he had at the moment and should have been sufficient. Any stronger, and he thought he'd shatter a fellow so brittle and fixed. "Good night!"

The Rooster turned on a back toe and continued pacing—

One hundred yards down the Liverbrook—

And then was thunderstruck to see the same small Beast ahead of him, frozen in the same position, this time squarely in his path, though not a sound had passed between.

"GOOD NIGHT!" roared Chauntecleer at this piece of sculpture, using bombast after all. "GOOD NIGHT!" from thirty paces, and then again "GOOD NIGHT" from a foot. "Good night!" as he continued downstream. Well, if the command itself did not inspire obedience, then the Rooster had to drop a detonation or two to force obedience, Roosterly-fashion.

Curious, however, that the Beast did not budge, no, not a quiver, despite the impact of Chauntecleer's nearest—

Good God!

There it was again.

One hundred yards ahead, still in that same egregious crouch, a tinder-box of tensions, an aggravation to the midnight Cock, a Beast in very danger!

Chauntecleer bore down on it.

Arguments flooded his mind.

This time the Creature moved: the tiniest, dreariest grin curled down his jaw from the cheek to the point of his snout. And he said, *"Tsssssst."*

"Ha!" snapped Chauntecleer. "So wire can make a sound. Ha! Can wire also untaut itself, and go away, and go to sleep? You can eat in the morning, with all the Animals—"

"*Tsssssst!*"

"What, you don't like that?" thundered the Cock. "What, you think you're something special? Listen to me, you insignificant Nit: neither you nor anyone else is special. Good night! Nobody's special; everyone's special; or no one would survive. Good-get-your-butt-out-of-here *night!*"

But suddenly a sort of fit seized the little Beast, a shuddering and a writhing within himself.

At once Chauntecleer feared that he had overwhelmed the fellow, and remorse—the same old, immediate guilt—poured through him. With all his heart he repented again his habit of hurting the meek, and his soul turned within him. He looked carefully and saw suffering in that slant eye after all, and he wanted to touch the Beast, to apologize and to feed him at once—

But this trembling was not a reaction. It was willful. And the little Creature was not so much suffering *from* something as suffering *toward* something. He was in a mighty struggle, all the while gazing at Chauntecleer; he was battling desperately to what? To do what? Why, to speak!

All the groaning and twisting and striving produced one word:

"Rachel."

And the Beast bowed down and sighed.

"Rachel," said a tender Chauntecleer. He picked the word up as a precious thing, since it took so much effort to create it—and since he had almost ignored this one of God's Creatures. " 'Rachel': a very important word, I see. The name of someone, and she is important. Are there others?"

Well, that was another nearly impossible task. But this little Beast was uncommonly tenacious. He fought hard and long, first to say, "Benoni," then "Twill and Hopsacking," and with a final effort, "Bird in her bush—so hungry—" Then he sat down in a haywire heap, faint for all he had accomplished.

Chauntecleer looked upon him and was moved. What love this fellow must have for a Rachel, so to sacrifice himself this way, enduring Rooster-attacks and overcoming even his own nature. Skinny could be very, very strong.

"You are a Coyote," said Chauntecleer.

The Coyote nodded.

"Coyote, forgive me for what I said before," said Chauntecleer. "You *are* special."

The Coyote shook his head.

"You don't know," said Chauntecleer. "But I know. You have done a remarkable thing for Rachel." He sat down before the Coyote, to put that one at his ease, to make amends. Here in the night he gave a Coyote his whole attention. "Therefore," he said, "this Rachel must be a remarkable Creature."

The Coyote nodded. His slant eye moistened. This was good conversation.

Chauntecleer pursued it: "And the Benoni whom you speak about must also be exceptional."

The Coyote nodded, almost to the point of smiling, now.

"And there's a Twill, I perceive. And someone of noteworthy beauty named Hopsacking—"

The Coyote was nodding with glad volubility.

"And a Bird," said Chauntecleer, "the only one whose name you haven't told me. Perhaps you'd like to chat a little with me," said the Rooster, further to comfort a Coyote, "and tell me her name, too."

And Chauntecleer succeeded. The frightened Coyote lifted his face in honest pleasure to the Rooster and spoke. He smiled and said two words which stunned Lord Chauntecleer no less than a spike to his brain.

The Coyote said, "Jug, jug."

"What?" said Chauntecleer.

The Coyote said, "No name for her. She can't talk. Poor Bird has no tongue." He smiled.

Chauntecleer did not smile. "You said 'Jug, jug,' " he said, drilling the Coyote with an immoveable eye.

The Coyote's smile slipped a bit before this intensity.

He said, uncertainly, "It's what she says."

The night stars loosened and began to wheel around Lord
Chauntecleer. The woods and the earth rose up to float about
his ears. The universe was tipping, and the Rooster felt as
though he would soon explode for the thing occurring.

He bit hard against his excitement and whispered hoarsely,
as carefully as he could, "Again," gazing at this Beast, this
oracle of God: "Say again what the woman says. Again."

"Jug, jug," whined the Coyote. Chauntecleer let a laugh slip
out of his solemn face. It sounded like a bark, and the Coyote
shrank. "Jug, jug," he stuttered, "and Tereu."

The Rooster's beak drove closer to a Coyote, so that a
Coyote fell closer to a freeze.

"And she," hissed Chauntecleer, the delight about to rup-
ture, "she's sad? I mean, *sad?*"

The shrinking Coyote nodded one minimal degree, and
that was the end of communications for the night—

—because the Rooster blew up. Lord Chauntecleer rose on
his wings, laughing loud and long and lustily, a geyser of joy:
"And you know where she is! And you know how to find her!
And here you are! My God, my God!" roared Chauntecleer.
He soared into the sky, he whose flight was usually lumbering.
He flew high enough to see dawn at the eastern horizon, and
his heart burst for the seeing of the dawn. He cried, "O my
dear God!" and he meant it.

Then he swooped to the topmost branch of the tallest tree
of the highest rise around, where he stood black against the
greydawn, and he, Lord Chauntecleer the Rooster, gleefully
took dominion of the world.

"JUG!" he crowed a new crow. His head went back—oh,
see the acrobat! His wings swept out. His lungs were brass, and
Lauds broke bright upon the gloom, and Animals were jolted
awake, and the sun himself seemed tardy:

"JUG, JUG—OH, WYRM, I'VE FOUND YOU OUT, AND
I AM COMING! MUNDO CANI, HERE I COME TO YOU!
TEREU! TEREU! *TEREU!*"

Twenty-six
Daybreak

"Mrs. Cobb! Did you hear that?"

"Aye. It woke me."

"What *was* it?"

"I don't know. I truly don't know."

"Should a body go investigate?"

"I don't know that neither, Mr. Cobb." A pause. "It could be dangerous."

"Could be. Could be. Probably is—"

Deep ponderings in the Squirrels' burrow. And then, a memory: "I saw lightning hit a master-elm, once," Pertinax Cobb said carefully. "The light blinded me, shot down the tree trunk in a flash—cut it, like peeling it, and such a boom went with it that I tumbled backwards. For a second all was quiet, like sleeping. But then, Mrs. Cobb, that there elm, she sang out. A screeching—a screeching, like I never heard before. And what should I see, but the elm tree splitting, heavy limbs on one side, heavy limbs on t'other, gone splitting slowly down the middle—screeching! That, Mrs. Cobb: that, I swear, is the sound I just heard again."

Pertinax Cobb's wife shuddered.

Cobb said, "It wants investigating, doesn't it?"

Mrs. Cobb said, "It does."

"I'm off," said Cobb.

She said, "Can I go with you?"

And he: "I should be grateful, if you did."

Down the Liverbrook in the dim greydawn stood a single figure: Pertelote the Hen, gazing southward. She was holding her breath, her wing at her throat, herself as silent as the ice. Waiting.

Two Squirrels crept toward her from behind—

"Chauntecleer," whispered Wodenstag. He didn't move.

Seven little noses were pressed together in star formation. Fourteen eyes were open to the darkness. Forty-two whiskers twitched.

The Brothers Mice were wide awake. Wodenstag had spoken first.

"Well, I think so, Wodenstag," said Freitag. "Chauntecleer."

"Crowing," said Samstag. "Far, far away."

"But when did he crow like that before?" said Freitag.

"The Rooster—the Rooster, he never crowed like that before," said Wodenstag, "unless it was when his children pleased him—"

"Oh, Wodenstag!" cried Samstag, the youngest of them all. "I am so happy. You should feel how my heart is beating."

Every Mouse began to wriggle. The star expanded.

"And do you know why you are happy?" whispered Wodenstag, full of awe.

"Why?" said Samstag.

"Because the Rooster is!"

Out of the earth flew seven Mice. Down the frozen Liverbrook they darted, around a bend and straight ahead, where they saw three Creatures sitting still, facing south. Their poor hearts were tripping away, yet they restrained themselves and with a grave formality took places behind a Ground Squirrel.

She turned and smiled a greeting upon them, then she pointed to the other Squirrel, so stiff beside the quiet Pertelote.

"Mr. Cobb's investigating," she confided.

And the Mice suppressed giggles of glee. What a marvelous occupation, to be investigating!

There was a Hawk whose head came up to the daybreak cry like a gun-hammer. His stern eye flared with the light of gladness, and his whole body trembled to soar.

Goats heard the ram's horn. Goats heard the trumpet which once had blown the battle-note so wildly that it cracked stone. Goats woke with that sound in their hearts. They took to their hooves. They stamped toward the Liverbrook.

The Pronghorn leapt straight from their sleep. The whole herd danced like raindrops on puddles—down to the Liverbrook.

The eyes of String Jack popped out of his head in opposite directions.

"What—? What—?"

The flanks of the noble Deer began to shiver.

The Sparrows chittered; Partridges made silly bubbles in their throats; the Jay plain laughed; the great camp of the Animals awoke in all of its sectors, and stirred, and wondered at the good feelings and the sweet anticipation running through them—and, grinning, they followed a general flow: rank upon rank, in tribes and families, by breed and by individual wish, they came and filled the valley of the Liverbrook. "What—? What—?"

But Pertelote stood the foremost of them all, stood silently in patient grace: waiting.

It was Chalcedony the crippled Hen who went close enough truly to see the woman Pertelote. And the sky was brighter when she came. She had no thought in her head save to sit near the kindest heart in this vast congregation—but when she saw the face of her Lady, the words flew out of her of their own accord:

"Ma'am!" wailed Chalcedony. "Ma'am, oh, ma'am! Why are you crying?"

Then came Chauntecleer.

That Rooster strode the Liverbrook as one in full possession of the land, his jet beak shut upon some glorious news, his tail a fountain, his white nails flashing, his eye clean, bright, and pure. Lo: he had arisen from his gloom. Who could be sad any more? He was the sunlight coming home, bursting twice his size. Who could look upon such a Lord and *not* smile?

White breath puffed faster and faster from Animals' nostrils. The excitement tingled through them. Someone giggled. Everyone waited.

But Chauntecleer leveled his gaze and took deliberate time to approach the one in front of them all. Pertelote.

Silently he stopped before her. He nodded twice.

With her eyes, which were brimming with tears, with her eyes alone the woman questioned him. She searched his face, and he did not flinch. He smiled; and he nodded.

She put out a wing and brushed his neck: *Can I touch you?*

He did not draw back. Again, he nodded.

So then it was that Pertelote lowered her head, and like a child moved very close to him. And it was *he* who swept her into a full and mighty hug, he who buried her head in his breast. Her shoulders began to shake; she was weeping, unashamed. The Animals saw that, and many of them, too, began to weep. But Chauntecleer raised his head above his wife. "Oh!" he said with a grand pride. "Oh, Pertelote!" He closed his eyes below the sky, and then this is what Lord Chauntecleer did: he opened his beak, and he laughed. The Rooster burst into a long peal of rolling, uncontrollable laughter. He breathed, and he laughed again. So then the poor Animals were crying and laughing both at the same time, whose mood had been so dreary till this morning—laughing because the Rooster laughed, crying because their Lady was so glad. And a new sound rose up above the land that day, a deep and throated, holy sound, the whole camp participating, none left out, none louder than the others. And this was the name of the sound: it was Joy.

"Ahhhhhhh, Chauntecleer!"

Twenty-seven

Morning, and Pertelote's Enlightenment

Now, lightly, Pertelote herself walked down the ice of the Liverbrook, carrying Chauntecleer in her heart.

"I've found it," he had whispered in her ear. "Pertelote, I have found my Something to do." These words were for her alone, since she alone had known the torment of his soul. "Be glad with me."

She was exceeding glad.

And he had asked her to go and comfort the small outlander that waited a half mile down-ice from them: "He holds the key."

She'd nodded at the request, and he with perfect love had kissed her. He kissed her. He gazed into the deepest part of her being, and he kissed her.

Then they had parted, Chauntecleer leaping like fire to the crown of the Stag Black-Pale, crying "Ho!" to all the Animals; Pertelote walking south in singular wonder.

Now, walking, she heard behind her the slow roaring of the congregation. That sound pursued her like the waves of an ocean, for the Rooster was calling to the Animals and they were answering. He was an orator, as in the old days, holding them by the mere force of his language, his vision, his desire.

"Ahhhhhhh," she heard: one giant throat, a completely harmonious veneration. They would follow him, and that was something. But that he was willing to lead them, why, that was something else again. Chauntecleer had *chosen* the office and was glad to be in it! Chauntecleer was alive. "Ahhhhhhh-men!" Dear God, thought Pertelote, bending her neck in the prayer: what gift has given the Rooster hope again? What "key" has accomplished his transfiguration?

Yet, there it was, just like the old days—

"Ahhhhhhh-men!"

When she lifted her eyes again she spotted the outlander, fixed between the naked, wintry trees. He was a Coyote, twisted into the most ghastly contortion, stiff and grinning at once, and flicking his eyes between the distant roaring and her own approach.

And here is the grace of Pertelote: that, in spite of all the glories of the morning, her heart went out to this Coyote, and she cared for him.

She paused.

"Are you afraid?" she asked.

Not a hair of the Coyote moved.

"Do you think that I might hurt you?"

Sticks and bones was this Coyote, thin as a razor, sunken eyes and hungry and, indeed, afraid.

So Pertelote sat down ten yards away in order to show that she meant no harm.

"No, no, none of us would hurt you, sir," she said, smiling. "Don't mind my tears. They are happiness, I assure you."

It seemed to Pertelote that a pitiful guilt sat in the corner of this Coyote's eye, as though he were asking, What have I done? But he said nothing. He cowered. Then the Rooster roared, and she saw the ears twitch to the distant declamation:

SOMEWHERE THERE'S A WAY, cried Chauntecleer. I HAVE DREAMED IT—

Ah, the Coyote was listening, too. So Pertelote said to him, "You're very important to Lord Chauntecleer. To all of us, really. Somehow, sir, you've given him hope again. Do you understand that?"

He blinked. For an instant the poor Beast truly looked at her, and she poured words into the opening.

"I don't know what your goodness is," she said, "but I think —I am convinced, sir—that I've been praying for you to come to us. And look! You have come!"

—DOWN TO THE NETHERWORLD, THAT WAY—they both heard the Rooster's cry—WHERE TWO BEINGS DWELL, ONE OF THEM GOOD AND ONE OF THEM EVIL—

"See? Do you hear that? Do you hear the strength in my husband now?" she said, and she thought she saw the ghost of agreement in his grin. Impulsively she spoke the frank truth to this stranger: "Oh, how I love him. I love him so much," she whispered.

He heard her. He dropped his eyes before her confession and relaxed—and dear Pertelote recognized the kinship.

"Why, you too!" she said. "You love someone too, and someone loves you. Isn't that wonderful? We're not such strangers after all—"

WYRM! the Rooster tolled that word like a bell.

And WYRM! thundered the Animals.

Pertelote heard, but Pertelote was also caring for the Coyote. "You didn't come here for yourself, did you?" she said. She rose and took three paces closer to him. "You came for someone else, didn't you? See? I can read the heart in you, and we're not strangers. Who is she? My beloved's name is Chauntecleer. What is the name of your beloved?"

The thin Coyote relaxed and sighed, and a thoroughly lonely shadow covered his face. Ah, the outlander! He was homesick!

MUNDO CANI DOG! roared the Rooster.

And the Animals answered, MUNDO CANI!

She heard. Part of her had never left that convocation. But part of her remembered homesickness and suffered with this Creature. "You are thinking of her right now, aren't you? And you can see her, too. Dear sir, let me see your beloved." The Coyote raised his eyes, and he and the Hen were looking at one another. "What is her name? Tell me her name," said Pertelote.

But in that same moment the blaring of the Rooster carried a dreadful message to Pertelote, and she went up on her toes as though stabbed. She was listening.

I WILL! I WILL! Chauntecleer was crowing. I'LL GO THAT WAY TO THE NETHERWORLD, AND I MYSELF WILL KILL THE EVIL ONE, AND I WILL SET THE GOOD ONE FREE!

The Hen staggered for a moment on two legs, then listed and sank to the ground. "Chauntecleer?" she wailed. She covered her head in her wing. "Chauntecleer?"

The Coyote saw all this and stood up.

Pertelote shrank. One sob, like a spasm, shook her, because she lay in a void.

Then it was that the Coyote spoke. "I'm," he said. "I'm sorry."

Not his fault. Not his fault—but Pertelote couldn't tell him that. She could hardly breathe. Not his fault—but she was drowning in her knowledge. *This* was his Something to do? Go down to Wyrm? Oh, that Cock! Then he was going to leave her after all, and who did he think he was, that Cock! That overweening Cock! So self-centered in his mopings and his guilt that no one, no one but himself could go face Wyrm! So blindly penetential that he could forget her, forget her heart! But she had *loved* him. *"Chauntecleer!"*

Incredibly, the little Coyote crept to her side, and touched the Hen lightly with his paw, and whispered, "Tssssst," with sympathy. Whispered, "Rachel."

The Animals were tumultuous in twice ten thousand voices: *AHHHHHHH-MEN!*

But the memorable word, and the one that Pertelote never forgot thereafter, was the little word of a kind Coyote, seeking some way to console her:

"Rachel," he said. "Her name is Rachel."

Rachel.

Pertelote started to cry.

Twenty-eight

A Day to Put His Affairs in Order

He had sworn an oath before heaven and all of the Animals, and he was persuaded that Wyrm had heard it, too. Now there was work to be done, and one day to do it.

Chauntecleer sent Black-Pale on a wide, magnificent run, while he himself rode banner in the antlers. They made a complete circuit of the camp, Black-Pale striking the ground with authority, the Rooster breasting the wind, his wings laid back, his eye narrow, his comb smoking. He was flame. This was a day of unspeakable sweetness for him, though there was sadness too: he was taking his leave.

He crowed constantly. He wanted to lift the spirits of his Animals in spite of the bitter winter; more than that, to convince them of strength and purpose and grandeur and color in their lives, to unify them with the sense of their own significance; but most of all, to proclaim the good news that the Rooster had changed. He'd taken hold again. He was in startling command. The times! The times themselves were changing—and by a single, extraordinary act he, Chauntecleer, would see to the health of the Animals forever. He was taking leave. But he wanted to leave them faithful and whole.

"Mundo Cani shall come out of the depths!" he crowed. "Then who can hurt you, when we have triumphed over Evil, face to face, in his own place? Oh, dear hearts! When Evil is dead, there shall be no Evil any more. And the Dog shall be the sign of it. Watch for the Dog. Remember that I told you to watch for the Dog!"

Bright, incendiary Rooster, scorching the land from the top

of a traveling Stag! And the Animals believed in him. They laughed. Their eyes were stars, their voices full of worship, and their hearts burst.

They said, "The spirit of God is upon him." Then who could resist his excitement?

None. Neither two nor two thousand. He asked none of them to go with him tomorrow, because the battle would be his alone. This time *he* would enter the breach. It was his obligation and his oath. But neither did he deny any happy heart the right to attend him, and many talked of going.

And Chauntecleer, flushed with leadership, could play it two ways that day: not only did he handle the Animals as a single body, he the head; but he remembered them one by one as well, individuals in need of individual attention. Having circumscribed the whole community, he entered it and walked among them, talking. And then it seemed that he was everywhere.

Gentle words for String Jack and his kin, who shied from noise of any kind, even the glorious kind.

He requested Sharpshin the Hawk to fly pilot for any that would run north with him in the morning. Sharpshin was proud to accept.

He suggested that the Goats take baths. The Goats announced that Hophni and Phinehas, their forebears, maintained a faithful sobriety from water of any sort. They were content to stink.

He noticed the Fawn De La Coeur, following at a distance but hanging back with a troubled eye upon her father.

He strengthened the will of the Sheep.

He encouraged the Pronghorn to closer quarters with other Animals.

He met the little Coyote on a lonely stretch of the Liverbrook, was mildly surprised to find the Beast alone, since he thought that Pertelote was with him, but forgot his surprise in the more crucial task of convincing the Coyote to wait, to stay. The poor beast was desperate to be home again. He seemed at the end of self-control. A little food was all he wanted, and leave to be gone. But since eloquence was lost on him, Chauntecleer tried friendship, first, and then the simple command that the Coyote had no choice but to wait. They would go together, at the right time. The strange Coyote cringed, both from the "together" and from the order "at the right time." But Chauntecleer allowed no debate on the matter—too much depended upon this Coyote's knowledge!—and the Coyote stayed, watched by two Deer. Oh, where was Pertelote to pet and to keep this Creature?

By the Canonical Crows, Terce and Sext and None, the Rooster ribbed the day, giving it a fine round shape. But each crow wounded De La Coeur, ever close behind them, and Chauntecleer felt sorry for her.

He declared a feasting for the evening, and food came out in abundance, and the Animals ate, and the chatter around their mouthfuls was happy indeed.

But while they ate, the Rooster spoke a different word to the Mice, whom he appointed to manage the larder in his absence. The word was wise, but it troubled them because it also seemed so final. They were just Mice.

"A little hunger today," he said, "is better than famine tomorrow. Tags, be as frugal as possible with the food hereafter. Enough to live on and no more." They were walking to the Hemlock, the Rooster and the Mice, and the Mice kept looking at one another, questioning.

"We don't know what the future holds, do we?" said Chauntecleer. The Mice all shook their heads. They knew very little of anything. "If," said Chauntecleer, "I say, *if* I don't come back again, then you must make this food to last a long, long time. I trust your prudence, don't I?" he asked, and they nodded automatically, but their eyes were very big. "And I trust your integrity, right?" They nodded. "And you are mature, now, and I respect your maturity, isn't that so?" Poor Mice, they nodded and nodded, and they blinked, and they nodded. They looked afraid. "Good," said Chauntecleer. "I know I won't be disappointed."

In this way he gave each Mouse a manhood. They couldn't

talk to him just now, having so much to turn over in their minds. But neither did they cry.

And so they came to the Hemlock. Chauntecleer sighed with a certain satisfaction. A good day. A good kingdom. Good, good Animals. It was going to be fine after all. They would fare well, and they would remember him, please God, with honor—

But then he noticed one little Hen alone, and it troubled him. Facing the stone cliff and shivering helplessly was Chalcedony, eating nothing of the feast. But she was the one for whom he had gathered so much food! No, he wasn't done, yet.

The Rooster went and stood beside her, a Rooster and a Hen together.

"Well," he said, "we are sister and brother for sure now."

She stared at him, astonished.

But he simply smiled.

"I did that," said Chauntecleer. "Oh, yes. Ever since the winter began I have been shivering just like you. See? The cold was in my bones. I know how you feel, Chalcedony."

She opened her beak and closed it again, gazing at him. Hoo! He was so close to her.

"But here's hope," he said. "I'm warm now."

She tore her eyes away and bowed her head. "It's not," she confessed, "so much as I'm cold, m'Lord. It's somewhat a different matter—"

"Shoosh, shoosh, Chalcedony," he said. "I know that. We are alike. I was cold because I was weak; and I was weak because I was sad. Like you."

Her head came up. He continued to stare at the wall. The shivering grew worse in her, and she marveled: "You? You was sad?"

"Me," said the Rooster.

"Oooooo," said Chalcedony.

Then Chauntecleer narrowed the subject. Directly he asked her, "Why are you standing here, so sad?"

She sighed and shivered terribly. The day was dying into

quietness, the evening heavy, now, and grey. It seemed as if the whole world were hushing to hear of Chalcedony's sadness.

Chauntecleer turned so that his beak was an inch from hers. "You can whisper," he said. Gentle Lord Chauntecleer.

And she did. "On account of—my beautiful Lady was weeping," she whispered. "On account of—I don't know how to comfort her."

Pertelote! Chauntecleer felt a sudden rebuke. Pertelote? He hadn't expected Pertelote to appear between them. He hadn't seen her all day long. He hadn't even thought of her, except once, and then in irritation. Chalcedony's goodness was better than his.

"Well," he said, "what if I went to comfort her?"

"No, I, *I,*" the little Hen insisted. "How often wasn't I the one was weeping? And how often didn't she put me in good cheer again? 'Tis once, just once, Chalcedony should do somewhat for her Lady." She sighed. "But there's not nothing in this body for to give, you see. That's the truth, and that's the sadness. I'm a cripple after all."

"You are my Hen," said Chauntecleer immediately. "You are my sister."

"Please, sir," whined Chalcedony. "Thank you for that, but I know what's true. I'm runted, sir. I'm nowhere near my Lady for worth. Do you think that you could go away now?"

Chauntecleer didn't move. He kept his head by hers, and the longer he stood the more distressed she became.

"Do I upset you, Chalcedony?" he asked.

"Oh, sir! Oh, sir! How could you think such a thing?" She jerked her head in confused embarrassment. "Did I make you think that?" Her tiny comb reddened. "No! It's, why should you spend time with me? This is no Lady here, nor nobody worth noticing. That's what it is." She was near tears. "Maybe you could just go away now?"

Chauntecleer looked at her with honest love. "I will be going away," he said quietly. "But I want it well with you before I do, Chalcedony. You are a good woman, and better than you know. Wait here. I've a job for you to do. No one can do it but you. Wait. Wait a moment—"

The Rooster backed away from the Hen, nodding his wish that she should stay just where she was, then turned and searched among the bodies of the Animals. They had begun, now, to buckle their knees and to lower themselves for sleep, though a general buzzing hung above them, and that was excitement. The lowest Animals lay in shadows. Chauntecleer looked for antlers, fourteen points, a minor forest—and he found them. Black-Pale stood still and silently. His daughter De La Coeur was gazing at him, as she had the whole day through.

Nothing had been said between them; that was clear. But there was much that should be said, and that was clear as well. Tomorrow was no easy day for either of the Deer. Both were suffering.

Chauntecleer went and touched the Fawn.

"Child," he said, "Will you walk with me? If you walk with me, you walk with a very wise Rooster."

Her glance went to her father, who neither restrained her nor set her free. The Stag was mute. He was not a Creature who displayed his feelings.

Chauntecleer said, "You love your father."

She tipped her head to one side and nodded. How young was she, and vulnerable!

And Chauntecleer said more quietly, "And you miss your mother, too."

The Fawn hung her head in memory. She missed her mother.

"You see?" said Chauntecleer. "I am wise. I understand these things. And I know even more than these. Come. Be brave, child. Let me say them aloud while we walk. Come, walk with me."

Slowly, at his gentle urging, the long-legged Fawn followed him, though often she threw backward glances to her father:

such pride and such a forest of antlers black against the dusk!

Chauntecleer said, "You heard that your father is going away tomorrow, though no one told you this. You guessed it. And you are right. He is. He will carry me north. Now, here is the hard part: you are afraid that he will not come back again. You think that maybe he will go the way your mother went. You don't say this, of course, because maybe that would make it come true. But you fear it. And then you would be left alone." Chauntecleer looked at her in the darkness. "Do I speak the truth?" he said.

She stopped and sighed.

"Do I?" he asked.

"Yes," she said.

"See?" said Chauntecleer. "See the things I know?"

She nodded sadly. Indeed, he knew very much.

"Now, listen to me while we walk," said the Rooster. They walked. "It's with me that your father goes. I will watch over him. I am very wise, De La Coeur, as you have said yourself; and I will send him home again. Do you believe this?"

With enormous eyes she blinked.

"Do you?" he said.

And she said, "Yes."

"Good," he said. "That's settled. But that's only the half of it. I know, I know, I know. The other half is: who will watch over you."

The Fawn drew a breath. Chauntecleer had touched every worry in her. He was a surgeon of the feelings.

"Please don't stop listening to me now, dear De La Coeur," he said, "because I have an answer for that too. I'm a very wise Rooster, you see."

They had come to the Hemlock tree, and they had to stop. There was nowhere else to walk.

"De La Coeur, child, can you say hello?" said Chauntecleer.

She nodded.

"Practice," he gently urged her. "Say hello."

She said, "Hello." She gave a silly smile.

"Good," he said. "Wait here." He went to the Hen Chalcedony, and he touched her. "Come with me," he said. The Rooster and the crippled Hen walked to a Fawn.

"Again," he said.

"Hello," said the Fawn De La Coeur.

"Well?" said Chauntecleer to the Hen, and Chalcedony curtsied, somewhat flustered to be introduced to this highborn child, the object of so much secret affection. "Hoo, sir," she whispered. "Is this right?"

But Chauntecleer ignored the question. "While I'm with your father," he said, "this Lady will be with you, and you will not be alone. Child, she is even wiser than I am and so much better in the eyes of God." Then, to Chalcedony: "Love her. Please love and care for this child, dear Chalcedony, with all your heart. Neither you nor she should be lonely, do you hear me?"

"Ooooooo," breathed Chalcedony. "Oooooo, my Lord! I don't know what to say."

"Say," said Chauntecleer, "that you have a daughter, now. Someone to comfort. Say that you are not nothing. And sometimes in the night, when you two are together, say, Chalcedony, that I love you. I do. I wish you believed it. I do."

He left them, then, and went to the other side of the Liverbrook; and he waited, his head bowed.

In a little while he heard first the Hen and then the Fawn.

The Hen said, "Does De La Coeur fancy a snack now and then?"

The Fawn giggled.

And Chauntecleer was finished. Oh, the leader loved his own.

Vespers.

Chauntecleer lifted his voice like a trumpet across the land; the frigid darkness took a glory, and all of the Animals paused in their night-talk. "Listen, listen," they said. "It's Chauntecleer." He sang. He sent their souls to God. Neither sleep nor the grave could trouble them then, for they were kept.

Did anyone fear the absence of their head in the days to come?

No more.

Did anyone think that they had no purpose in the world, or love?

No more.

Was anyone ignorant of the name of Mundo Cani, soon to stand among them, living and loving them again? Was anyone too fainthearted to cry "Wyrm! Wyrm!" in a curse, to taunt the Evil One in his own lair? Why, even the Sparrows spat his name, then giggled. And the Hens above all yearned for the Dog to come and touch them and weep at their whiteness.

Could anyone suffer the hopelessness of the dreary winter?

No more!

Chauntecleer, trumpet of the imperium, convinced his entire land of possibility, and then of peace.

He blew one keening note so long, that women found themselves to be sobbing before it was done, and their husbands held them, and the whole congregation of the Animals closed into a universal hugging—and so they entered the darkness, and so began the night.

Only—Pertelote was not on her branch. Pertelote had not returned.

Twenty-nine
Night

The Lady had spent her day in loneliness.

As soon as she realized the magnitude of her husband's ambition and the consequences that must come of it, she couldn't so much as speak to the Coyote. Talk simply wasn't in her. And she dreaded to face Chauntecleer. And everything else in existence diminished. Ten thousand Animals were nothing, nothing. She wanted only to be alone.

"I'm sorry," the Coyote had said.

She couldn't thank him. She couldn't ask how much he loved his wife, Rachel. Love had become such a cruel thing to her. She left.

Altogether dazed, she wandered the Liverbrook south through the woods, and south until it met with Wyrmesmere, the sea now frozen to its bowels, humped and yellowed and silent. The cold goes deep, my Lord. Then she walked westward on the plains. She brushed the stones with the tip of a wing. Her face was numb. Her heart was numb. The cold goes deep, my Lord. In time she came to the old earthwork, the wall her husband once had engineered against the enemy when hope and a certain warmth had bound them all together. There, on a whited ruin, she sat down, and she sat merely.

For the rest of the morning she held her peace.

But at noon, under a grey sky, while picking at her feathers, she suddenly threw up her head and wailed, "He wants to fight Wyrm. What then? O Lord! O please, my Lord! The cold goes deep, my Lord, my Lord."

And she burst into tears.

She was angry with Chauntecleer. It seemed that she hated him, hated him for his childishness and his everlasting obsessions. She wept until her throat ached and the tears went dry and the sobs came in separate spasms; and this was several hours.

In the afternoon she wrapped her wings around herself. All alone and softly, she sang:

> "—made love to me so slow and sweetly,
> Sighing names, he came discreetly
>   Home;
> And I to him gave children after;
> I it was had cried through laughter,
>   'Come'—"

She closed her eyes. What would she do with all her memories? Ponder them?

But then, in the darkness, the beautiful Pertelote heard the distant vespers of Lord Chauntecleer. That trumpet shuddered her as well as any other, its last, longest note literally taking her breath away. It must have reached to the end of the earth. And he, she understood, was persuaded of his holy enterprise. He was bounden to it. He was crowing creed.

So she said, "We've had our tears. Enough. Enough." She lifted her head. She stood up with slow resolution.

"It is his decision," she declared out loud. "His honor, his purpose, his dignity. So. I will not trouble him with my troubles. So. So, I will accept him now as I did at the beginning: Chauntecleer is Chauntecleer."

The Hen walked to the site where the Coop had stood before the war. She measured the ground from one corner and found a hollow covered by woven branches and sealed in ice. With a sudden strength, she smashed the ice; and then she picked the weave apart by jerks of her claw. When she had torn a hole in the earth-pocket, she drove her beak into it and withdrew two utensils of leather and metal.

Yet, for all her resolution, Pertelote could not help despising the taste of that leather.

This one night Chauntecleer did not seek solitude down the Liverbrook. He sought Pertelote. This should not be a night alone; he wanted her body next to his, and forgiveness if she could give it, and the assurance when he left tomorrow that there was peace between them—

But he didn't know where to look for her. The wood and the world were huge after all. The sky was starless. He stood still, a doubtful Rooster on the ice.

She had ever been a woman unto herself, quiet, private, and never truly claimed by the land. By the marriage, yes; and by motherhood, when that was a reality; by friendship, but not by the land. She could have gone anywhere.

Pertelote, born and raised in another place, a woman al-

ready when he met her—Pertelote carried memories in her
that he would never know. She'd never made much of her
past, except that it had been difficult and that it was over. Yet
because a part of her was secret from everyone, the Lady
always seemed something of a sojourner in Chauntecleer's
land. Not his. She was not *his* Hen, but wholly her own. Then
she could be anywhere.

He shouldn't have neglected her during the day.

He shouldn't have taken her for granted.

He stood on Liverbrook ice a perfect fool, paralyzed by his
ignorance. He had no idea where to look for her, and the
world was huge, and the night was empty without her.

"Pertelote?"

Then a little sound touched him on the back of his brain.
It was so tiny that he didn't hear it. He suspected it. He
screwed his eyes to the darkness.

"Hello?"

Tink.

There: downstream the Liverbrook. There. And not ice
only. The ice had grown so old it lost its crystaline quality. It
sounded lumpish and wooden these days.

Tink.

That was not ice.

Tink, tink.

Chauntecleer went to his toes and stretched his neck. He
cocked his head to stare with one eye and then the other. The
sound was regular and ringing, delicate, metal on metal.

Pertelote? "Pertelote? Is that you?"

Who else would come with such a delicacy? No one! Chauntecleer allowed himself to grin. He didn't deny a flush of joy,
and he began to run toward the noise—

And here came a darkened figure, walking slowly the bends
of the stream, beautiful, sure-footed, sure-spirited: Pertelote,
indeed! Two straps hung from her beak, two metal pieces at
the ends of these, striking one another as she walked: *tink.
Tink!*

"Oh, Pertelote," Chauntecleer cried, overcome by the woman's goodness, her simply being there. He choked.

She said, "I thought you'd want these. I've polished them for you."

"Pertelote," whispered the poor Cock.

"Sit," she said. "Sit down, sir, and let me have your ankle."

He sat. He loved her. He loved her touch, but he could only shake his head.

With efficient skill she bound a terrible spur to Chauntecleer's lower shank, a gleaming, reaching weapon named Gaff. By this weapon he had killed the Cockatrice. She drew the leather tight with her beak. To his other leg she tied another, this one named the Slasher, no less fearsome than the first, and a yank made it tight, and then she herself sat down, silently.

She was done.

When he could find his voice, the Rooster said, "Then you approve?"

Pertelote's own voice was not missing. Nevertheless, she waited before she spoke. And then she said, "I ask only that you do not do this thing in madness. That you are not mad, Chauntecleer."

"Touch me," he said. "Do I feel like a child or an idiot?"

She didn't touch him. She said, "It's not the Cockatrice. Wyrm, this time. You are going to fight Wyrm himself. Do you know what you are doing?"

"Yes," he said.

"That he *is* the Evil One?"

"Yes," he said.

"And what the consequences of such a fight must be?"

"Yes," he said. "Perhaps I'll set Mundo Cani free."

"Perhaps," she said. She closed her eyes. "But that's not what I mean."

"No," he said. "That's not what you mean."

"Say it," she said. "Say it aloud."

And he said, "I will die."

She said, "Yes." She said, "Thank you." And then her whole body shuddered, but her eyes stayed closed, and she did not cry. "You will die, Chauntecleer."

Neither touched the other for a while, because what were they, now that the truth was spoken? Husband and wife? Widow, corpse and comforter? What were they doing here? Remembering? Cherishing? Taking leave?

Chauntecleer was the cause of this. Therefore, Pertelote had to speak first, because he didn't have the right. When she did, it was in a diminished voice.

"Tell me the worth, Chauntecleer," she said. "Tell me the need."

And he was conscious of the depth of her question. For both of them, the Rooster chose his words with scrupulous care.

"For righteousness," he said. "And as for me, for penance."

He thought through his answer. So often Chauntecleer had acted in passion, afterward justifying the act. This one time, for this extremest venture, it was necessary that he explain himself first and clearly.

"My life has been a shameful thing, Pertelote," he said. "I've been a sickness in the land, and who's to say that all our sorrows don't find their source in me? It is wrong, wrong, that Mundo Cani moans in hell. It is wrong for him, wrong for the earth, wrong in the order of things. And it is *my* wrong. And what can I do about it?—"

He stopped. He wanted to speak few words, not many. He did not want to protest, only to explain.

"Unless I die," he said slowly, "then all this life is a death. Do you understand that? But if I sacrifice myself, then this life was something after all. I need to plead forgiveness. I need to do *one thing right*—and the best thing of all! Otherwise," he said, "how could the Animals live in peace? Otherwise," he whispered, "how could you love me?"

Pertelote fairly wailed in her anguish, "But I do love you!"

"I am someone now," he said.

"No!" she cried. "I loved you all along, no matter *what* you thought you were! Don't scorn me so much as to think I've been blind. I knew you, and still I loved you."

"When I ignored you?"

"When you ignored me, of course! You were here, weren't you?"

"Pertelote!" he said sharply, stopping her. "This is me. *This* is me. This is Chauntecleer, finally! This is the way I should be. I've taken an oath. I've challenged Wyrm in a sacred vow, to fight him. By the grace of God I now have the chance to find him and to fulfil the oath—to be! In dying I will *be*. This is me. This is my being, now. This is my purpose, my justification, my goodness, my goodness, to fight and to die—"

"*Ahh!*" gasped Pertelote as though she were falling, and Chauntecleer rushed to her. He caught her in his wings, wrapped her all around and hugged her tightly from the ice, from the night, from tomorrow, from the terrors of this sinful world, from fear. He had a boldness in his heart, now, and by that boldness he wished his wife a perfect peace. Oh, God! It was so good to be holding her again. And when she allowed it, when finally she shaped her body to his own, he nearly wept for gladness: he was her husband, protector again! He squeezed her till he trembled.

And in this wave of loving her, he whispered, "Sacrifice." Almost divinely he murmured, "Sacrifice. It isn't madness, is it?"

She didn't answer him. And still, she didn't cry.

He rocked his beautiful Pertelote and whispered a litany of names. "Lord Russel the Fox," he said. "Him. The Wee Widow Mouse. Nimbus and Beryl, that humble Hen. And the Rat Ebenezer, whom I do not forget. And the thousand, the meek and the faithful thousand. And the Turkeys—" He chuckled to himself. "Our children, too, the Pins, the First, the Second and the Third: they shall none of these have died in vain when I have met their murderer. Is that madness?"

She shook her head. "I hear how you name them, Chauntecleer," she said. "I hear how deeply you care for them. But you always did. But this thing, this obsession—'' She stopped.

Slowly Pertelote returned his hug. He felt the warmth coming to him as a gift. He felt her cheek upon his neck, caressing him, and now the tears did run from his eyes, for she had chosen; he had not demanded.

"You are my husband," she whispered. "I am your wife. I love you, Chauntecleer. *That* is not madness."

"O mighty God!" the Rooster cried. "Watch over this woman! Never, never let her go!"

And then, while they clung to one another on the Liverbrook, their backs to the weather, he said, "You sang to me once in my desolation. Do you remember?"

"I remember," she said.

"Do you think that you could sing to me again?"

That night Compline was a tender shock for all the Animals. It woke them, gently, then composed them for a yet more blessed sleep.

It was sung in a woman's voice.

Pertelote did not crow or cry out or lift up her voice in the treetops. It was crystal, ringing clearly of its own accord, completely clean. Her soul was a crystal bell.

> "—For safety I commend my friends,
> Their spirits, sleep, and all their ends,
>   To God;
> And him whose life myself I live,
> His name Sweet Singer, *most* I give
>   To God—"

Chauntecleer inclined his ear and swallowed. It was an exquisite benediction, to hear his name within her prayer, as though he were eavesdropping upon her love for him. When the singing had died from the sky, it continued to wring his heart.

He did not sleep that night. He did not dream.

Thirty

John Wesley

One of the reasons why John Wesley Weasel grew so long and narrow was to keep him from getting stuck. Maybe the Creator expected that Weasel-brains would figure they could go anywhere and that Weasel-kidneys would know no caution, so that a Buggar like John Wesley, charging forward with a purblind courage, might find himself in straits, as it were, and stuck. Half-way down a burrow, and so forth; midway through two rocks. So, what the Creator did: he gave John Wesley a skull-bone bigger than any other part of his body; he shortened the legs and lengthened the tail, and he loosed this oddment to Weasel-devices hoping, since no one else could restrain him, that his own head would. Well, if the head-bone didn't fit, he'd be stopped right there at the beginning before matters got worse, right? And if John Wesley *could* get his head through anything first, why then the rest of him would follow like *hoopla!* and happiness, right? To gauge him against his own fine qualities of daring, courage, pluck, and fearlessness, God gave John Wesley Weasel a fat head.

And it worked reasonably well in the physical world.

It failed in the spiritual.

More times than a Weasel liked to remember he'd gotten himself stuck in tight situations, and sometimes he could brazen his way out, but sometimes he was plain stuck and discomfited.

Once his head did not prohibit him from loving a Mouse. A fool thing to do, to love a woman of *any* stripe—but a Mouse? And then he'd acted moony, lounging at her door,

puffing his chest, suffering the irritations of her seven children, suffering them in silence, mind you, "sparking," as he
called it. "Sparking the Widow." This was the situation, a
pleasant one, he admitted at first, and worth the bother, because the Widow had a touch of ferrety spunk herself. Oh, yes!
She'd brought her children a monstrous piece from the mountain regions downriver to Chauntecleer's Coop, and that by
herself, and a Weasel could admire Weasel-notions, even in a
Mouse, and in a woman. So John Wesley slipped into a situation pleasant—at first.

Then came the sticking. The Wee Widow Mouse was murdered by a sliding Basilisk, and John was the first to find her
dead, and all at once he was stuck, squeezed in his grief.
Nobody told John about grief! No, he couldn't scream the
aching out of him. It stays. No, he couldn't fight nor murder
nor slaughter the aching out of him; and though he scorched
the battlefield that day, and though he killed a countless host,
himself inspiring the Animals unto victory, he lay down that
night still aching. Nor was it the loss of his ear that caused this
aching. It was the Wee Widow Mouse. Dead. And the aching
didn't pass.

See? No way out of that situation, except maybe time. Time,
busyness, action, no thinkings since thinks buggars the brains,
noise.

But even in these latter days John Wesley will notice one of
the Brothers Mice in a certain pose, Freitag laughing, Samstag
crying, and suddenly he'll feel the pressure of his grief for the
Widow: stuck. Still stuck, even though God gave him this fat
head. . . .

And now, in the northern regions of the world, it had happened again, and the world was in a bad way. Old and gloomy
memories were troubling him, and he moved with a slow step
among the pine, frowning. It was an article of faith with him
that thinkings buggars the brains; yet here he was, thinking.

He tried a few short punches to cleanse himself, rising on

his haunches: "Do and do for you—" It didn't work. Do what and for who?

Despite his head, John Wesley had sort of got himself stuck again, this time in a totally unexpected pinch, but one of his own making nonetheless: he had discovered lonesomeness. Worse, he felt it, and this gave him pause. It made him think, as it were. Because this was no mere want for company; John Wesley had felt a cold and total solitude, and in that moment he believed in endings. Endings: only so many Critters in this universe, and few at that. Endings: one by one the Critters die. Endings: but could be *all* could die together, and then there would be a universe, turning, turning silently—but no Critters. . . .

"Hoopla!" shouted John Wesley in a pine forest, as loud as he could, to shake these gloominesses. "Hoopla! Hoopla! Hoop—"

Well, what had happened was, John Wesley had sort of come to an end, bumped into one.

Not only, in his vigor, had he cleared the territories of their populations, leaving himself to scramble alone while others went south for dinner; not only was he truly tired from the labors, and maybe that made even a Weasel vulnerable to contemplations and philosophies (seeing how seldom a Weasel is weary unto idleness); but also, John Wesley had traveled, finally, to the northernmost regions of the continent. He had walked out onto the utter wastes of the tundra, when all the stars were a shower in black heaven, and all the white around him cold and ghostly. He had seen his own paw, dark upon the ancient glacier. He had heard and felt the polar wind. And nothing, nothing in this vast, impassive realm either cared or knew that a Weasel was there. It dawned on John Wesley like thought: nothing *could* care, because nothing here was alive, except for himself. He had come to an end. He stood in it. Ice below, ice-pieces suspended for stars above, and only the emptiness between. John Wesley shriveled; he had another thought: that his own little life could wink out and then the world would be deserted, left to the wind and the stone and the ice alone—

"Hey! Ho! Try me, yo! Weasels sucker Buggars—oh! Gives to butts a hundred cuts, and says, 'Please pass the sugar, Oh!' " Thus he recited now in the pine forest, stomping his hind paws, beating his fore-ones together, raising up his fat head. "Hey! Ho! Bite me, yo! Weasels whirling fast and slow, Whips you raw—jaw, paw and claw, then sits to see how fast you go—"

No good. Taunt songs, bawdy songs, and he was stuck. He sat down.

Well, John had escaped the tundra as soon as he felt its haunting on his spirit. He'd run to the green, south to the forests and some thin light again. But even so, he ran slower than usual, and memories began to bear him down, and the death of the Widow, which he hadn't openly considered for so long, saddened him; and it was strange, but the old ache was in him again, almost as though grieving and the northern cold were one and the same. He thought he saw what the Widow might have seen in the instant before she died, and he thought, "Oh, Widow. How lonely!" And he thought, "Why-come someones couldn't be with you then?"

"Ho-kay!" roared John Wesley Weasel in the middle of a pine forest. He leaped up and raced on short legs in a hard, tight circle. "Do and do and do for *you*, John Double-u!" And he bellowed at the top of his lungs: "Thinkings buggars the brains!" He stopped and thrust his paw high in the air, declaring, "Times for John to go home. Now!" He sat down, frowning.

Stuck.

Who knows how long a Weasel, on first descending into melancholy, stays there? No one. Not even John. One thing for sure: he wouldn't blame his Rooster any more for gloominesses, since he found out what powerful things they were, even to overcome a Double-u. John Wesley thought that thought most solemnly—but then it became the last thought of his gloom, and suddenly he was delivered.

He heard a living voice:

"Do and do for you, Double-do!"

His hair stood up.

A piece of rust went flying over his head. John Wesley sprang for the hollows beneath the pine and crouched, three-quarters hidden.

But there was no one in the forest. Dead logs, ice-locked; rocks out-cropping. No one. He stretched his neck—

Suddenly *behind* him the voice announced its position, yelling, "Hoople-la!"

He snapped round but saw nothing.

Then closer, from the tree at his left, the voice sang, "Gives someone what-for! Hoople-la! Hoople-la!"

John twisted into knots. By Gaw, the devil was quick! Three cries from three places and never a dash between! John's heart had begun to pump: a little fear, a little admiration, a great, huge rush of excitement: WAR!

Well, and if this was war, then let the warrior emerge. What kind of a bloody warrior hides? Not John Double-u, whether he knows the foe or not!

By Gaw!

His head low down, his lip curled back from a row of needle-teeth, John Wesley Weasel stepped to open ground. Flashing his eye all around himself, he drew his legs together, humping and hardening his spine, tightening like a bowstring. His claw closed on the earth; he found a footing. At the bare glimpse of a throat this Weasel could spring and slash it. He was a deadly weapon, and he knew it.

Slow, slow he delivered the challenge in a hiss. "Show. Some ones show him damn self to me—"

But "Show!" sang the voice from the left-hand tree. Then, as quick as sin, it shifted and sang from the right: "Damn self. Hee-hee!"

Hee-hee?

What it was: there were two, three enemies, and John was surrounded, and it was their territory, not his, and they knew the terrain, he didn't, so every advantage was theirs—hot damn! John *liked* them odds! Black thunder was his face! He was feeling better.

"This Double-u," he hissed, "he fights like a fighter. Teeth to tooth, in the opens. Come out, Someones! Kill or bloody be killed by John—"

"Hee-hee."

Hee-hee, for God's sake! Who giggles at battles? At threats? At John?

John threw himself into his viciousness. He extended his long body and roared, "See me? See John? John's built to go in hidy places, Buggar! Fang first, and death in his mouth!" He began to crawl toward the left-hand tree: target—

"Hee-hee!"

Oh, those giggles were intolerable! Oh, this Weasel trembled, the bolt so close to shooting: "No protections, no! You don't comes to John? So! John, he comes to *you!*"

John coiled—

But in the instant before his launch he heard the wail, "NO! NOT THEM!" A new Critter come! "ME! ME! KILL ME!"

John spun on his tail and saw a full-grown Coyote limping toward him from the east, unguarded, unable, desperately abject: by her hindlegs alone she was pushing herself ahead, her cheek and chest both on the ground. What? Cripples came to fight him?

He turned toward his target again, and found his anger somewhat off the rhythm. He hesitated.

"Please," the woman whined. "They could outrun you. And even if you eat them, they're a mouthful apiece. I'm dinner for several days!"

What kind of a war was this?

"Hee-hee!" That giggle again! "Hee-hee" and "Hee-hee" from points north, west and south of the Weasel. John was growing bewildered by this sort of aggression. Might-be a truce and some talking together—

All at once the gigglers appeared and began to charge at him, and John Wesley was thunderstruck:

"Babies," he murmured. Fluffy, rusty, delighted with the scene that they had caused: "John was going to slaughter— baby Coyotes. Gaw!"

The closer they came, the more the woman panicked: "HERE! FIGHT ME! FIGHT ME!"

So she was the mama. But he was no fighter no more. He turned to her for help. He took a step and said, "Mama Coyote —" But then he had another shock:

Straightway the woman leaped a full nine feet through the air, a strong, spectacular flight away from him, astonishing grace. Nevertheless, when she hit ground again, she twisted into crippledness and crawled all broken back to him—

Poor John, his wits were gone. No: he wasn't gloomy any more, just confused. And tired. And might-be he *should* be alone.

"Mama Coyote, she doesn't need to worry, no," he said delicately. "John goes away now, ho-kay? Goo-by. Goob—"

But he had forgotten the baby-attack on its way.

The brother of the bunch, utterly fearless, tumbled forward, knocked a Weasel, and stuck his nose into John Wesley's mouth, crying, "Hello? Hello?"

"Benoni, no!" The woman rushed between them on healthy legs.

"Right! No!" gagged the Weasel, spitting fur.

"Why couldn't you stay at the Den?" She cuffed a sister.

"Right! At the Den!" the Weasel approved the discipline.

"I can't"—while she cuffed the other—"watch and forage both!"

"Right!" roared the Weasel. "Can't. Goo-by! Goo—"

But, "Do and do and do," sang this little Benoni, happily plucking Weasel-whiskers, one at a time.

"Ack! Get!" bellowed the Weasel, snatching back his whiskers. "John needs them things!"

And "Get!" he howled at the sister who was sniffing his behind, the most indefensible part of his anatomy.

"Get! Get! Get!" he pleaded with the sister who was licking all his old scars with maternal compassion. "Mama Coyote, doesn't you see to your childrens?—"

But Mama Coyote was no help at all. She'd changed again. She was plain sitting on her haunches, her muzzle stretched up to heaven, her eyes shut tight and running tears—and she was laughing. Laughing.

John, under full attack, was on his own. "Doesn't," he roared, "Mama Coyotes spank them bratlings?"

She shook her head. She couldn't speak for laughing.

"Doesn't Mama Coyotes *worries,* that bloody warriors swallows childrens down?"

Then language burst from the woman. "Soldiers," she gasped, "who stomp and sweat—in your own backyard—look —ridiculous!"

John Wesley Weasel, bloody warrior locked in battle with babies, suddenly saw himself stomping and sweating, glowering, threatening, glooming about such things as end-of-the-world, solemn about lonesomeness and death—John Wesley Weasel suddenly saw himself ridiculous! So he said, "Haw!" loud as a horn, and that's how *he* laughed. "Haw! Haw!" roared John Wesley, on account of his silliness. And "Haw!" because, by Gaw, these here babies liked him, and he liked to be liked.

For the space of a day, by the grace of God, the Weasel forgot hunger, the winter, the world and all. He had a vacation.

"What's a Double-do?" asked Benoni.

"Fearsomenesses, threats and storm-spits," growled the Weasel, "what gobbles childrens."

"Ha!" cried Benoni, marshmallow Coyote. "Double-do knows about the Witch with No Stomach?"

"Ha!" cried John Wesley. "Is my mama."

Benoni laughed. Private stories shared make friends. "Double-do! You only got one ear!"

"John's mama freezed one off for sassings."

"Double-do, do you got courage?"

"Courage is braveness. John gots braveness, you bet! Beats little Buggars' headses in."

Benoni presented his head to find out what beatings-in were like.

"Rips out little Buggars' gizzards!"

Twill searched her whole body for a gizzard which could be ripped out.

"Bites tails to make some garter-straps!"

Immediately, three tails were in his mouth.

"Ack!"

Oh, what a pleasure on a very cold day. And Mama watched, grinning. And Mama it was who invited a tired warrior to rest in their Den at the end of it. And a warrior was glad again.

So easily John Wesley's head fit through the hole into their Den. And so domestic was the Den itself, like a little hut against the weather. Where babies are, where women sit, the fighter can't be brutal any more.

John lay relaxed while Benoni Coyote gazed at him with unabashed interest.

"So," said the Weasel.

Benoni nodded solemnly. "So" was a fine thing to say and to hear.

"So. Might-be," the Weasel began, "little Benoni, he doesn't know from what is a bloody warrior."

"Warrior," said Benoni, nodding. A manly conversation.

"Is mighty, is a warrior. Fights fights of goodness and noblenesses."

"My papa is mighty," Benoni declared.

"Benoni gots a papa?" John Wesley scrutinized the pup. He thought backward a moment. "Is skinny?" he asked. Benoni nodded. "Sometimes stiff as wood? A wooden Critter?" Benoni nodded. "Ah, well, John, he thinks he met Benoni's papa once."

"Then you're lucky, aren't you, Double-do?" said Benoni.

" 'Cause he's stronger than Bears and faster than Hawks, and he could beat the Witch with No Stomach. Mighty."

"Okay," John thought it wise to say. "A mighty Coyote."

There was a nice silence in the Den. Rachel combed her daughters' coats with a motherly claw. Benoni sat fixed, staring at the Weasel. "Double-do?" he whispered. He had a new question in his head.

"What, little Benoni Coyote?"

A very important question—for the pup squirmed round until he'd put his nose to the Weasel's nose, and he took John Wesley's face between his paws.

Very earnestly he said, "You're my friend now, right?"

"Ack!" said John. He began to clear his throat. That was his answer.

"And do you love somebody with a very big, big love?"

The Weasel thought of a Rooster, his melancholy Lord. But he said, "Don't squash John's face, okay? No kissings! Warriors hates kissings, okay?"

But Benoni had another matter on his mind, so deep and serious that it made his eyes seem old indeed.

"Please," he said, "when you go, if you meet my papa again —please tell him to hurry home. Tell him Benoni loves him with a very big, big love. Double-do, tell him that Benoni misses him."

Thirty-one
Dreaming Still

Lord Chauntecleer set a remorseless pace for the journey north. He himself took a grim position in Black-Pale's antlers, riding the high bounds without a word. As fast as the Stag could travel, so fast did Chauntecleer wish to go.

One thing alone was left for him to do, and how he was constrained till it was done!

Animals traveled in his train, like the tail of a comet: other Deer, Goats, the hasty Hare and Pronghorn, Sheep, Cats on their own recognizance, Wolves in the wings. The fire in him had burned them, too. But inspiration isn't capability, and some of them fell back, too tired to continue. Pertinax Cobb got as far as Chalcedony's valley of Cicadas, where he collapsed panting. He dragged himself to the side while hooves and paws pounded past, and he thought, "Well, I can't go back again. What would Mrs. Cobb think of me if I did?" He thought, "I'll wait here. I'll wait till they return—"

The hardier Animals kept pace. A band of Creatures wound through the woods; broke open to the frozen grasslands; bowed their heads before a bitter wind; fell silent, save for the rhythm of their running, under a low, forbidding sky; slept dead and close to one another in the night, but rose in the dim morning, rose to their aching legs, rose again and followed the blazing Rooster—and ran.

It was because they chose to follow that he led—not because he chose to lead them. Their hearts were on him; but his was on the thing ahead. Chauntecleer: he was oblivious of the hardship they endured. He raced to his baptism. They merely ran. But they believed on him. So they ran.

Animals galloped behind him. There was only one who went before. Yet this one had the Rooster's attention, because he had a map in his head, and he was the key. A Coyote, utterly terrified by the trek and its intensity.

Sometimes the strange Coyote would fall down. He would twist around and bite his own shin, and this was no soft bite. He'd break flesh and draw blood. Then Chauntecleer would talk and talk to him in a low voice, and the Coyote would get up again to a nervous trot. But his tail was ever between his legs.

One noon the Beast doubled over and vomited all the food he'd eaten at the Hemlock. It lay steaming on the ground, and

the Coyote seemed to regard it with immeasurable sadness.
Then Chauntecleer, since talking availed nothing, touched the
point of the Slasher to his buttock, mounted the Coyote himself and rode him a while, beating his wings for speed. After
that the Coyote withdrew into a daze and took them straight
to their destination without another lapse.

Chauntecleer wore his weapons. Again and again, unconsciously, he felt the heft of Gaff and the Slasher, bound tightly
at his spurs. He was feeling his readiness. He was feeling the
skill in him and the fight to come, the strength of his cause and
its certainty. Nothing prevented him any more but the getting
there.

He breathed through his nostrils. His beak was a nail in this
outrageous winter; his eye was lidded and hard. He took the
black Stag's bucking leaps without a word.

But his heart was screaming, *I am going to kill you, Wyrm!*

Ferric, that skinny Coyote—Ferric simply couldn't comprehend the thing that he was doing. All he could think was that
the consequences would be terrible.

He had gone to get food, and he was bringing back instead
a host of thundering beasts. Run he never so fast, they were
always right behind him, closing in with all their weight and
all their teeth on the little Den that held his wife and children,
who hadn't a hint of what was coming. Rachel! He thought of
Rachel's smile and Rachel's confidence in him. Benoni, too.
Benoni, wondering why his papa was so weak, so craven, and
so scared. For Benoni he would be mighty. For Rachel he
wanted to be a calm provider. But what was he doing? Why,
he, Ferric, *he* was bringing the doom upon their heads. He.
He! None other.

So when Rachel appeared in the air before him, whispering,
This is the truth: mighty among all of the Creatures; when that
woman smiled, Ferric fell down in an agony of self-loathing,
and he took his own leg between his teeth, and he bit it to the
bone. Who else was there to punish? No one. Himself.

But the Rooster would murmur with fire in his eye, "Jug, jug," and all of his images would fade. There was only the driving Rooster and himself. "Bring me to her who cries *Jug, jug,* and I will set you free," the Rooster would promise, and Ferric would feel the lure of that freedom. "Till then the world depends on you. The peace of the universe rests with you. Go. Go. Go—"

Once, astounded by his own bravado, the Coyote had lied. He took the whole procession in the wrong direction, for three full hours making a slow turn to the right, enough to angle them away from his pitiful family. He planned to take them nowhere, and then they could kill him if they wished.

But suddenly there came a dreadful whistle from the sky, the shriek of accusation, and down from the heavens dropped a Hawk, stooping at a wild speed. He landed. He revealed their divergence from true north. And Ferric Coyote threw up.

He vomited every precious bit of food reserved for his family. Neither could he swallow it again. He could only stare at the loss in sadness, because now he had nothing for the children that he loved, and the very reason for his going was gone.

After that he lost himself as well. Motion became automatic merely. A sting in his buttock made him move. The Rooster clutching at his shoulders judged him. And instinct took him home.

He didn't want to think.

Chauntecleer is dreaming.

Curiously, he's glad that the dream has returned, proof of the expedition.

With all his heart, with all his soul and might, he is crying aloud, "I am coming!"

But there is a difference in this dream, and it rather distresses him, since everything should remain the same and nothing change to trouble his purposes.

He can see.

Far, far away, walking on some celestial sphere as though she is walking in the valleys of the moon, Chauntecleer sees the Dun Cow, one horn at her head, one horn gone. Oh, she is so distant! He could use her nearness now.

Are you—he wants to call—Are you the woman of sorrows after all?

But he doesn't call anything like that, because he can't see her face; because she is walking yet farther away from him, as though refusing to acknowledge him, and he is hurt by the coldness of the gesture; and because in this dream, in this sublunar sphere, he's calling something else.

"I am coming!" roar his throat and mouth. "I am coming!"

Almost he cries to the Dun Cow his perfect explanation: It is my destiny, my worth, my goodness; I can't do otherwise—

But suddenly the dream is strangled by a single word from Wyrm, arising like the fog:

Come.

And Chauntecleer wakes.

Thirty-two
The Canyon *Lough Derg*

John Wesley's eyes popped open, awake, alert to a sound.

Clop.

The woman Coyote woke second, raised her head. The pups snored.

John Wesley stood up.

"Wait," said the woman. Coyotes *do* freeze; Weasels break cover and fight. There was light outside—

Clop.

So: an uncertain hoof at the rim of the canyon, someone finding footing. Then there were a number of hooves clattering, and several someones descending the steep fall of stone. So.

A figure passed. The woman drew breath sharply: "Ferric!"

Wooden Coyote, thought John Wesley. He'd glimpsed a thin Beast grinning meaninglessly, skulking downstream with his tail between his legs. Is Ferric? Poor Ferric. Poor little Benoni—

Immediately the legs of an enormous Stag crossed the Weasel's vision, and other legs in forest. These, too, were familiar. John stuck his head outside—and was struck dumb, a Weasel speechless, so shocked by the sight that he truly could not catch his breath.

It was his Rooster! It was his Rooster, riding that elegant Stag in the exact same canyon where John was, but how could this be? It was his Rooster! *Look* at his Rooster. By Gaw, look at him! Why, he was glorious now. He was huge and proud and golden, and grim as a Lord should be. His comb stood up like a castle wall—oh, *look* at that mighty comb! And his beak, it gleamed like jet. And his nails flashed whiter than the lily. And he had weapons on! It was his Rooster, by Gaw, the same Lord Somebody-Chauntecleer that he remembered from the first bright days of vigor, conviction, and we-can-do-any-things, anythings: *that* Rooster! Him! Come back again!

Rooster! Rooster! Poor John couldn't get his mouth to work. Rooster! He couldn't declare the marvel that they should bump into one another in a northern canyon. And the black Stag was galloping downstream—

For one horrible instant the Weasel feared that this wonder was all a dream. It was too perfect. But then imperfection happily kicked him in the butt, and he knew it was reality: the Deer behind Black-Pale struck and nearly crushed John Wesley, the Goats, the Sheep, the swirling hooves of Beasts. He fumbled back into the Den. And this is how glad he was for the reality: he didn't hold this beating against a single soul. No, he came up grinning, forgiving them all.

"Mama Coyote," he coughed, he laughed, he gestured outside and downstream. "Is my Rooster, my Rooster come back again!"

Neither could Rachel speak. She stood pressed against the back wall, all of her children beneath her, a staring terror in her eye.

Benoni said, "Mama?"

The plain brown Bird leaped frantically, branch to branch in her thornbush. Her body switched and fluttered; her claws snatched and released three twigs in a second; but her head held steady, because she was watching an impossible arrival. Down the gorge, splashing and stamping behind a crouching Coyote—a herd! Toward her directly and without a pause, as though *she* were the destination, but how could that be?—a herd of Beasts, strangers. And in the front walked a coal-black Deer, and in his antlers trembled a flame—

The Bird couldn't control herself. She could not hold still. She thrashed around the bush as though flying on a tether, though she couldn't fly; in fact, she was piercing her flesh by the broken points of wingbone, and bleeding. This was such an enormity, suddenly to be watched by so many eyes.

The Beasts halted some space from her.

What? What? She watched them back.

The fire on the Deer spread its wings and sailed down to the ground in an easy circle. It was a Rooster. It was a Rooster of vast dignity and strength and a penetrating eye. He moved toward her, he alone.

His eye fixed her like a charm, and she stilled. He yearned to know something. What? He came unhurried. She was his total attention. Oh, he draped her altogether with his looking, and it was not cruel. It was—it wanted to be—familiar: do I know you? He tilted his head to the side in a motion of perfect pity, and even her heart went quiet to see that. Do I know you?

The Rooster paused at the bush, his warm eye level with her own.

"Woman," he said aloud. "Are you sad?"

What a question!

Sad? Self-consciousness burned her from the throat to the breast, and she fluttered, and sadness did in fact overwhelm her—a sadness that rose from this moment and the loneliness of such an audience: embarrassment. A sadness that reached backward through her isolated life in this place, to the memory of the obscenity that kept her here, guarding a hole, the stain that stained her. Sad? What right had a stranger to such a question? Do I know you? She never intended to be sad in public. Sad!

She cried out at the Rooster.

She cried, "Jug!"

"What?" he said.

"Jug!" she cried, hopping in the bush again, angry that he could so quickly draw her out, he and his sympathetic eye. She told him to leave her alone. But she had no tongue. Therefore, "Jug" is the only sound she made: "Jug, jug! Jug, jug! Jug, jug!"

Instantly the Rooster was transfigured, and the brown Bird silenced. He swelled like a thunderhead in heaven, startled with lightning, and he began to rumble. No! I *don't* know you! He was magnificent. He was frightening.

"Coyote, you are free!" he crowed. "Go!"

But the tone of that crow only drove the Coyote into a heap against the farther wall and ice.

"Woman," he crowed to the Bird. "There is no need for your loneliness. Look: I've brought you brothers and sisters and cousins and friends!" He meant it. The Bird perceived that he truly meant to abolish her loneliness—but the gesture was too grand, and she was only diminished.

"You!" crowed the Rooster to the herd that stood wall to wall in the canyon. "Oh, you whom I love—farewell! You are a holy nation, truly. Believe that. And we have suffered our troubles together, and you have been so dear to me, so dear that I cannot say it. But I go, now, to redeem those troubles forever. You will do well. You will do so well without me—"

Some of the Sheep looked stunned by those words, and their soft faces melted in sorrow. "I ask only two favors in remembrance. When the winter is over and the times are sweet and green again, please give a thought to me, and know that I caused that for you. I will be in the grass; my own breath will be the spring breezes. And this: tell Pertelote that I love her. Farewell!" crowed the Rooster a ringing crow. And then, more softly: "Farewell."

This glorious Rooster turned, then, and walked in water to the side of the bush and behind it. He stood a moment in the shadow of the portal, the hole that sank so deep into the earth.

And the brown Bird realized what he was about to do. He was going down there.

No, she wailed. *I'm sorry I yelled at you! No!* she wailed.

But what she said was, "Jug!"

He took a step toward the darkness.

She leaped from the bush to his back

Oh, you don't know the Evil that waits for you down there!

But what, in wild frustration, she said was, "Jug! Jug!"

He shrugged her off.

She sprang to his back again, and this time she drove her beak against his skull, puncturing flesh. He didn't fight or hurt her. Neither did he stop. He bowed and plucked her from his feathers with an iron claw and laid her on the ground, and was gone, swallowed by the earth.

With all her heart the woman calls to him, in dread for him, and desolated because he will not answer; but she should have prevented him, because she is one who knows the Evil.

Woman, she thinks she hears his distant voice: *What else do you want me to do for you?*

Come back! she wails.

But she is hopeless. For all she can cry is, "Tereu!"

Thirty-three

And Down

Light-headed and frightened at once, Lord Chauntecleer felt his way along the pitch-black, twisting corridor. He followed a falling water. He did not stumble, since all of his senses were tuned and acute. He was ready, now. And he went without a doubt: this was his dream awoken. This was the real. Wyrm was below.

"God, give me the strength!"

He held one secret in his heart which released him unto this endeavor and lent him a limitless power: that he was willing to die. Nay, death itself would be his victory! Then what could Wyrm do to him? Evil had lost its threat, and he was free.

"I am coming to kill you, Wyrm."

Down. Down. Feelingly down—

In the utter depths, then, where the walls had widened into a massive yawn, and the roof was vaulted monstrously high, and the air was fetid; down in a cathedral of silence, where his claw had found the stone substratum, Chauntecleer the Rooster had come.

Gaff struck stone and made a spark, red and dying.

Night in this place was perpetual.

Wyrm's lair. It stank of Wyrm.

One violent shiver passed over the Rooster, the last in his life, for this one was anticipation of his final offering. Then that was all. He prepared. He raked the darkness with sightless eyes. He drooped his wings. He arched his back. he sucked the loathesome air into his lungs; and he, with all his being, all his

long collected hatreds, his vengeance, his vengeance, crowed:
"WYRM!"

He echoed the earth-tunnels with that challenge and
shocked the ancient silences. It was a living voice he issued:
"WYRM!"

Ah, said the air. *Finally.*

Chauntecleer raised the Slasher, trembling with readiness.
A light appeared above him.

He whirled and stared at it. It was thin as thread, and green.
Soon another hung beside it, and another, and each was writhing as though it were alive, but none was longer than an inch or
two, and all of them glimmered mid-distance in the darkness.

The glowing spread. Chauntecleer watched it spread like a
rash, slowly; but he would be as patient as eternity.

Yet his body screamed with the thing to come.

Sing, said the air.

The light itself dimmed and said, *What shall we sing?*

Of death, said the air like pressure around him. *Death already
dead.*

"Wyrm!" cried Chauntecleer. "Show yourself!"

A million million tendril lights lit up, and all the little lights
were taking shape. They formed a titanic head with a mouth
as wide as a chancel, locked open on a huge, sardonic laugh.

"Wyrm—"

Behind that head there lay a winding body, serpentine, like
the vein of the planet that runs a thousand miles through
mantlerock. And all of the light was pulsing.

"Wyrm."

Chauntecleer thrust his wings wide to either side of him. He
set his mind, now, and he rushed for speed, and he took to the
air. He soared upward in the chamber, higher and higher until
he curved near the ceiling, five times higher than that head,
and the carcass lay below him like a river.

Chauntecleer sailed to a precise zenith.

This was it.

"Now!" he shrieked. "My life! My vindication!"

And he dropped.

Like the Falcon, with his wings laid back, his claws against his chest and Gaff and the Slasher turned to a lethal strike, Chauntecleer shot his body, his body the bullet, down to Wyrm. He would drive through the skull! He would pierce the skull and die in the monster's brain!

"Wyyyyyr—"

But he didn't.

It was a marsh of rot that he plunged into. It was an oily, putrifying meat. Chauntecleer took the concussion, spun an instant, then leaped up on Wyrm and fought. He stabbed and riddled the skin; he scored it with brilliant speed, deep, deep, digging to bone before the monster returned attack, like digging in mushroom—but none of it mattered.

The corpse didn't move. It didn't bleed. It didn't cry out. It didn't react. It didn't fight back, though Chauntecleer assaulted with a devestating skill. It lay inert.

It was dead.

Wyrm was already dead!

And suddenly Chauntecleer stood still on his skull—alive.

And what was the light that surrounded him, green and glimmering, as passive as the grass? Why, worms. Little worms! An infinity of threadlike worms, eating the flesh of the enemy—how long?

"What are you?" shrieked Chauntecleer, stamping his claw. He touched bone. He had burrowed to bone. "Where are you? Where are you that I can kill you?" He waved his wings around himself in futility. "Wyrm? Wyrm? WYRM? IS THIS YOU?"

Chauntecleer, panting, slumped to the edge of this continental corpse and looked over to the ground, but there was no answer anywhere. The earth and all its passages were still.

"Oh, God," he murmured. He fell. He slithered down Wyrm's cheek and cracked himself on stone. "Oh, God, don't take this away from me. Not this."

John Wesley's eyes were shining. Each new word increased his excitement.

"Who?" he said.

"Wyrm," said a Goat.

"Naw!" said John Wesley Weasel. He beat his paws together. "Naw! Naw!" He could hardly believe his good fortune. "Where?" he said.

"There," said String Jack, staring at the hole behind the bush where the stream was swallowed. Indeed, all the Animals watched that hole.

"Naw!" cried John Wesley. "There?"

The Hare nodded solemnly.

"Rooster, he went down there?"

The Hare nodded.

John grinned. "For fightings with Wyrm? *Wyrm?*"

The poor Hare nodded.

"Naw!" John fairly exploded, grinning till his cheeks split.

But there arose from that hole such a shrill, sustained, and distant battle-crow, that the Weasel fell on his back and roared with laughter. Nothings, nothings, nothings in all the world could ever match this act for glory. And his Rooster had conceived it, and his Rooster had gone and done *done* it! Hoopla! Who else but his Rooster? Nobody else, by-cause no one was *like* his Rooster.

"And whats," he cried, "what does Buggars do now?" He grinned like the sun on all of them.

Black-Pale-on-a-Silver-Field answered, "We wait."

"What?"

"We wait. Lord Chauntecleer chose to go alone. We wait for a Dog to come up—"

"Dog?" said John. He ran to the portal and gazed in. "Mundo Cani Dog?"

"Get back," said Black-Pale with strange quietness. "We wait."

John Wesley looked at him, at all the Beasts, and saw that none of them knew his joy. "What-a-hell?" he thought to himself. "Somethings is wrong?"

But "Wait," he said. He could do that.

His eye lighted on the Coyote crouched in an icy corner, and happiness leaped in his heart.

"Hey!" he cried. "Hey, wooden Coyote! John, he gots a message for you." The wretched Creature didn't so much as lift an eye. So John went straight to him and gave him a happy cuff. "Hey. Wooden Coyote, he's papa to a little Buggar, right?" No answer. No response. "Well, lookee: John chatted with that little Buggar; and that pup, he says, 'You see my papa,' says he, 'you tell my papa—' " John grinned: good news. " 'You tell my papa, Hurry home.' Little Benoni Coyote," said John, "he loves his papa."

The Coyote heard. The thin Coyote began, without a motion, to cry.

Well, that was more than a Weasel could stand.

"What-a-hell!" he roared, turning to all of these taciturn Beasts. "Why-come Critters is so sad, so gloomy right now?"

It was Black-Pale who answered, quietly, "Lord Chauntecleer isn't coming back."

"What?" said John, eyeing the Stag.

"He went down below the earth to die."

"What? What?" John Wesley rose on his hind legs, a dull cold gripping his chest. "The Rooster, he *what!*"

Black-Pale whispered it like a litany: "He's gone to die."

Again and again and again, desultory, Chauntecleer struck Gaff against the stone, making a dead-metal sound, while the massive mouth above him laughed no sound at all. It looked as though he were trying to chip a basin in the floor. Perhaps to catch some liquid in. Tears. Blood. Shame.

Like hot wax he allowed the knowledge of his shame to run through him, and still he had no words for it. Wyrm was dead. What was there left for him to do? He'd sold his whole life for this moment. He'd bought sweet death and an oblivion. But Wyrm had beaten him to it. So what was left for him to do? He had promised the Animals—

"Oh, Wyrm!"

—he'd sworn an oath before his Animals: how grand he had been then! He had committed his worth and all his purpose to this single task, and he had declared it absolutely in the presence of Pertelote. This is Chauntecleer. This is Chauntecleer. This is the Savior, finally, of the whole world, O glorious Cock. But Wyrm was dead already. And the wretched Cock alive. So what, with his miserable life, was there left for him to do?

"Oh, Wyrm. Oh—"

Look. Look! There's Pertelote! Or the shadow of her—O my wife. Standing in darkness, shaking her head with a cold, condemning reproach: *I asked only that you would not do this thing in madness—*

Chauntecleer started and wailed, "Pertelote!"

Chauntecleer bellowed mightily, "Oh, hideous—! Oh, fire and fury—! Oh, *Wyrm!*"

He leaped to his feet, trembling. Little worms dropped from him. Little worms had been crawling underneath his feathers. He didn't notice. He turned. He confronted the monumental corpse in its mansion, and he shrieked, "Can I pretend that I killed you? No!" Chauntecleer doubled with the violence of his words. "I can't even pretend I did the deed! Because look at me. I'm still alive! There was no sacrifice! Will nobody," he cried, and he whirled high into the air, blasted by the winds of his humiliation. He was beginning to understand. "Will nobody come and kill me here?"

It looked like madness. But it was a Rooster totally mortified. He flew. He circled thrice in the vault, beating his wings mercilessly, going nowhere.

Then, suddenly, Chauntecleer flew with a lancing skill straight for the swelling that once had been Wyrm's eye. He hit it. He attached himself to it. By rapid slashings he tore the flesh and raked it with his claws and shredded it as though it were a curtain—till the membrane gave way, and he tumbled inward, landing in the alcove of Wyrm's skull where the eyeball had rolled so long ago—

"Oh, no!"

There before him lay the last, most painful grief of all. Even his passion turned against him and accused.

For here, as though awaiting him, lay the bones of the Dog, Mundo Cani.

Bones.

Only the bones. Great shin-bones of a fleeting speed, stilled. Ribs that had contained a mortal heart. A head without eyes. A nose—

Chauntecleer began to pat his wings together, like a child, whining, staring, disbelieving.

"Mundo Cani, Mundo Cani, Mundo Cani," he whined high in his throat, a child, "couldn't you wait for me? Didn't you know how much I loved you? How can I tell you that I loved you, now? Mundo Cani, Mundo Cani—"

Dead, said the air. *He died within three days,* said the air. *Didn't you know that?*

Chauntecleer bowed his head. Deep spasms passed through his body as though he would vomit. But he was changing, like the chrysalis.

He raised his head again; and in that alcove crawling with worms, he began to pick the individual strings, the worms, from his beloved, one by one. Slowly he cleansed the skeleton, delicately laying each green tendril by. In the light his eye and his manner seemed all at once serene.

"I am going to die beside you, dear," he said.

No, said the air around him. The air sighed. The air spoke.

Who knew whether Chauntecleer heard it?

"For no good," said Chauntecleer, now cradling Mundo Cani's skull. "For no good at all, but because I love you, I will stay here till I die—"

No, you won't, sighed the air.

"—and because there is nothing left for me. It is as though I am dead already." He rocked the Dog. He lifted up his head, his eyes closed. He was mother to these bones. "You and I and no one else. Alone, alone in our grave, forever. And I will sing for you—"

Ah, Galle, you are still the fool, heaved the air of the alcove, the air of the caves, the air in a dry sighing. *I am dead indeed. But I am not consumed. What do you know of death? The Dog knows more than you do, and I learned from him. I watched him die. I saw the better part of him resolved into the air. Gasses, more than gasses: he floated out of himself as spirit. Spirit, Galle, unconfined by flesh, the very penetration of will and free being. I saw, and I chose that way for myself. Galle, behold: I have died. I have gone out of myself as spirit. I am the Dark. What is the shape of darkness? I am the Cold. Where are the limits of coldness? And I may be the penetration into whomsoever does not deny me. Let the living but breathe me in, dear Galle, and I live! No, you are not alone. I am here. I suffuse the subterranean regions, cold and dark, am everywhere below. Waiting.*

Who knew whether the Rooster heard the sighing of the air? He bent in his round closet and kissed the Dog's skull. He stroked it lovingly. He, too, was waiting. He caressed the eyesockets of Mundo Cani. He whispered, as though it were the conclusion of all things. "Wyrm is dead."

Indeed, Wyrm is dead, the air blew lightly, like a breeze. *No body and no name attaches to me any more. I am Evil, the thing itself. Breathe, Galle,* sighed the air. *Only just breathe and receive me, and I shall abide in you, something of your soul. Oh, Galle, isn't this a wonder? When you leave this place, then I go with you. You, Galle, you are my escape! You, who set your face against me! And in time, like a spirit into all the Keepers, the very soul of the community, I shall escape you as well.*

Spiritus Mundi! sighed the wind in a clear, whispering gale, endless as eternity. It really did rush through the tunnels of the earth. It blew throughout the huge room where Chauntecleer sat round his bones, protecting them.

Then, *Ecce!* whistled a mighty wind through the throats of stone: *I shall be free! I shall darken the face of God, and all creation shall grow cold! Ecce, ego facio nova!*

Only just breathe me, Cock.

But Chauntecleer covered a skull against the wind and whispered his sorrow and his consolation together. He said, "Sweet Mundo Cani, I love you—and Wyrm is dead."

Thirty-four
A Ceremony of Innocence—

John Wesley Weasel had instincts for the darkness and speed underground. When the black water flowed straight and downward, he swam the water. Where it boiled, he slithered rock. And down. And down, breakneck.

What harried him was the wind.

The farther down he went below the earth, the louder grew a whistling, premonitory wind, and the air in this tunnel was a sucking thing. It was a greater motion than he understood, like breathing.

But down, because his Rooster shouldn't die. What did the Rooster think? Did Rooster think that nobodies would stand by him? Rooster, gone in his lonesomeness. Gone to do things alone! Fight Wyrm! Fight Wyrm! What-a-hell, fight Wyrm and planning *already* to die! Is no fight, a dying fight: is hopeless! So what's a-matter with Rooster, gone to die?

John flung himself through the blackness.

And down—

When the tunnel suddenly opened, John Wesley bolted out onto a wide escarpment and tumbled. He rolled down stone until he hit an absolute floor with his left shoulder. The jolt shuddered his joints, and he was dizzy a moment.

He'd fallen into a measureless cavern. The wind fairly

roared in this place—like a living thing, the haunting of the Netherworld. John had no second thoughts about this wind: he feared it. He despised it. He was an Animal who knew the malice of yellow tornadoes and sudden squalls in the afternoon. They were unnatural. But this was unnatural *on purpose,* alien altogether.

"Rooster!" he cried.

Far ahead of him was a sort of glowing, a livid shadow of astounding size. He blinked to see it, but it was vague. Therefore he threw himself across the stone the better to see.

He ran, and his poor heart kicked inside of him, because the shadow took shape—as huge as the razorbacks low in the mountains, and still, and longer than sight could follow; softly green; a head like a mesa, the mouth wide open, and maybe this blasting wind rushed from that mouth. Wyrm.

John Wesley Weasel paused in awe. Wyrm, you are so big!

And so wicked.

The very stillness of the monster, in so violent a wind, was treachery. John flat hated what he saw.

But what he saw: like an endless bluff, it was not moving. It seemed a mere thrust of landscape, a long green cliff that overhung him, impassive, calm and—dead.

Dead!

John Wesley choked on the wonder. "Rooster!" he cried. "Oh, Rooster, what you done *done!*" Dead. John wanted to laugh with his whole heart at the miracle. This was impossible. Who kills great Wyrm? And singlehanded? Dead!

He stood on hind legs, leaning against the wind, and he pierced the roaring with his own triumphant cry: "Rooooooooster!"

Then all at once it seemed that the monster turned its eye, and John shrank from that horror. Too soon glad—don't never be too soon glad. The horror went deep. John Wesley would not shake it until he'd left this place for good. Nor did it matter that there was no eye at all in the head of Wyrm, that it was a darker figure moving to look outward from the socket. The dread was in John now.

The figure peered a moment into space, then withdrew into the cavity and sat.

It was Chauntecleer.

Chauntecleer composed himself and sat. Like being home. What. What. He *likes* it here? What?

"Rooster! Ha-ha!" cried John Wesley, truly delighted. "What you done! Oh, so brave, the thing you done—"

Again, the Cock inclined his head—but so casually.

"—but is time, now! Time, now, for Critters to go," he called, truly fearful. "Come, Rooster! Buggars be so happy to hear the things all done. Come. We go!"

Chauntecleer said something. John Wesley could not hear him for the wind.

"What?" he cried.

The Cock bent back his head and crowed. It was little in the rushing wind, but John heard it and was thunderstruck.

"Save yourself, John," crowed the Rooster. "Go away."

"What? Rooster says what?"

"Go away! Go away!" the Rooster crowed in Wyrm's skull, blackness in his eye. "Leave me alone!"

John Wesley was bewildered. And angry, suddenly. "Why?" he cried.

Like a lamentation, the Rooster crowed, "I've found the bones of Mundo Cani. Here are the bones of Mundo Cani. I'll stay with the bones of Mundo Cani. Go."

"Bones!" cried John. "What is bones? So bones is buried. But soon some wickednesses here makes bones of us. *Come* and we go!"

"No!"

"Why?"

"Because I am going to die here."

Oh, John hated the ceaseless blowing of the wind. The Rooster said it! Said what they said he said. Said he's going to die here. No! Rooster, he's not going to die here. And it never was a question, even, whether John should leave without him. By-cause, he loved his Rooster.

"No need!" John announced. "No need for dyings.

Rooster, he can strut and be proud. Lookee," cried John Wesley. "Wyrm is dead—"

Then came a crow of shattering agony: "I did not kill him. He was dead. God took the glory from me. It is gone. It is gone."

The wind lulled, as if a climax had been passed, and the silence that followed was funereal.

John's heart bled inside of him. By-cause, he loved his Rooster.

"Rooster," whispered John. "Oh, Rooster. He doesn't needs to be Lord-and-General-of-all, no. Not for John, no. Only just to come home again, and might-be rules a little bit. Please just rule a little bit."

But Chauntecleer had bent his head. He was singing. In the silence the Weasel heard him singing softly to something in front of him. Bones.

"Rooster?"

Songs that rhymed with Mundo Cani, odd lullabies in this dank and cruel vault.

"Rooster? Doesn't you talk with John no more? Rooster? Which somebody gots fur on him still? Does bones, or does John Double-u?"

Quivering melodies sung in the nose, like an old, old woman.

"Who loves you, Rooster?"

The songs resolved themselves into a plainsong chanting. No ending to them. But it never was a question whether John would leave this place without his Rooster. And maybe the quiet was worse than the wind. And John was a Weasel who could not *not* act for long. And this had been too long, by Gaw!

"Hoopla!" he cried all suddenly.

He took ten steps toward the darkness, turned, and charged the very jaw of Wyrm.

"Hoopla!"

Up the cheek of the monster he scrambled, screaming

Weaselish war-cries. He gained the socket-ledge and flung himself inside. Chauntecleer had just begun to turn a bland eye toward him, when the Weasel—"Hoopla!"—threw him a body-check, grabbed the leg-bone of Mundo Cani, yanked it free, and hurled it into darkness. Tail-bones went flying next, like dice skimming the stone—

"Don't!" the Rooster shrieked.

Shin-bones, ribs, a pelvis cavorted through the air. John cleaned house.

"Wretch!" screamed Chauntecleer. "What are you doing?" He sprang himself into the darkness. He sank out of sight. But a rattling below was the hectic Rooster gathering bones again. "Mundo Cani! Mundo Cani!" he wailed.

The wind began to blow, swelling like laughter.

Finally the Weasel seized the skull itself and the Dog's crumbling nose. He pushed it over the edge and leaped after it. So, the Rooster loves his bones, does he? So, let him chase his bones!

"Dog's head! Dog's head!" John Wesley sang, and he kicked it. "Here goes a Dog's head!" He struck and punted the skull like a ghastly ball. He drove it as fast as he could across the stone. And then he hooked a paw through an eyehole and dragged it up the escarpment. John had an instinct for darkness. As though by feel he found the tunnel again.

There was bloody rage in the Rooster's voice behind him. John didn't mind. He was behind him, after all. "Fire and fury, Weasel!" cried the Rooster. John didn't mind. He heard his Rooster slam himself against stone, trying to find the tunnel. John didn't mind that either.

"Dog's head!" he sang, climbing against the current and pulling a hollow skull. "Dog's head!"

Three apparitions exploded from the hole. The Animals were appalled by each and each.

A skull came skidding out, grinning, deathly.

A Weasel appeared, harassed and panting. He nearly collapsed to catch his breath, but a Rooster leaped into the light and attacked him. The Animals stumbled backward. Chauntecleer swiped savagely at John Wesley, slashing his haunch. Gaff opened a long wound. The Weasel did not defend himself. He took off running as best he could upstream, coloring the water with his blood.

But the Rooster was fixed on that Beast.

His comb was torn from his brow, his beak stove in, and someone thought he saw a tear in the Cock's eye. It was no tear. It was a threadlike worm dangling from the tear duct.

Chauntecleer streaked to the neck of Black-Pale and drove his weapons into flesh. "After him!" he commanded. The Stag reacted to the pain. He lurched like an engine and bounded where the Weasel went.

The Animals caught that intensity. Some crime had been committed. Some shivering excitement was in the air. And blood flowed in the water.

They followed the Rooster. This was no mindful choosing: he came and he left with a blistering passion; passionately they jammed the canyon behind him, running, galloping, making of themselves a wild stampede—

John Wesley both heard and felt the pursuit, for it troubled the bedrock. He was racing the ledge, now, rounding bends and pumping his little legs like springs. His lungs were raging. His left hind leg was numb. But he dashed the canyon, John Wesley Weasel, some precious distance ahead of the herd.

Oh, he had infuriated his Rooster. He'd done that before. But never before had Chauntecleer hacked him for it. Poor John Wesley! He didn't know what he'd done. But his Rooster was up in daylight again. He'd done *that.*

There was the canyon's end. But he was a broken Weasel and could not climb giant steps. A dying Weasel.

At the last instant he cut right and dived into the Coyote's Den, sliding across the floor to the back, where he curled into a ball.

Two pups were knocked aside. Mama Coyote shied to the

wall away from him. Well, he was bleeding and looked filthy
with combat. "Shh!" John Wesley put a paw to his mouth and
made the only sound left to him, for he had no breath. Shaking
his head, he warned them, "Shh. Shh."

But who had counted on the courage of Benoni Coyote, the
great and innocent heart of that pup?

"Double-doo!" he said. "You're cut," he said. He put his
paw on the helpless Weasel's shoulder. There was such sympathy in his manner.

John Wesley gulped at the air. "Shh. Shh."

"It's the enemy," said Benoni.

Furiously the Weasel shook his head. He tried so hard to
talk.

But Benoni stood up, foursquare on his paws, his fur like a
nimbus. He had a grave expression on his face. He knew this
was no game. "Me too, Double-doo," he said. "Mighty like my
papa, a warrior like you."

He turned and went out.

His mama gasped. Then she blazed the Den with a mother's
cry, *"Benoni!"*

And in a flash she was behind him.

With all his might John dragged to the doorway. And then
he had to hump his back to keep the other pups, bleating their
fears, inside. But this is what he saw:

He saw the careening charge of the Animals, caught in a
narrow strait, and who could stop them?

He saw a mother snatch her child in desperate jaws, and a
great black Stag rise rampant above them, trying to stop, the
furious Rooster at his neck and the driving weight of Animals
behind. How could he stop?

The stampede poured past the Stag. The first Beasts twisted
themselves aside, but the latter kept coming, and the mama
was down below them all, saving her child by crawling toward
the wall. But a hoof stunned her, and a hoof wounded her, and
the continual passage of hooves beat her down, and one of
them killed her.

And this is what John Wesley saw:

Benoni Coyote, caught in his mother's jaws; but he could not free himself however he wriggled, because she was dead.

"Mama?" His mouth formed the word. "Mama?"

The Animals swirled in the narrow canyon, full of brutal confusions.

The Stag still reared above the mother and child.

Chauntecleer cut his spur into Black-Pale's muscle.

When the Stag came down, then, in the midst of the turmoil, his hoof hit something soft. And something snapped. Then Benoni rolled free of his mother and lay still. And her mouth was open, but his was closed, a bit of tongue protruding; and his eyes were closed. Benoni was dead as well.

That is what John Wesley saw.

The terrible bugling of the Stag, finally, froze all the hearts in the canyon. Oh, Black-Pale began to bugle a primitive grief. The Animals drew away from him, and there they saw the murders, and then they understood. Soon, they began a moaning too. But Black-Pale's cry was inconsolable.

Still bugling, he threw his body hard against the ice of the canyon wall. Once. Twice. Three times. Deadly blows, till the Cock was shaken free and fell. Bugling still, Black-Pale mounted the stones at the northern closure and bounded away.

The Animals followed.

The Rooster was left behind to pull himself from the stream. He stood lost a moment. He looked at two bodies lying in a certain peace. Then, consciously, he did not look at them. He left. He took himself slowly downstream, the opposite of the others.

All of this—with two babies behind him, now clutching each other in silence—is what John Wesley saw.

He began to cry. Weasels can cry.

And white, and lightly as forgetfulness, touching torment like the wings of angels, it began to snow.

> *Here ends the third part of the book of our sins.*
>   *Oremus!*
> *Illumina, quaesumus, Domine, tenebras nostras—*

PART FOUR

NOW, THE SERPENT WAS
MORE SUBTLE THAN ANY
OTHER BEAST

Thirty-five
The Snows

It was snowing, now, in a steady, silent dead-fall, filling all the little burrows of the earth, drifting mildly, blanketing everything with a kind of white amnesia.

Maybe God said, "Let it snow."

Maybe God had meant it mercifully.

But for Pertinax Cobb, who lay in a foreign hole because he couldn't keep pace with the Animals but wouldn't go home without news, for Pertinax beneath the snow, it was oppressive, and he felt so lonely.

The snow kept whiskering the ground above him, like some mammal sniffing the darkness. It sifted across a quiet earth, pretending to be as light as ghosts; but that was a lie because it was heavy after all and made his hole a tiny pocket. He felt the drifts above him. He was a Cobb cut off.

That would have been just fine, if there had been two Cobbs together. Many a winter he and Mrs. Cobb had gnawed nuts in a chamber five feet below the cold, and he had told her stories, and half of them were fictions, but she would say, "You're wonderful, Mr. Cobb," so the fiction had had its truth. But Mrs. Cobb was nowhere near him now. He missed her. And the whispering snow made him miss her the more.

Pertinax was homesick.

Mrs. Cobb was a very important person. He knew that now.

When it snowed at the Hemlock, the Hens and the Mice woke up in wonder. They walked grinning onto the pillowed Liverbrook, making tracks and marveling at the cleanliness. They were very quiet a while. Oh, holy snow!

Change itself was welcome in the Fimbul Winter.

But then the Brothers Mice made miniature plows of themselves, and they raced around to scrawl some complicated designs in the whiteness. They squealed in perfect delight. So then other Animals joined the fun, because what do you make of snow? You make fun!

Down the Liverbrook slid some Squirrels; and Squirrels shook clots of snow from the trees.

Sparrows played lancet games in the twigs.

The dumpy Partridge cried, "Dear me!" scandalized at herself for acting so silly.

The Fawn De La Coeur tried to romp in a broad field of snow. Chalcedony the Hen watched her, doubtful. And when the Fawn went down in a white explosion, this Hen was sure she'd seen an injury: children are so careless! But when the Fawn clambered to her feet again, breathless with laughter, why, the crippled Hen cackled till the tears ran from her eyes. Children are such a blessing! And this was the first time she had seen the child to laugh. Oh, the times, they were improving.

It snowed a gentle snow upon the earth, and Pertelote looked on in silence. She was grateful for the gladness of her sister. But she did not laugh.

She was mourning Chauntecleer.

Pertinax felt a tremor. Instantly he was alert. He felt another and another until he knew it for a steady rhythm, and then he was sure of his facts: someone was coming.

He punched his way to the surface of the world, popped out, and sat like a question on top of a drift. He looked north and gasped at the sight, for the valley had gone so lovely in the snow. It was a deep and dazzling bowl, an amphitheater all white and silent, and old, and old.

"Hoo!" said Pertinax at such grandeur. The snow had made eternity visible.

But someone was coming. There was that thrumming, thrumming through the ground—

Aye! *There!* See? News!

At the northern rim of the valley a Beast appeared as black as a midnight memory. It sailed the lip, then descended the long fells, bounding beautifully, kicking white clouds behind it.

Pertinax ran a step sideward, then stopped to watch, ran for excitement, then watched again. News!

Marvelous speed in that Creature! Majesty, and a marvelous large head. No! 'Twas a great rack of antlers on him, laid back because his face was raised. Yes! A Deer. Pertinax stood severe and squealed inside his chest: the Animals were coming home again!

Cobb, the Ground Squirrel of hypercuriosities: he'd get to hear it first of all. And then what? Then he'd tell it to Mrs. Cobb, that's what.

That Deer, that messenger, never slacked, but bounded twenty feet a leap, his forelegs knifing softer snow, his hind like pistons whirling snow into the air.

Pertinax couldn't stand it. He cried out, "Bring us the news!" And he ran to stand directly in the Deer's path. So up the near side of the valley lunged the Deer, and Pertinax saw mucus streaking a black flank, and blood on the shoulder; and Pertinax heard the *woof* that came with every landing; and Pertinax knew his name—

"Black-Pale-on-a-Silver-Field!" he cried. "Stop! Tell me the—"

But the Stag did not stop, did not even hear the cry.

The Stag burst by him, destroying the world in blizzard and blindness, thunderbooms beside him; and Cobb went tumbling backward; but Cobb caught sight, through the cloud, of Black-Pale's eye—and Cobb grew cold.

He stared at the Stag's retreating, until the woods had hidden him and the crystal cloud had sunk again. He stared till the land was quiet. There was a memory nagging his mind.

"His eye," said Pertinax. "It was like—"

Once in a drought, the Squirrel had gone down a narrow

shaft which should have ended in a reservoir of water. But the bottom was dusty, hollow and dry; and the Squirrel despaired.

"The eye of that Deer is an empty well," said Pertinax. And he said, "The news isn't good news, is it?"

This is the way that it was in the south: the snow fell fine and beautiful, with a soundless flake. There was the sense of mothering come to a drowsy child, someone tucking the world to sleep. Animals were thankful for the featherbed.

But in the north, those several nights, the snow was a dissatisfied hag: bitch-winter beating the earth with her stick. Bitter crystals blew hard and horizontal so that the Animals lowered their heads and turned away. If someone tried to see where he was, his eyeballs stung for the trouble, as though punished for looking—and he saw nothing anyway.

So the Sheep simply stopped on a hillside—the lee side, they hoped, but they didn't know. They were leaderless, and their own poor senses had been whited out. They pressed together in a flock, all of them hanging their heads, not one of them lying down, for fear that he might be covered and smothered and lost forever. Or, maybe Sheep were just too stunned to think of lying down. They'd walked into this weather standing up; they'd wait the weather standing up still. They stood, leaderless. They stood like plain cattle in the blizzard. They packed their tails against their anuses and stood motionless. And this is how submissive the Sheep were: they didn't so much as shake the hoarfrost from their faces. Their own breathing bearded them; their exhalations froze, and the white beards grew, because no one told them to move.

It's a perilous thing, to be leaderless and obedient at once. When there's no command to obey, then "No" becomes the only command, and a heartless one: *No* to instincts, *no* to boldness, *no* to newness even in this witching weather; then *no* to survival, and *no* to life. Don't move! How do you know your movement isn't for the worse? Then stand still and hang your heads, Sheep, Sheep! And the harder the storm blows, the meeker the Sheep. The worse the conditions, the more they yearn to obey. Therefore, this blizzard fixed them.

Leaderless, there was nothing to do but nothing.

Leaderless, they just stood still, and the Hag shrieked all around them, cursing them, beating them with her stick.

Leaderless, Sheep are lost.

There was one Creature untroubled by the blizzard and the extremities of the north. Boreas the White Wolf had an eye as cold and pale as the ice, and a paw so wide it walked the drifts, thick-shank fur, a powerful neck, and a heart impervious to · hostilities or friendship, either one. Boreas trod snow as if he were the snow, carelessly. And he moved of a perfectly free will through any wind of the winter.

Boreas stood on a high ridge, watching the dispersion of the Animals. If he helped none of them, it wasn't because he wished them ill; simply, he had another purpose on his mind, and nothing disturbed his purposes. He was interested in the state of one being only. Let the others pass.

Now Notos, the Black Wolf, came slinking behind him in spiteful misery. He blew on his knuckles. He hated the knifing wind. "Let's go," he growled.

"Did you see it?" Boreas asked, not so much as flicking his eye.

Eurus and Favonius and the grey Chinook stepped closer.

Notos swore an oath. "I can't see nothing, I don't care for nothing, I'm freezing to death, dammit! Let's—"

"I saw a weakness." The White Wolf heard what he wished to hear. Presently he was deaf to complaints.

Chinook said, "I saw it, too. Let it be."

"No. No," Boreas mused slowly. "There's a crack in the Rooster. There's a flaw somewhere: him, his mind, his rule, his authority, I wonder. I don't know; I wonder." He swung his head round to look at Chinook. They were shadows in the unobstructed wind, their fur in whorls; but their frames stood firm. "And how deep does it go, I wonder?" said Boreas.

Notos, finally, spat a filthy word at the both of them and started off in the blizzard.

Boreas finished his thought first, saying, "The times are changing, count on it." Then he raised his eyes after Notos. "He thinks he's going south," he said.

Eurus and Favonius shrugged. "He isn't," they said.

"Well, go with him then," said Boreas. "The four of you, take your way to the Rooster's land again, and watch for the flaw. I'll watch for it here—"

Boreas lingered alone on his ridge thereafter, allowing the wind its ripping of his coat. He didn't move. He wanted to assess the Rooster. He wondered, coolly: what the possibilities. . . .

At the dying of the blizzard and the bare beginning of dusky light, String Jack grew bold. He put his face out of the snow and looked around. Then—slowly, slowly, since all the world had changed—he crept forward on a blue, sculptured land. He hopped carefully across the crusty snow, feeling estranged and endangered: this was a world too smooth to be true, its valleys and hills ceramic, and the silence too mystic. He didn't know where to go. He'd lost his bearings.

String Jack had passed the storm in a personal hole, as had all of his kin, here, there, and everywhere; and now he went looking for them with greater and greater panic, because he could not find them. The world had changed, and the family was scattered.

Smells were gone; so he felt as though his nose itself was gone.

His stretching ears heard nothing.

And what did his eyes see? A stark and lifeless land.

No, it was worse than that. He saw statues! He saw on a hillside statues of the most unnatural sort of Creature: they stood five-legged, the fifth leg where the head should be, and no head at all! And there was not just one of this mutant breed; there was a whole herd, frozen, timeless.

String Jack's ears popped up like exclamation points, indeed. Then he canceled them straightway, afraid that they'd been seen. And then he canceled himself, in a high-speed decision to quit this museum—with his relatives or without them.

The world had changed!

How could a Hare understand what he couldn't name, or approach what he'd never seen before? All he could do was escape. All he could be was afraid. And all had to be handled alone—for strangeness and fears divide the closest of kin. . . .

Of course not: these were no abnormal beings that the Hare had seen. They were Sheep, mere Sheep. But the frost on their faces had frozen like stumps of ice to the ground, and they were every one imprisoned in their low servility, bowing down with no other choice left to them. Their heads had turned to legs—or so it seemed at a distance.

The storm was over, and still the poor Sheep stood. They could neither lie down nor walk, though in this more peaceful weather they might have chosen either—to rest, or to go home.

Ice-locked! Slave-locked to nothing.

Lord Chauntecleer had brought them north.

But Lord Chauntecleer was not taking them home again.

The Sheep were abandoned to the tendencies of their own natures. But Sheep under Sheep are under no one, and freedom for them becomes captivity.

They didn't even bleat. They stood on five legs and waited. Bowed down.

In the same dim, morning light, Boreas saw him. From the ridge the Wolf looked down upon the singular Cock, Lord Chauntecleer, passing southward all alone.

Alone the Rooster went, but not at ease. He was dragging something after him with a great deal of effort. It didn't slide well, whatever it was, and the snow impeded it. It moved by yanking, or by pushing; and often the Rooster swept it clean with his wing.

Suddenly, while the White Wolf watched him, Chauntecleer jerked erect. He issued a short cry, immediately cut off; then he doubled down and coughed. He thrust his head forward, coughing violently as though strangled. His wings thrashed the snow on either side, till a final wretching spewed up an enormous gorge. Chauntecleer crowed and attacked that gorge, moving with such force and clean direction that Boreas shook his head. "No, not yet," he whispered. "Not weak enough yet."

Below, the Rooster stood still a moment, by habit ruffling his feathers after a fight. He sighed and returned to the cargo, his sledge, and push by push drove it southward ahead of him.

Boreas slipped the ridge, then, and descended to identify the Rooster's adversary.

Worms.

They were worms. Two score worms as thin as thread, each one cut precisely in the middle, a single drop of blood for each, and the blood, though dark—it was not red.

Boreas lifted his head to gaze where the Rooster went.

He heard the coughing again. Then, distantly, the cry.

He said, "The times are changing."

Thirty-six

With Safety of His Innocence

John Wesley had no use in his left hindleg, now, at all. His movement was handicapped and heavy. And the night was dark, the darker for the snow falling. But he could not bear to

see the two Coyote bodies simply sink in snow. He couldn't
bear for snow to sift into the mama's mouth or to drift on
Benoni's face. They lay near one another on the terrace where
they died, exactly as the Animals had left them at leaving. It
was up to John, now.

The babies Twill and Hopsacking had fallen asleep against
each other, tired for staying in the Den and waiting for their
mother to come. That was a goodness, that they slept.

So John had gone out.

He had pulled himself to Benoni, and he was stroking the
child to brush the snow away, and he was thinking that there
should be some place, a fine and private empty place, for
Benoni and his mama to lie together; he was thinking, Why
couldn't he find such a place, or was there such a place in all
the world where nobody would hurt them again. He was thinking these things when Ferric came.

"Oh," said Ferric, and John saw him, and he stopped stroking the baby.

The Coyote stood with his side to the wall, as though shy.
A Bird slipped from his back. The Coyote put his cheek to the
wall, too, and closed his eyes. "Oh, no," he said.

John said, "Papa?"

The Bird huddled in the snow.

The Coyote pushed and pushed himself against the wall as
if it would give way for him. When he glanced at the bodies,
he pushed harder. All at once he stood straight up with a busy
expression on his face. He looked at Rachel, and he said,
"One—" He looked at Benoni, and he said, "Two—" Then
he looked with infinite questioning at the Weasel, and poor
John didn't know what to say. "One," whined the Coyote. It
was a terribly important number. And the next was worse.
"Two?" He pleaded with John: "Two?" John felt pity and an
utter helplessness.

"But Papa," he whispered, "what's for a Double-u to say?"

"One!" begged Ferric, nearly desperate. "Two!" Who
could understand him?

Suddenly he ran to the Den. He thrust his head inside and

stood still. Then he backed out again. "Three," he said. "Four," he said, thinking long about these numbers.

"Oh, Papa!" John Wesley cried too loud. "Is okay. Them babies is sleeping!"

"Sleeping?" said the Coyote, fixing John, the Savior, with a hungry stare. "Sleeping, do you think?" He came to John. He looked directly into John's eyes. "Do you know Rachel?" he asked.

"Um, yes." John dropped his own eyes. "Is Mama Coyote, yes," he said

Ferric said, "Please, what is your name?"

"Um. Well. John," said the Weasel.

"John," said the Coyote with true fervor. "John, is Rachel sleeping, too?"

The Weasel mumbled, "No."

"Oh, please, John!" The Coyote's eyes were burning him. "Not sleeping? What else is there? If she isn't sleeping, then what is she, John?"

"Wooden Coyote, doesn't you know?"

"Rachel is my wife," said the Coyote as though this information might assist the Weasel. "Nothing ever troubles her. She doesn't worry about anything. She smiles."

"Wooden Coyote," said John. "Don't."

"She knows how to laugh."

"Wooden Coyote!"

"What?"

"Rachel—she's dead."

"*No!*"

"Oh, wooden Coyote—oh, yes. She is."

"Do you," said Ferric, still glaring at John. "Do you know a pup, a brave pup named Benoni—"

John Wesley Weasel simply turned and began to drag his useless leg away.

"—he is my son," the Coyote continued to talk to the spot where the Weasel had been. "He is my— He is—"

John passed the darkness of the Den. "Oh, Coyote," he

whispered to the night, "John, he is so sorry for all we has done to you."

But there was a silence behind him. He turned back and saw that the thin Coyote had finally looked upon his family. As gently as the snow itself, he was dipping his snout to the woman, Rachel, stretched upon the ground. Tenderly, he licked her face. Tenderly, he washed her. Then he stopped with his nose on her forehead. He began to shiver. He drew his lips back until it seemed that he was grinning, his nose pressed to her brow. But he wasn't grinning; his voice was thick. "Rachel," he said. "I'm so cold. Are you cold, too?"

John Wesley wanted to race up the stone steps and away, screaming curses at the universe. But he bowed his head instead.

Then the scream that came—it wasn't his own.

The poor Coyote wailed, "Benoni! Benoni! Why is your tongue stuck out? Couldn't someone put your tongue away? Oh, Benoni!"

John tried as hard as he could to get to the steps, wounded by the Coyote's cry, feeling his own tears start at his eyes.

But, "John!" cried the Coyote again in the night. "Where are you?"

"Here, wooden Coyote," he said.

"Is Twill sleeping? Is Hopsacking sleeping?"

"Yes, wooden Coyote."

"I mean, *sleeping?*"

"Yes, yes, wooden Coyote. Yes."

"Don't go."

"John, he gots to go."

"Please, John, please! There's something you have to tell me."

"Oh, wooden Coyote, let John go."

"Just one more thing." Ferric bounded toward the Weasel, then immediately turned away, dropping his head between the bodies and the ground itself, but unable to look at the Weasel any more.

"What, wooden Coyote."

"Tell me—" Ferric ceased in shivering. "I'm sorry. I'm cold," he said. Indeed. The blizzard was just beginning above them, and the wind said *Oooooo* in the Pine.

"Can you tell me again," said Ferric humbly, "what Benoni said about his papa?"

John Wesley choked. Poor John—he was stuck all over again, and what was he to do? "Benoni says, he misses his papa," said John, and they both began to cry together. The Coyote lay down to weep. John looked at the furry pup-form, lying like his father, one and two. "Benoni says, he loves his papa with a very big, big love."

Ferric wept, "Thank you, John."

And John Wesley wept, "Is nothings, wooden Coyote."

When Coyotes howl in the dead of night a long and plaintive wailing; when they round their mouths to the empty sky and sing shrill notes, this is what they say: they say, *Son of my sorrow, where have you gone?*

They are the voice, lamentation and bitter weeping; they are weeping for their children. And they refuse to be comforted for their children, because they are not. This is the way of the world. The children die.

John Wesley heard that howling when the storm began. He heard it in spite of the blizzard, in spite of the pine around him, in spite of the fact that Ferric was wailing from the bottom of the canyon Lough Derg.

He heard it because Ferric was wailing to heaven itself.

Thirty-seven
Home to Coma

Black-Pale-on-a-Silver-Field—he thought no thoughts whatever while he ran. It was an impulse of the heart that drove him. It was right to go fast, that was all. It was right never, never to stop. It was right to reach the extremities of physical exertion, to crack his lungs in the run, to hear a mortal rattling there, to taste the blood. He asked no farther than rightness; just now the rightness was all, no reasons, no reasons.

But there was a reason. In fact, there were two.

Barely felt at the tip of his hoof, but tingling there however hard or often he struck the ground, was the sensation of a soft snap. Black-Pale was fleeing the name of that feeling. He was escaping the remembrance of the act and the title that should attach to him forever for what he had done. But names and memories are swifter than wind in pursuit. Therefore he couldn't pause, not for an instant; and therefore he ran as fast as he possibly could: he was racing thought itself. And he sought fatigue, and he wished to be tired, and he wanted to drop, unconscious before his body hit ground. But God had given him a remarkable heart, both noble and strong. He ran. He accomplished a marvel, though no one ever knew it: aground, in snow, the Stag ran faster longer than the Hawk in the air could fly, a grueling, unrecorded marathon.

And the reason why, all thoughtlessly, he tended toward the Hemlock was: he wanted to see his daughter. He never once thought this yearning through; it was too dangerous to consider. Yet in him was the terrible need to see if she was still all right. More precisely: to see if she was still alive.

Mindless, then, the Stag broke into the camp of the Animals, woofing a hollow, wretched breath, stamping the ground because he could not be still and because he was seeking his daughter. His nostrils hung whips of mucus that lashed him when he threw his head from side to side, seeking. The mucus was strung with beads of a startling red.

"Have you seen her?" he rasped to no one in particular, would have heard none if any had answered. But the Animals simply stood aside. He looked fanatical.

"Have you seen her?" he asked with greater intensity, rushing among the breeds. The intensity grew in him because his own words told him why he'd come: for her. Thought was waking, and with it a true panic for the Fawn.

At the Liverbrook, finally, he abused his lungs once more, swelling them past their capacity. He threw himself rampant, the better to see, the louder to cry, and he bugled all down the stream to Wyrmesmere: "De La Coeur! De La Coeur! Where are you, De La Coeur!"

"Papa!" Her tiny, surprised bleat. She was behind him.

Black-Pale came down twisting himself so that he could see her. Already by the time his forehooves caught the ground, his mouth was closed; and something else was beginning to close.

"Papa! Oh, Papa, you're back!"

The child was so happy she could hardly walk straight, De La Coeur his daughter, dappled, alive and blameless, and—O God, who can understand these things?—and a knife in his very soul.

She came to him sideways like a pup in her excitement, laughing in her dark eyes, because he was her father and she was his daughter, and he was home again.

No such child would in like manner meet the Coyote at his Den. Homecoming there would be a different thing. And why was this? Why would a Coyote weep to be told that his child was dead? And why, please. Say it, please.

Because Black-Pale-on-a-Silver-Field had with his own hoof killed the child!

Murderer!

"Papa! Such things I have to tell you, my aunty and me!" De La Coeur closed the distance between them. The great Stag lowered his head, almost as it were for battle, presenting his antlers; but then he swung it to the side—

"Oh!" the Fawn gave a tiny cry. "You're cut. Aunty, Papa's been cut. And his neck and his shoulders, how deep!"

The Fawn and a crippled Hen together approached Black-Pale, full of concerns for him. Before they reached him, in a restless gesture—a nearly threatening gesture, if any had thought that possible—he jerked his body backward. Here was the tragedy. Here was the knowledge that flooded Black-Pale now: he could not look upon his daughter, no, not with his eyes, because he was a murderer; she did not know this; he did; and what had he killed? A child.

He pawed through the snow to the ice of the Liverbrook, his head still cast to the side.

"Papa, let us put a salve—"

Crack!

Black-Pale struck the ice with his guilty hoof.

De La Coeur hesitated a moment, confused.

The shock of his strike shook something loose inside his chest. Black-Pale heaved out his breath, and with it came a dollop of the brightest blood, impossibly red in white snow.

This time De La Coeur's concern was no minor daughterly thing; it was scribbled with true fear, and she came forward in low voice: "You're not well. It was hard on you, Papa. But Aunty—"

Crack! Crack!

Twice more, with all the might in his shoulder, all the weight of his great body, Black-Pale struck the ice, the same hoof, the same place.

The Fawn pulled herself up short. Ice chips hit her. The expression on her face began to show its own pain. "Papa?"

Crack!

And even while he splintered and chopped at the Liverbrook, his breathing bubbled up more and more blood. He was digging a hole. He spat in the snow around him.

"Oh, Papa, look at you!" wailed little De La Coeur. "You are so hurt. Can't I—"

Crack!

"Can't I come to you? What is the matter?"

Crack!

"Won't you look at me? Papa—"

Crack!

"Papa!" bawled the poor Fawn, bending forward and thrusting her head toward him like any Calf: "What did I do? Why are you mad at me?"

And when, with a final, tremendous blow, the Stag broke through and rammed his leg to the shoulder in icy waters, she cried, "Aren't you glad to see me any more? Papa?"

But this is what Black-Pale was doing: he was trying to cleanse his hoof of the blood of the baby, to shock from it the feel of a backbone snapping. He'd splintered utterly that hoof. He'd compacted his knee and fractured the shin. And now the water was numbing it all—and still that snap, and still the soft sensation lingered, indelible forever: *murderer!*

Black-Pale put his face into the snow. He spoke.

Not to answer De La Coeur, nor even to address her. It was as though she weren't there. She began a keening, heartbroken moan. She couldn't help herself. She was just a child.

It was to the Hen that Black-Pale spoke. He said, "She calls you aunty." He said, "Well and good. Now let her call you mother." He said, "She needs a parent. She needs that goodness. She is your child, now, forever and ever till the end, your child—"

This was the last thing he said.

While his daughter watched him, he withdrew the offending leg from its bloody puncture in the brook; he stood shakily and began to walk away to the south.

Suddenly De La Coeur raised her voice to the highest sorrow she had inside of her and cried after him: "But what did I do wrong? Papa! Papa! *Papa!*"

He didn't stop then. He stumbled farther and farther. And then it was the stumbling alone that dropped him. For a while his legs continued a walking motion, though he lay on his side; but this was because he'd been granted his heart's wish. He'd slipped into unconsciousness. God had created him a noble character, Black-Pale-on-a-Silver-Field, so that he could not countenance a treachery, not even when the sinner was himself. Coma was his refuge.

And in this way the child became the mother.

De La Coeur never left her father's side again, but nursed him day and night, while Chalcedony looked after both of them. The Fawn continually wiped blood from her father's muzzle and sang to him when he was wracked with coughing. She could do this without his denying it now, could love him anyway, because he was unconscious.

Thirty-eight
In the House Alone

With Chalcedony and the Fawn De La Coeur, Pertelote ministered to Black-Pale. She brought him simples and nursed the wounds on his neck and shoulder. But his lungs were too deep in the great black body; and his heart was deeper still.

While she bound the shivered leg, she said, "He said nothing?"

"No, Lady. Nothing," said Chalcedony. "Or something," she said, "But not so's we'd understand—" And she paused.

Pertelote completed the sentence: "—understand what happened to Chauntecleer."

"Aye. Nothing of Lord Chauntecleer."

This was not the return that Pertelote had expected. Some

heroic triumph, maybe—though she had, in fact, prepared herself for failure; she was not convinced that her husband could defeat Wyrm in his lair. Some sadness, certainly—because she'd imagined a thousand deaths for the Rooster and dreamed them nightly. But sadness can be consoled. She had not anticipated so grieved a Creature as Black-Pale was, nor such determined self-destruction. She pierced the swelling of his fetlock. The ruptured blood ran out, slow, purple blood from his beautiful tool for walking. She caressed the leg. She thought: he is so honorable and so desolated. She thought: he carries a secret in his breast. But his mouth and his eyes were closed together, now; he would not be telling it.

She looked at the overheated bustle that Chalcedony was making of herself and had the grace to smile. The Hen was embarrassed to feel so pleased under these circumstances.

"Something," Pertelote said to her sister. "What *was* that something that he said?"

"Ooo, Lady," said Chalcedony. "That the child was mine. That I'm to be her mother. What d'you think of that?"

Pertelote returned the question. "What do *you* think of it, Chalcedony?"

The crippled Hen sat down at gazed at De La Coeur, the child of aristocracy, and of the melting eye. "I say," said Chalcedony, "I don't know. It's an uncommon request, surely, and maybe not fitting for nurses to be mothers. Ah, Lady, but I love the child. So therefore I say, deep in secret I hear myself saying," whispered the Hen, " 'And why mayn't Chalcedony have a pretty child of her own?' Ooo, Lady."

Pertelote went to the little Hen and hugged her.

"The heart has reasons," said Pertelote. "Sister, I say the same."

Cobb came home with an illicit air about him. But he had always been straightforward. Pertelote was not encouraged.

Jasper the fat Hen, greasy in her busy motion and rather pouncing in her question, saw him slipping to the Liverbrook.

"Well!" she shouted: hail-Squirrel-well-met. "Glad you're back! What happened, then? Everybody fine?"

The Squirrel looked smitten by the ambush, unable to answer for himself. He peered past all the Animals till he caught sight of his wife, then he lowered his head and sneaked toward her.

"To the hole, Mrs. Cobb," he snapped.

She said, "It's so good to see you again, Mr. Cobb."

He said, "Yes."

She pressed her paws to her chest with the same sunny smile that was always reserved for him. "Well," she said. "Tell us the news, Mr. Cobb."

He said, as though he knew, "It isn't good news."

"Oh, I'm sorry," she said. "What happened?"

But the Squirrel turned taciturn and barked with a louder irritation: "To the hole, Mrs. Cobb!"

So then, nothing was learned from him but negatives.

Pertelote's spirits slipped a degree.

She had kept the crows in Chauntecleer's absence, though in Pertelote's throat they were songs.

This night, as always, she sang a Compline of peace, but she wasn't sure whether to believe it. Hard it was to roost alone at night. Harder to think that this condition would last forever. But hardest of all was not to know. Something *else* took place. How could she shape the future while she remained ignorant of *what* else?

Near the end of Compline a presence was circling the night sky above her as silently as the Owl; but she felt it. When she was finished, then, she went to find it. Never, never did Pertelote shrink from knowledge.

Sharpshin the Hawk sat on a stump. He did not greet her but perched with his shoulders hunched, his beak hooked, his figure dark and stern. She took her place below him.

"Sharpshin," she said.

"Lady," he answered.

"You came back," she said.

"I did. For the moment."

"But you didn't dive from the sky."

"I didn't."

"Was that because of the snow?"

"I can stoop in any weather, Lady."

"Ah," she said. "Yes, you can."

He sat still above a field of infinite snow, volunteering nothing. She felt lonely. She felt, somehow, judged by the Hawk that would not look at her, and this was, perhaps, unfair since she knew nothing of events—unkind, because she had to ask to discover them. Yet this was the very reason for which he came, to be interrogated. It was his obligation. And she was obliged to ask.

She did.

She said, "Please, sir. What happened in the north? Was— some— good accomplished?"

"Wyrm is dead," said Sharpshin.

Oh, what extraordinary news! She turned and grinned at him. But, oh! What a deadly way he had of delivering it. Her happiness was not his. He gave it and he judged it at once, the frowning Hawk.

"Dead?" she whispered, wishing some other attitude.

"That," said Sharpshin, "is what the Weasel screamed. And the Weasel saw."

"John Wesley Weasel was there?"

"The Weasel. The warrior. He's everywhere, isn't he?"

"Wyrm is dead?"

"Dead."

"And how—" Pertelote hesitated. Everything depended on the next question—too much for a single answer. Too much of the present and all of their future. "How is Lord Chauntecleer?"

In very waves the Hawk's severe opinion came down. He did not answer immediately. In spite of herself, Pertelote looked at him with piteous desire. Well, it was her husband after all! She saw that he was considering how to speak.

Finally, "Living," said the Hawk, and that was all. "Living."

Pertelote caught her breath. Chauntecleer had *not* died! Wasn't that a good thing? A wonder? And shouldn't someone rejoice?

"He's coming back, then?" she whispered.

Sharpshin said, "I do not know the mind of the Rooster." He blinked, closing a subject. The blink came from the back of his head. "These are the facts. I've communicated them to you," he said. "Now: I've one thing left to do, and then I'll be gone." He spread his wings and by slow strokes flew midnight to the north. He left her by the stump in a snowfield.

But there were so many questions. What of Mundo Cani? And where was someone to celebrate her husband's life? His triumph? Wyrm's death? Wasn't it a good thing that Wyrm should be dead, a marvelous accomplishment? Lord, the present was so obscure: what would the future be?

And why, if Chauntecleer was somewhere alive, did she feel so close to tears?

That night Pertelote paced the beaten snow of the Liver-brook.

Wodenstag Mouse woke up with a sharp premonition and with joy. *He's here!* he thought. *The dear Rooster's come home again!* He smiled without moving another muscle. He stirred no other Brother in the burrow. He allowed delight to flow through his little body a while, and then a warm contentment, and then the warmth alone, and then sleep.

All night the pacing above ground encouraged dreams about the golden Rooster.

But by the morning Wodenstag had forgotten his dreams. Therefore, when he crept across the snow to the Hemlock, he couldn't understand why the plain whiteness disappointed him so deeply; yet he wanted to cry. And when he saw Pertelote alone on her branch, that loneliness seemed a greater grief than yesterday. Why? He felt so bad, but he didn't know why.

Then Pertelote saw him, and they looked at one another in

a sort of privacy, the Hen and the Mouse, each one knowing that the other knew so little. They shrugged together. They gave each other silly smiles, grateful, each, that someone saw the sadness and didn't ask the reasons, since they had none. With their looking alone they said, *I'll watch over you. Will you watch over me?* And both of them smiled again, and that meant *Yes* and *Thank you,* both.

How good, to have a friend!

How necessary.

The day to come was not a kind one.

The Goats came home. The Goats stamped into the camp, heedless of the various rules or properties of other breeds, heedless of the quiet. The Goats came shaking the snow from their coats and braying a list of their misfortunes. The Goats —permitted some swagger and some allowances because of their adventure—or else, perhaps, because of their misfortunes? Who knows? What are the sources of pomposity? How does a demanding spirit justify itself? Or does that even matter?

The Goats came.

They were tired. Mark how tired they were.

They were cold.

They were, they were bound to announce, less than pleased with the whole trip, from which they had received one lousy moment of excitement and diarrhea. They drilled the snow with brown holes to prove the latter claim, and cried out, "See? See?" each time they did.

And they were hungry. Breakfast!

Where was their breakfast?

Well, that was the job of the Brothers Mice, who took their duties seriously; so Wodenstag and his brothers brought roots for the Goats.

Exactly two Goats ate all the roots, snatching them straight from the Mice with their blocks of teeth, and no thanks out of their mouths.

The other Goats, however, filled their mouths with speeches about selfishness and demanded *their* breakfasts at once, since they had done no less than those two and were probably twice as hungry.

It bothered Wodenstag to bring more food than was absolutely necessary, seeing the emptiness growing in the bins; but he did. The Brothers brought roots again, garnished with a little leaf.

They arranged the foodstuffs prettily for the returned adventurers.

And then they were mortified by what the Goats did

They stomped on the food. They kicked it through the air. They ground it underneath the snow. And they urinated on it. On food! *Food!*

Wodenstag said, "I thought you were hungry."

"You thought that because we told you that," said the Goats. "We said 'hungry,' " said the Goats: *"Haw-*ngry! *Haw-*ngry! So what did you get us?"

"Your breakfast?" said Wodenstag.

"An insult!" brayed the Goats. "You insult us with these tiny piles of foods. What do you think we are? You think we are low as Mice? *Haw-*ngry! The tribes of Hophni and Phinehas need substances for their guts—but this! We loathe your worthless food!"

Poor Wodenstag tried to explain: "But everybody eats the same—"

"Hey! Hey! Do you think we are everybody?" brayed the Goats.

"Oh, no. You're Goats, to be sure—"

"Then bring us eatings fit for Goats!"

"Which is—?"

"Lots!" they roared. "Lots and lots! *Haw-*ngry!"

Well, that was more than Wodenstag could handle. But he couldn't just give away food according to Beasts' requests, or no one would be eating soon. Well, and he thought that the Goats could be dangerous, so then he was frightened, too—

He went to Pertelote, and his brothers followed in quick scamper over crusty snow.

"It's not your job, I know," Wodenstag began, apologetic over his inability, "but—" His brothers had no such apology. They were simply outraged by the Goats' behavior, and they said so in squeaking tumult. "Honk-ry!" they mimicked the Goats with distaste: "Honk-ry! What kind of a way is that to talk?"

Then Samstag blurted the most scandalizing thing of all: "They *peed* on the food!" he squealed, and all the brothers fell silent. What could anyone say about such vulgarity? Nothing.

Pertelote sighed.

Wodenstag felt a rush of pity for that sigh. It wasn't just a passing problem they'd brought her, was it?

Pertelote said, "Thank you, Tags. I'll see what I can do."

Then the Hen walked in a certain dignity to the Goats' field, where she paused. Wodenstag crept up behind her and saw what she was seeing: it was simply amazing how fast Goats could befoul a place. There wasn't a patch of smooth snow left, not a place to lie down in cleanliness. He heard Pertelote sigh one more time, then he himself shrank from the command and the anger that flashed from her.

"Stand still!" she cried. "Don't move!" she cried. Goats blinked their slotted eyes at this sudden appearing and, for the moment, stood still.

Pertelote, glaring at them, dug below a yellow snow with unconcealed disgust. She pulled out a root both damp and salty. Then, like a vulture clutching carrion, she took to her wings and flew at the most outspoken Goat. Suddenly she dived for his mouth. She jammed the root into it. She stung his nose with her nails so that he sucked the root inward, and she cried, "Chew!"

One or two other Goats began to leer at this fellow's discomfiture, but she flew over these with nails for their snouts as well and the hard command, "Shut up!" They did. She was suddenly an iron Lady.

"Chew it," she repeated to the first Goat. "You'll eat what you get, do you hear? And if you don't like it seasoned, don't season it."

The Goat lowered his head, as if to spit the stuff.

Straightway Pertelote bolted for his neck and gripped him there in a very strong claw and hissed, "Lord Chauntecleer has two weapons, sir. If you spit one-half that root, Gaff will cut you here." She drew a line from his ear to his shoulder. His head came up with that line. "If you spit the other half," she hissed, "the Slasher will cut you here." She stabbed his jugular.

The Goat ate the root.

To them all she said, "Surely you don't wish me to give Lord Chauntecleer a bad report of you, do you? Surely you will live according to his rules till he comes back—won't you!"

"Well," muttered the Goats. It sounded like "Waaaaal." "Well, if he can slash a Stag, then he could slash us, too. If he can kill a baby, he'd kill anyone—" Their manner of acquiescence—it sounded like snot and was meant to sting. It did.

Wodenstag saw Pertelote go rigid.

Stiffly, silently, by an amazing self-possession, the Hen stalked from the Goats' field and into the woods. The Brothers Mice came quietly behind, and so they walked some fifty yards, white snow piled at the trunks of trees, each twig its line of white.

All at once she whirled around, and she cried, "I know what he means, 'Slash a Stag.' I saw that. I don't understand it; I *saw* it. But what does he mean by 'Kill a baby'?" She glared at them. Wodenstag only bowed his head. He had no answer. They both knew that.

"Lady, thank you," said Wodenstag, "for having a talk with the Goats."

The expression in Pertelote's face relaxed. "I hate this," she said to Wodenstag, but there was the ghost of a smile on her woman's beak. "Did you see what I did? I threatened them. I made them eat—" She shook her head and waved her wing and smiled. "I hate this."

But that was the last moment of smiling that day. Wodenstag watched her do marvelous things for returning Animals, all the while suffering her own private torment.

In the afternoon a flock of Sheep arrived nearly dead from exposure and exhaustion. Pertelote went out to meet them because she'd seen a Hawk circling in the distant sky and knew it for a sign. At her coming, the Hawk departed without a word of farewell. Pertelote sighed.

Her heart broke for the Sheep, though it wasn't only their condition that troubled her: it was their abject debasement. They showed no will whatever of their own. She walked, and they walked. She stopped—even on a whim—and the whole flock stopped without a question, stopped and would have waited there until they dropped. It was as though they had no mind any more, or else believed that they deserved no choices, as though they should live in perpetual punishment. They would not so much as bleat to be whipped. So, what had they done? What had they been led to? What were they not speaking of? Dear God, what caused this killing of the soul?

"Gentian," Pertelote said to the Mice when she'd brought the flock near unto the hemlock. And with a yearning heart she said, "The herb will ease their insides, Tags. Go get them gentian."

She noticed Wodenstag gazing at her before he left. He had a dear, sympathetic eye. He said, "The Rooster can't be far behind, Lady."

She released a sigh so sudden and deep that it surprised herself. "Oh, Wodenstag!" she said.

Cats despised the snow. They shook it constantly from their fur, for when it melted it made them wet. But everywhere was snow. They couldn't put a paw down but that it touched snow. They couldn't raise their faces except the snow flew into them.

Cats returned in a villainous mood, breathing curses on any who thought to find pleasure in the snow, on Hens and Sparrows and Mice and any who'd merely accommodated themselves to the snow, on gladness and laughter and joy, on the Partridge because she was clumsy. Nor did they wait to see the effect of their curses; it didn't matter; it wasn't vengeance but a pure vexation of the spirit. They held the world in derision, and any who trusted in the goodness of the world they judged to be naive.

Nor did they come like the Goats in a herd. Rather, they rambled singly through the camp of Animals so that there was a general deflation of goodwill and universal unease.

"We've seen your 'goodness,'" they sneered when Pertelote urged on them the goodness of the other Creatures and asked some kindness in return. "We've seen 'goodness' to its core. It has a maggot in it."

String Jack rushed to the Hemlock, harassed.

"Lady!" he panted. "Lady!" He sat up and struggled with the words. More than ever his eyes denied each other. "Seen my sister?" he pleaded. "Seen my cousin?"

But Pertelote had to admit that he was the first Hare to return.

"Yep. Yep," he chattered, panicked. And then, as though unsurprised, "Well—"

Pertelote's heart went out to the fretful Creature. She said, "Perhaps Lord Chauntecleer is with—"

"Oh, Lady!" String Jack exclaimed as if that were a very uncertain suggestion and probably not to be desired. Then he said, "What'll I do? My kin! My family!" In distraction he started a little run to the south. He stopped, whirled, and finally darted to the north again.

He was gone, and he took a part of her heart with him.

Pertelote was being whittled by her ignorance, smaller and smaller to nothing. What? Had Chauntecleer defeated Wyrm? Or what? What? What was she to make of all this?

The Pronghorn, the trip-spring Antelope, came more skittish than ever before. And here was a strange thing: once the voice of a child had been able to calm them. Now the voice of a child sent them flying in alarm. And they couldn't bear even to be brushed by the flank of another Creature. They took no comfort in a Hen's clucking. And the night itself, when it descended, seemed a pall upon their heads. But they could not run from the night. Worse than that, a Wolf would howl in the distant gloom. They were everywhere menaced and nowhere safe.

And Pertelote was helpless. She sang a Vespers for hearts she couldn't understand, and then it was the Brothers mice who whispered in their hole to one another, "Did you hear? The Lady is lonely."

Thirty-nine
Relic

Chauntecleer was alive. Chauntecleer the Rooster was *twice* alive and coming home.

There was himself. And there were in him the worms.

Himself: since every other holy task and every other cause for living had been stripped from him, he'd settled on one final purpose, and he gave it his whole attention, and he meant to see it completed, and he called it *love*. By the most strenuous effort, Chauntecleer was bringing the skull of Mundo Cani home again. A mean proof. A nasty proof, perhaps. But proof enough that he had indeed descended to the Netherworld, and perhaps Pertelote would count it for something.

No! It wasn't a nasty proof at all! It was the right and proper thing to do, to give this Dog an honorable burial—his head, at least. Oh, how Chauntecleer loved the Dog! How precious, then, the relic of the Dog's life! And if anyone wanted to measure the length of his love, why, they had only to look at the Rooster's exertion, his ruination, his *self!* Look at his toes, gone swollen both purple and black. They were frostbitten and likely gangrenous. There was no feeling left in them. And the snow, the everlasting snow piled up against the skull to push back when the Rooster pushed forward. Snow clouted the skull's mouth. Snow extruded from its sockets. Snow fouled his good offices and wore him down to death. But the harder the going became, the more certain was the Rooster that he would get that skull to home, and show that skull to praiseworthy effect, and finally bury that skull as it ought to be buried.

Having nothing else in all the world, the Rooster spent himself on this one thing only.

And so long as it consumed him—so long as he could with passion curse the snow and the trouble it took to drag a skull, so long as he truly suffered in his person pain in the progress, so long as he delivered *all* his intellect to the problem of burial, and his expectations to the welcome Mundo Cani would receive, and his pride to the little glory that might redound to him—then he could not think of the deaths of a Coyote and her offspring. Could not. Was unable to.

No, he could not think of these. He didn't.

Himself: Lord Chauntecleer the Rooster crossed the snows of the prairies, pushing a bone ahead of himself.

He had his token.

But the worms: within him writhed another life, a wriggling in his nasal passages, a multitudinous crawling in his chest, in the muscles of his shoulders and in his gut. Chauntecleer had come up from the cellar of the earth infested with a congregation of threadlike worms—green, when they slid through his mouth, irritating when they twitched in his lungs.

They had thriven on Wyrm-rot. Now they thrived in him.

He hated them, even as he hated the deterioration of his being: these things were the same thing. And both were answered by the same expediency: labor, labor, labor hard, and he could ignore their squirming inside of him.

Can anyone wonder then why Chauntecleer became so zealous for a bone? Or why he swore so violently whenever it lodged in a drift? He lifted furious eyes to the grey and sifting heavens, convinced that God was against him, and balled his claw; but then he'd whisper devoutly, "No. No, God cannot deny the righteousness of this deed. Not this deed, too." And he'd bend himself still more to drive his Mundo Cani home.

But the worms: it was worse than that they simply lived in him like parasites. They seemed, as well, to sing. And the song was *in* his ears, in the itching canals of his head, deeper than he could thrust a nail and twist it. They sang at the center of his thought. And what they sang were interpretations, how he might see and understand the behavior of other Creatures.

This was the more insidious horror. Because when was it his thought, and when was it theirs?

Several times as he thrashed his way homeward, Chauntecleer had looked up to see that he was being watched. Barely visible through the grey curtain of snow stood a Wolf—white, the heart of the snow, regarding him.

See? sang the worms—or, he thought it was the worms singing. *Enemies.* And the worms in his heart would squeeze him exactly like the feeling of fright. *You've enemies, Cock, and they are watching you.*

And when he was fool enough to listen to them, he'd groan, "No," out loud, like talking to himself. "You were born in hell. No, you don't know the truth. No, you don't know my Animals."

Oh? sang the worms with perfect assurance. *Look at their faces, Cock. See if there's any love in them. See if they don't slit their eyes, conceiving evil against you—*

"They are good," the Rooster would bellow, sound to drown out thinking.

They are treacherous.

"I don't believe it!"

But you are the best of them, and aren't you treacherous?

"I will not believe it!"

You will. You will. Sing, sang the worms, *for a Lord betrayed—*
When, in that first night the Rooster had spied the white
Wolf on a ridge above him, the worms had gone so hectic and
his denial so savage that it came to choking. They wadded in
his lungs like tension, hissing, *Watching you with all his spite.*
And he had opposed them by beating on his own chest; then
he coughed a ripping, explosive cough and expelled a fist of
worms into the snow. This was the first time he'd seen them
alive, waving their tendril heads. In a rage he attacked them,
dividing them with a fierce dexterity, piercing them singly,
slaughtering by tiny bites each worm at the midsection, loathing the soft pulp of their skins, and feeling, when he was done,
one moment of grateful relief, as though the vomiting were
good—

But *Sing.* The song still troubled his mind. *Sing for the Rooster
observed.* And he had looked; and the Wolf still stood on the
ridge, observing. But he repulsed the thought and returned to
the Dog's skull, reminding himself of its significance, and he
wore himself to death dragging it, and then he did not listen
to the vile voice inside.

It worked! Labor and labor and labor hard, and he could,
by God, be deaf to insinuations. He could be good.

Can anyone wonder still why a Lord would be obsessed by
a relic? A dead thing?

In the night before he came to the hemlock, Chauntecleer
raised his voice and crowed to the vacant skies and to the
dead: "Wyrm," he crowed. "I will not do your evil! As long
as I love the Dog and serve his honor, I cannot do your evil!"

He said "Do—*Do* your evil." He might as well have said, if
he were speaking the deeper truth, *Be.*

That night he trudged the last night home—so wearily.

Forty

Beside the Nest, and Pity in Their Breast

So it was first of all Wodenstag Mouse who crept out of the hole and across the snow like a thief. Next, Donnerstag Mouse. Then one after the other, Sonntag, Montag, Dienstag, Freitag, and last of all the youngest of all, Samstag.

Not that Pertelote recognized each tiny face. It was midnight. They looked like nothing so much as purposeful hairballs. But she'd known Wodenstag by his manner and had counted the rest. Besides, the thieves were gathering at the root of her Hemlock, and as their number grew, so did the noises of one telling another to shut up.

Mice and a midnight raid.

Pertelote had nearly tucked her head beneath her wing again when a change in the noises drew her attention and a curious activity held it. No, it was a very daring activity—for Mice. While six stood semicircle, staring straight up with their noses, their mouths hanging open, the seventh Mouse had begun to climb a tree. He had all four legs extended as wide as they would go, like a daddy-longlegs on the wall; each paw had its little nip of bark; and he was trembling so furiously he looked like a plucked rubber band. But his expression was earnest. And somewhere inside of him was the conviction that he could climb a tree, and somewhere, too, the notion that he *should* climb a tree.

Pertelote forgot, for the moment, the torments of the day in watching this tiny test of fortitude: *Well, can you do it, Wodenstag?*

The Brothers whispered upward, "Are you going to fall? Should we get out of the way?"

But grand efforts are always performed in solitude. Wodenstag answered them nothing. What he did, stuck to the trunk of a tree: he trembled. His chin drummed the bark like a woodpecker—and lo! His eye lit up. It must have been the chin-drumming that imparted him a flash of insight, because he suddenly called, "Bite the bark!" And Pertelote felt a little cheer in her throat. *"Bite* the bark. There's the ticket!" Wodenstag bit the bark. So then he could let go successive paws to move them higher up—and what is that if it is not climbing? Why, it's climbing of the finest sort! Pertelote wasn't tired. She was enjoying a miniature triumph. *Bite* the bark! What a breakthrough.

So then up the tree trunk, one by one, with instructions from Wodenstag on a branch above, and encouragement from Brothers on the snow below, a constant buzzing of grunts and information, Mice climbed the tree. A string of thieves up a tree. And how they patted Samstag, and how they praised that youngest Brother when he had gained the branch with them. How they congratulated one another all around—and then!

Then they turned in unison to look down the branch itself, and the Hen at the end of it. So that stilled their jubilations.

"She's probably sleeping," they said in dreadful quiet.

"So much the better," said Wodenstag. "She needs to sleep."

Pertelote experienced a true softening in her breast, and her head inclined for gladness. Why, the Tags were thinking of her!

So Wodenstag came balancing along the branch, picking his inches with monumental care. And after him, frowning severely, Donnerstag. And Sonntag, and so forth, all staring at the wood in front of them as if the staring itself were gripping. And then this is what they did: they lined up next to Pertelote, side by side, sitting on two legs (aye, *there* was the peril: two legs) and facing south the same as she. And then they were done. This was it. This is what they came for. As solemnly as worship they sat still.

Rather, they tried to sit still. In fact, they had all begun independently of one another to rock. Forward and backward, in an effort to keep their balances, like round-bottom pepper-shakers. Too far forward ("Whoa!"), too far backward ("Whoa! Whoa!"), but all done with the greatest solemnity and an air that it was right to be here; no other place to be, amen.

Pertelote the Hen for whom they had come, she could only shake her head. There was a pressure in her heart that might have been laughter or might have been tears, either one.

"Tags," said Pertelote.

"Ah, Lady. Ah, Lady, we didn't mean to wake you up," whispered Wodenstag as though she were still sleeping. He began to pat her side.

"But here you are," she said.

"Yes," he said, simply because it was the fact. "All of us."

"What a remarkable thing for you to do."

"It isn't easy to climb a tree," said Wodenstag.

"Whoa!" said Montag. And Sonntag said, "Whoa!" spinning his forepaws like whirligigs.

"But it's night," said Pertelote.

"Yes," said Wodenstag, patting her, patting her. "And a very dark night, too, I think."

"Aren't you going back to sleep?"

"Whoa!" said Dienstag. "Whoa!"

"Maybe we could sleep right here," said Wodenstag. "We thought that this would be a very good spot for a sleep."

"Whoa! *Whoa!*" It was Freitag who tipped too far backward, too far altogether. Up shot his hind legs, and down went the whole mouse, plump into a snowbank.

Pertelote seemed the only one to notice his departure. "I don't suppose," she said, "that it's easy for a Mouse to sit this way?"

"Roosting," Wodenstag explained.

Samstag went over head first—*"Whoa!"*—and plopped into snow.

"We talked it over," said Wodenstag. "We agreed that this would be an excellent way to sleep sometimes."

Donnerstag dropped.

Freitag had begun to climb the tree trunk again, whispering, "Bite the bark."

"Whoa! Whoa!" said Montag and Sonntag together. They had locked arms.

Wodenstag himself still patted Pertelote. Sometimes he clung to one little feather; but then he patted her again.

"Why, Wodenstag?" said Pertelote. "Could you tell me why you decided all these things?"

Samstag was on his way up the trunk again, and Freitag on his way out the branch.

"Yes," said Wodenstag.

"Whoa!" roared Montag and Sonntag together. Together they hit the snow.

Wodenstag kept his earnest composure. "To keep the dear Lady company," he said. "She's got no easy day of it, and at night she's lonely—don't we know that? So we said— Whoa!"

Wodenstag's turn. He flew out to emptiness. But he caught a feather and so was left dangling from her breast. "So," said Wodenstag, gazing down at the ground, "we said, 'Let's keep her company.' We have us. But she has no one special just now. We thought that we would give her a little bit of us, and since she can't fit in the hole, we came to roost—"

Pertelote sobbed. It was *both* tears and laughter in her heart: she sobbed through an absolutely dazzling grin. And the sob felt good, but did no good for Wodenstag, who lost his grip and punctured the snow beside his brothers.

"The carefullest, kindest friends I know," sighed Pertelote, "so special to me indeed." She spread her wings and sank to the snow herself. Instantly all the ascending Mice became descending Mice, and Pertelote purely laughed.

"Don't you think," she said, "that you could sleep on the ground tonight, if I sat with you?"

"Oh, Lady!" cried Wodenstag. "What a fine idea!"

"Well, and what if you nestled beneath my wings? What about that?"

Little Samstag couldn't stand it. He began to laugh at the top of his lungs because his gladness was so great.

And Freitag said, "Just like the old days!"

And Pertelote whispered the nearly unspeakable profundity of Freitag's words. "Just like the old days," she sighed.

Then under her wings seven separate paws took to patting the down of her heart and her love, and she was not alone. Wodenstag popped his head out with an afterthought: "Don't feel bad you sobbed and I fell," he told her. "It's okay if you cry."

It was okay. She did cry. Pertelote bowed her head that night and wept the blessed tears of consolation.

Forty-one

No One Left but God

The Jay broke the morning. The Bluejay shocked it with yelling—streaking the woods, startling Animals, causing a sour consternation, then hopping the hemlock as though Hens should be as wakeful as he, and should move.

He yelled, "I saw him!" He squawked with egregious self-importance, "Me! I'm the one. I saw him first. The Rooster's coming! Haw!"

Pertelote's breathing stopped. Her emotions were huge and had no word. She wanted with all her heart to run, and at the same time to hide because she was so frightened. She walked.

She walked through the camp seeing not another Animal, and she did not notice that they crept into line behind her and that soon she was the point of a whole procession, flattening the snow in perfect silence.

She took the higher ground north of the Hemlock. It was an unconscious eye that followed the Jay's flight; her conscious eyes kept scanning the white horizon, seeking a traveler —and who would he be when she saw him?

But wouldn't he be Chauntecleer? Her husband? Why should she even wonder?

Too soon, there he was, standing alone like a nomad in the wilderness of snow.

By an effort she did not pause, but continued toward him. And he watched her coming. Pertelote went to meet a mystery with her heart in her throat.

Oh, Chauntecleer! Oh, Chauntecleer! What happened to you?

His comb hung sluglike and blackened on one side of his head. And when she could see them, his eyes appeared raw. His body was thin and yellowed from a very long labor. One claw was raised as though in pain, its toes thick and gnarled —and he was gazing at her so steadily that she flinched. And she did stop. Three feet before him.

The woman said, abashed, "Hello."

The Rooster did not answer, as though considering her greeting.

Pertelote felt guilty at her hesitation. How much he must have suffered! She called on all the love that dwelt in her for this husband of hers, and in a rush of affection she said, "Chauntecleer. You're home again. You came home after all." Impulsively she moved to him, to kiss him—

But he stood stock still.

"I did something, Pertelote," he said, his voice as bloodless as the snow.

So she didn't kiss him, though the need to trembled in her.

Tenderly she said, "Was it a good something?" And she said, "Are you glad?"

How hard he scrutinized her! She dropped her eyes.

"Not much of a something," he said. "Better than nothing," he said. But he made no move to unveil before her the north, the past, the truth of his excursion, himself. He was sealed in a solitude as hard as ice.

"Well," she said. She tried to smile for him, though it faltered. This was like a meeting between strangers and an examination too cruel, since she didn't know its purpose—and besides, wasn't he Chauntecleer? And wasn't he her husband? "Well," she offered the smile, "what did you do, then?"

Immediately the Rooster said, "I brought him home again. What do you think of that?"

Pertelote whispered, "Him? Who?"

"This is very, very important," said Chauntecleer intently. "You must see the importance of this."

Pertelote nodded. It was obvious that something consumed him. Even in ignorance, because she loved him, she said, "I do, Chauntecleer. Who?"

His eye took light. "Mundo Cani," he said.

"You—" Pertelote returned the gaze, astonished and feeling a prickle of hope. "You brought Mundo Cani with you? You found him, Chauntecleer?"

"Yes," he said.

"Where?—"

"Right here." The Cock moved. He bent, and with that poor crashed head of his he began mightily to thrust in snow. He scraped snow with his claws and threw the snow aside. He swept it with his wings—and there appeared between them, grinning, its eyesockets hollowed, a skull.

In spite of herself, Pertelote gasped.

But now the Rooster fairly rammed his face to hers. "This is so important, Pertelote. Don't say no. Don't make light of it. Don't be afraid. I am not mad. He's dead. I know he's dead. And what's this? His skull, that's all. It's only his skull. And I know this, too, that he died in the war, he's been dead a long time. But I'm going to bury him, Pertelote. And all the Animals will mourn him according to every propriety under the sun, and that is not wrong, it is not foolish, it is not nothing —*it is right!*" He paused, panting, glaring at her. "What do you think of that?" he said.

And he waited for her answer.

Pertelote was dizzy with confusion. It *was* Mundo Cani, and something of sorrow lurked in her to see his head all stuffed with snow. And it was not wrong to bury a friend. But it was strange. All out of proportion. Yet it was *his* desire, and he was her husband: this was Chauntecleer before her, crying her approval.

She said, "He was in the Netherworld?"

"Yes!" he said.

"So you truly went down below the earth? You, Chauntecleer?"

"Yes!" he said.

She was trying to find some premise, some rational footing for herself. It was as though *she* were digging in snow. "Wyrm was there?"

"Yes!"

"You saw Wyrm?"

"Yes!"

"And Wyrm is dead?"

"Yes!" he cried. "Yes! Yes! Yes!"

"And that is the something you did?"

"Pertelote!" he cried straight into her face. "You're avoiding the question. Do you see the importance of burying the Dog with ceremony? Do you?"

She felt so beaten. She whispered, "Of course I do—"

"You do?"

"I— Yes, I do."

He broke into a magnificent grin and roared, "I knew you would. No one is wiser than Pertelote!"

There was for her a thrill in his enthusiasm. So then, all she had to do was to agree with his convictions. But—

"Is that all?" she said. "The Animals are suffering some memory. Black-Pale—"

"Pertelote!" roared her husband in a sudden high good humor. "That's all there needs to be!" Then he bethought himself. "Oh, look at me, look at me," he clucked, struggling for calm. "I'm forgetting the little things, ha-ha! I'm forgetting to hug my wife, now that I'm home again. Pertelote: can I kiss you?"

The Rooster was a whirlwind!

But a kiss would be a good thing. It could be a starting-place. And he was her husband. Pertelote tried the smile again, and she said, "Yes."

He brought his face toward hers in gentleness. But in the instant before she closed her eyes, she saw a worm slide from his nostril—thin, wavering and green. In horror she watched while it twisted on itself. And then another dribbled from his ear. And she shrank backward, wailing, "Chauntecleer!"

"What!" Immediately he stiffened again into his suspicions, glaring at her.

She couldn't take the revulsion out of her face. She felt like vomiting. His very feathers rippled with the motion of a myriad living worms. "You—" she gagged. "You're— Oh, Chauntecleer!"

"I, what? I'm, what? I wanted to kiss my wife. What? What's that?"

"I can't kiss you," she whined the truth.

Sickened, Pertelote turned away. At once she saw that they were not alone, that Animals, Animals stood in silent ranks behind them back to the woods, watching, and all of it was on a stage. In public she was rejecting her husband!

Pertelote felt so wretched.

She turned back to find his gaze hard, cold, and frozen again. In the time of her turning twice there had come a world between them, a gaping universe.

"But I do love you," she cried. What was she to do?

"So," said the Cock. "She loves me. So. Then let her help me. Let her assist me with this one important thing, and then I'll trouble her no more. Take the front end of the skull," he commanded.

Abjectly, Pertelote went to the head of Mundo Cani and with a shiver gripped the hollow of his nose. She made ready to pull, her own head bowed.

The Rooster watched her, unmoving.

Then he accused her. "You think that I am guilty, don't you. With *all* of these Creatures here, you think it's my fault, don't you? They talk of lives and murders and mothers and children. They seek a scapegoat, and it's me, and you believe them, don't you?"

What could she say? She didn't understand a word of this. Without so much as raising her head, she said, "I don't."

And then she felt a brutal thrust into her stomach. The Cock had taken his place behind the skull and had driven it forward. "Pull!" he hissed.

She pulled, though she had no wind.

He pushed.

The Animals fell away from them and made a path, a sort of aisle, a ceremonial double file for the husband and his wife and the skull between. This, then, was the homecoming of Chauntecleer the Rooster.

"Pull!" he hissed.

She pulled, unable to look at anyone.

And he pushed.

See? sang the worms in the Rooster's ear. *Do you see how they look at you?*

Chauntecleer answered nothing.

And she above them all! sang the worms. *Did you see the loathing in her face?*

Chauntecleer drove the Dog's skull forward with power, answering nothing.

It's a conspiracy, Cock, they sang. *There's none of them does not*

*blame you: murders and mothers and children, these at the center of false
promises. And here is something to consider, that when you are no longer
lovely, you can't be loved again. Do you truly think that you are lovely,
Cock?*

So sang the worms through the whole complexity of the
Rooster's being.

But he gave all his attention to the one thing precious in his
life. He spent his strength on Mundo Cani's skull, forcing it
toward its burial.

Chauntecleer was home again.

Forty-two

And Then It Was a Pity

That same night Chalcedony the crippled Hen heard the
Rooster's Compline and knew he had returned. She was by the
Stag and De La Coeur, the child, now, of her heart. They
stood their huddled watch on the lower Liverbrook at the
southern edge of the Animals' encampment. She couldn't
leave them.

She heard the Compline and was not comforted, because it
seemed a foreign note against her ear and it did not name her
name. It did not recognize the distress of Black-Pale, whose
breathing humped his entire body. And it did not silence the
Wolves.

All that night the Wolves prowled the darkness, calling
bodiless to one another in falsetto howling—far in the north,
from the western and the eastern regions, and then so close
in the wood beside her that she rose to her claws in defense.
Not comforted. Chalcedony felt beseiged and naked. She had

a child to save, and that child had a father failing. They were a pitiful three against the darkness and the Wolves—
—and the wind.

In that same night the wind arose with a finer fury, and then it seemed that all the forces had combined to terrify a Hen. The wind sprayed snow-crystals like arrows.

No, not comforted. The poor Hen didn't sleep at all, nor did she tuck her head beneath her wing. She watched with her eye wide open to the darkness. She watched on the windward side of the Stag, as though she might protect him. She listened to the howling, and she watched.

And then it was a pity, come the morning light, when the Hen found that she was blinded on one side.

The wind had frozen her bare right eyeball as hard as a marble.

Here ends the fourth part of the book exactly writ.

Libera me, Domine, de morte aeterna,
in die illa tremenda:
Quando caeli movendi sunt et terra:
Dum veneris judicare
saeculum per ignem.

PART FIVE
THE SUN OF RIGHTEOUSNESS, WITH HEALING IN HIS WINGS

Forty-three

Bereaved

There was a day when Ferric talked a continual, frenetic patter to the brown Bird while pacing outside the Den on the canyon stream that finally had turned to ice with the rest of creation. From morning to night he chattered and laughed and wept with himself, back and forth, back and forth, pausing only for the new thought, the next memory, to rush in, then spilling that one, too.

He told her how he had met Rachel.

He complained of Rachel's carelessness, then caught himself and apologized and cried a while and praised her openness to all the world.

He described how they had come to the canyon and remembered aloud his hesitations.

He talked at interminable length of the wonder of her pregnancy and of her perpetual peace, her smile. He begged the Bird to believe that he had laughed once, he had done the right thing once, and he demanded whether she didn't think that Rachel was glad that he had laughed, and whether he hadn't done one thing right by her, and surely Rachel had noticed, hadn't she? And she loved him, didn't she?

And oh! could she tell stories!

And what a tenderness she had with children. She knew their ways by a merciful instinct.

And had he told the Bird about her smile, that Rachel had perfect teeth in a slender snout and a smile that could make him cry?

And then he said, *Why did she have to die?*

He pressed his head to the canyon wall, then, and drew his lips back from his teeth and suffered a speechless pain. Let no one think it was merely emotional: this was physical pain in the pit of his stomach, and he couldn't breathe, and he couldn't talk any more. He slumped to the ground with his paws against his gut, and his tail and his legs jammed in.

He had talked himself to the point of her death, and her death had entered into him, a hard reality.

He had chattered the whole day through. But he hadn't fed his children.

There was a day when Ferric lay in the den in hopeless silence.

If he had slept the night before, then he woke without moving a muscle. He had merely passed into consciousness. His eyes opened; that was all. And the morning, the afternoon and the evening all found him in exactly the same position.

If he had not slept the night before, then it was uncommonly long that he could lie inert, and his despair was unimaginable. The women whispered. The women—a Bird and two daughter Coyotes—went about with a hushed fear, avoiding him.

Neither did they eat.

He hadn't fed them.

There was a day when Ferric prayed.

He stood at the lip of the canyon, wailing unto God the misery of the whole world, and the greyness of it. His head was tipped to high heaven, somewhere on the far side of the cloud, and he asked whether God punished the wicked: "Do ye? *Do ye?*" Whether the proud are ever brought down, whether the heartless ever know what they have done, and do they sting for their sins? Do they wish they hadn't done them?

He wailed: "I know she isn't coming back. I know the forever of it. I know the body frozen in the grave—it's not her. But what can pay me for it? Do you comfort the little Creatures? Tell me the reason. Maybe the reason can comfort me. Oh! Oh—"

In all these days the Bird and his daughters feared for him, because it seemed that he was close to dying himself. He had always been so frightened, so craven. This was a change, as though something had burst inside of him. He had always said "Tssst!" as his sharpest comment. Now he was reckless. Now he uttered whatever came to his mind. Ferric Coyote was at the extremity, bereft of a wife and a son, talking or lying or crying to God.

Even in his sleep he moaned, "Benoni!"

But in all these days he did not feed his children.

And they were sickening.

Hopsacking sighed often, though she did not tell her papa. Her nose dried and began to crack. It made little prints of blood when she touched it to the snow. Her eyes ran a yellow rheum which crusted on the lids and blurred her vision. But she didn't tell her papa, because he was sad. And she was past the aching for food. And her tail was a miserable string.

She was the first to lie down and not think about getting up. This was probably the way of things, now: for both her mama and her papa to go away, but in different ways. Soon she wouldn't mind at all any more. . . .

"Papa? Hopsacking's sleeping."

Ferric rolled his eyes from his sorrow and saw Twill. He said, "Good," and closed his eyes again.

"Papa?" Twill nudged him under his chin, lifting his head. "Hopsacking's sleeping."

"It's good," said Ferric without opening his eyes. "Let her sleep."

"No, Papa." The pup was urgent. "But she's sleeping. She sleeped last night. And she sleeped yesterday. She never waked up to talk to me, but we always talk, Papa, but she didn't. Hopsacking's gone to sleep. But I want her to talk with me. What'll we do?"

Ferric tried to bring his attention to the child. There was a close smell in the Den and heaviness in his limbs. He was so empty and so tired.

"No one else talks to me, Papa, just Hopsacking since Mama—" She broke off confused. Some subjects were taboo. "Well, but you always looked at Benoni, and now you think about Benoni, but there's only just Hopsacking for me and me for Hopsacking, and she told me she was hungry, and then she went to sleep, Papa. Wake her up. Please just wake her up, and I'll let you be. I'll go 'way again. It's okay. You need to think about Mama. It's okay. But I need Hopsacking now—"

Ferric felt the insistent nudging of his daughter. His daughter. He had a daughter, and she had a brave little nose. For a moment the very touch of her caused contentment in his soul, because there was a piece of family left, and if a piece, then a family still. Well, this was a kindness he hadn't noticed lately. And Twill had spirit in her. And wasn't that like Rachel? She was the daughter of Rachel, too.

Suddenly this meant very much to Ferric—that Rachel walked in her children. And if he looked into her daughters' eyes, he could find her there. So was she gone?

He put out his paw and laid it on Twill's back. Like a waking convalescent he smiled on her, groggily.

But she said, "Papa!" She was not smiling. She was grim. "Hopsacking's *sleeping!* She said she was hungry, then she went to *sleep!*"

A thought gathered in Ferric's mind, like a tiny cloud. Then it swelled and then it stormed in him. Hungry!

He rose and turned to the other child, surprised at how close to him she lay. He called her name. He slid his snout under her and lifted, but she was loose sticks. She flopped down again. She was light and so sinfully thin! Her mouth sagged open, and her tongue lolled out. She made no complaint.

"Hopsacking!"

Rachel had named her. Oh, God, how could he take the name away again?

"Hopsacking!"

It was the protruding tongue that broke him. This was like Benoni's tongue. Then here it was, all over again. But he couldn't rage against the wicked now, because *he* was the wicked. How long had it been since he'd brought his daughter food?

"Hopsacking, please, please wake up!"

Her tiny breath smelled like decay. This was the death-scent. Why hadn't he gone to bring her food? She didn't wake up. Well, he didn't have to eat. He deserved not to eat. But the child was innocent and should have eaten. She didn't wake up. So what were the reasons, then? And why did some of the Creatures die? On account of other Creatures—like himself. Don't ask God why. You *know* why! But she wasn't waking up!

"Rachel! I'm sorry!" cried the poor Coyote, trembling and dizzy, and half of that was emotion, but half was his own malnourishment, because neither had he eaten: they were a den of starving souls. Now, under the effort, he felt what pitiful strength he had, and he nearly swooned. Oh, what a condition he'd allowed them to come to. He could hardly walk straight.

Twill's eyes were big, watching him.

He bumped her, leaving the Den. He thought, "I'll get some food." He climbed the great stairs but stumbled and slipped down. All of his limbs were rubber. So what then? Were they all going to perish in the end? Why hadn't he gotten food when he was able? One by one he took the stairs again—but who could find food in this damnable winter? Where did he think he was going? He had daughters. He had daughters! How cruel of him, to neglect his daughters!

Ferric, don't look for murderers anywhere else.

At the rim of the canyon he heard the panicky whine of Twill below, "Papa, can I go with you?"

He looked down and saw her tiny frame. Perhaps he said no, because she cried, "But are you coming back this time?"

That undid him. Go, should he go? When did going ever benefit his children? Stay, should he stay? But then they might

as well lay down to die. And who would talk with Twill then?
And did she think that he was running away from them?

"Oh, Rachel!" he wailed. "Oh, Rachel, what am I going to
do? *I need you!*"

He turned to the forest, and there, bulking between the
Pine and himself, was a Dun Cow walking toward him. He saw
her mortal eye under one horn only, and he fainted.

Forty-four

The Very Soul of the Community —*Spiritus Mundi!*

Chauntecleer said that he needed his rest, and then he
perched unsleeping on the lowest branch in the Hemlock.
With a baleful eye he looked at and did not look at his Animals. They were aware of the presence, and the meek among
them crept on a snow that had been windswept to the crust,
looking and not looking at him. They simply did not know
what to expect from that riven countenance. There was a black
striving and a tension in him, as though a dark sun radiated
black-light from his thought. They were stricken and uncomfortable.

Sometimes the wind would gust great scrolls of snow into
the air, and it would catch the Creatures from behind, invert-
ing their fur and sneaking to their skins. They were cold; and
now, at the returning of the Cock, it seemed that the Fimbul
Winter would last forever. They were hopeless.

Worse: the Wolves that roved the outland borders did so
with intent. No longer were they a remote and vaguely disqui-

eting menace. They went with a quicker step, now. They
showed their fangs to Animals who wandered out of the camp.
By growling, by the direct threat of the eye, by urinating a
pungent, stinging scent, they frightened Animals inward to
the core of the encampment, which was the Hemlock. On four
sides the Wolves were tightening the territory. It was a siege,
for Boreas had said, "The Cock is home, and the Cock's malingering. Now is the time." In the deadly whiteness of his eye
and by the might of his shoulder, Boreas patrolled the north,
and the wind blew cold, and he did not mind. All up and down
the western border ran Favonius, and the wind blew, and he
sent his howling with it. It was a northwest wind, made powerful on the prairies. And Eurus closed the borders of the east.
And Notos lurked the south. To Notos blew the odors of the
Animals. Then Notos, more than the others, gnashed his
teeth, because he smelled food, and he was hungry; starved,
and he was impatient; the least restrained of the pack was the
black Wolf Notos, and his red eye burned perpetual discon-
tent. To him the wind blew envy, and he was full of craving.
Chinook, the Grey Wolf of long endurance, took the whole
circuit round and ran communication among all the Wolves.
Boreas demanded of her, "Why can't I hear his voice in the
south? I know the west and I know the east. I feel three sides,
but not the fourth. Why doesn't Notos call?" And Chinook
said, "His head's low down. He's thinking his own thoughts
now."

It was a siege of ordered and cunning intent. A noose.

And the consequence was that Animals pressed inward on
one another slowly, hardly noticing the cramping of their
numbers, yet suffering the distress of it nonetheless. Close
quarters nerved them.

But Chauntecleer had said that he needed his rest. He
perched on his branch doing nothing.

And Pertelote had lost her will to care for or console the
Animals. Not even her sweet voice sang faith to their souls,
nor did she try to control the selfish behavior. She had tried

once more to talk with Chauntecleer. She had tried to explain her rejection at their meeting, that it wasn't rejection, though it seemed to be, and that she loved him still. He had listened in silence and then demanded again the kiss, but she couldn't kiss him. She couldn't bring herself to kiss him, dear God! But this time it wasn't only the obscenity of parasites that disabled her; it was that he *demanded,* and it was the cold scrutiny of that demand. So then he had dismissed her, saying that he needed his sleep, and she had gone to the wall behind the Hemlock and wrapped herself in her wings and grieved. Tomorrow she might rise up again. Tomorrow she might find love for the Animals again, and faith to console them; she was a woman of deep capacities; she had survived unspeakable shocks to the soul. But today, *today,* she grieved and had to seek healing for herself. Therefore she did not go to or discipline the Goats when she heard the new eruption of their vulgar language. Nor could she find it in her to comfort the Brothers Mice, who squealed and squealed but could not stop the Goats. And she heard the despoiling of a food bin. She heard the Goats break in with their vestigial horns, ruining the food. She heard their Goatish outrage at how mean the larder was after all, since they'd believed the best had been kept from them. She heard, but she thought in her sorrow, what could she do? If Chauntecleer did nothing, what could *she* do? His inertia gave the lie to her previous threats: no, he *didn't* cut them from the ear to the shoulder. He was taking his rest. Pertelote felt the trouble of unraveling events—but today, today she was disabled. There sat Chauntecleer on his limb, her husband whom she could not kiss, and below him lay the hollow skull of Mundo Cani. All she could do was to make her world a tiny place, sufficient for herself alone. She wrapped her wings around her body and grieved.

So the Animals were left to their own devices, stricken and hopeless and cold, unnerved and hungry, despairing, because the Fimbul Winter would last forever. They had looked to the blessings of the northward expedition. And then they'd

looked to the coming of the Cock again. He had come. But
there was no healing in his wings. So what was left to hope for?
And what could change their miserable existence?

Chauntecleer was taking his rest.

Then into this troubled congregation of the Animals there
came a terrible word which seemed, when it was heard, to
name the times like a title underneath a picture: That word
was Death. No one was surprised to hear it. But for some it
was the end of trusting and the motive to handle matters on
their own: for some, the end of faith; for some, the realization
of fears; for others, the justification of selfishness.

From ear to ear the message blew like a chill wind: Black-
Pale-on-a-Silver-Field is dead. He never woke up again. He
never made another sound. There was a long, harsh rattling
in his throat, and then nothing. He died. Was it his time? No,
it wasn't his time to die. He was a grand Beast, beautiful in his
blackness, noble in all his manners and stronger than most.
No one deserves to die, but Black-Pale least of all. This is
horrible! This is the confounding of everything right or good!
This is wrong. Oh, this—

All of the eyes, all of the hearts of the Animals turned
toward Chauntecleer, then, with a true beseeching. They
yearned for a crow. They wanted only that he should be their
priest, one soul undismayed by the shock of death. He didn't
even have to explain death, or this death: just to crow as he
had crowed before. Just to relieve them and give them leave
to break down and cry. He had done that in the wars. He had
done that even when the death before them was the death of
his own children. He knew how to crow the Crow of Grief. It
was not unnatural that they should look to him. Now, today,
all helpless in a nearly universal turmoil, today when they
lacked even private resources to withstand the loss, it was
absolutely necessary!

But Chauntecleer grew conscious of the thousand watchful
eyes and the silence. He stiffened on his branch. He raised his

head higher and higher while thoughts seemed to whirl behind his eyes. Like a ramrod went his back. Defensive was the tension in his wings. His glance shot everywhere over the congregation of the Animals. Then he opened his beak and he crowed. But he didn't crow to heaven. He crowed like fire against the Animals.

He crowed: "WHAT HAVE I EVER DONE TO YOU?"

And they were smitten.

This was not the Crow of Grief.

It was as though the earth had opened up beneath their feet.

See? sang the worms, tumultuous in his mind. *Isn't it worse than a dream and worse than all your imagining?*

The Cock was raising his head from the sleep that had not come to him. He'd felt, before he heard it, the dying of all sound around him and a growing silence. And when he looked, he saw a horror. Everywhere the Animals of his ruling stood still, stock still; and all of them were gazing directly at him. He was the center of their staring, as though he were an alien suddenly dropped among them.

What do you suppose, Cock, this trial is about? sang the vindicated worms. *Why do you suppose they turn on you? What is the accusation behind a thousand eyes? Do you think it's gone to hatred yet? Or is it mere distaste? And how will you argue their goodness now? There is not,* shrilled the worms in unholy jubilation, racking his soul with the blatant proofs of it, *there is not a one among them who does not know what you have done!*

Mice, and Hens, and by the cliff lay Pertelote, the humble Sheep and all the Birds of the air, and Squirrels and Cats and Goats and Deer—all of them stared silently at him and him alone. So then he was an exile after all, judged publicly for all his sins.

When will they bring out the stones? sang the worms. *When will they show you the execution of their conspiracy and stone you? Finally, Cock, at the bottom of things, this is the truth that controls the universe: that everyone hurt, hurts back; that everyone cut, cuts back and double.*

And it has a name, cried the worms inside of him. *Its name is Chaos.*

But Chauntecleer fought the maundering worms. He tried to find one thought to refute them, one refuge from the horror they insisted. But this was the only thought that the Rooster think and believe, that he hadn't sinned against these, not these, at least not *all* of these. He hadn't cut them all. He didn't deserve the condemnation of them *all.* That wasn't just.

And so he crowed a bloody, desperate defense:

"WHAT HAVE I EVER DONE TO YOU?"

And the worms sang, *What? What? Did you think there is justice in Chaos?*

The wind blew. The Wolves howled, tightening the circle. The Animals lay down in misery.

And no one—not even the quick-eyed Pertelote—saw that the Rooster in their midst had begun to cry. Chauntecleer cried with harsh, unsatisfying sobs.

Two things grieved him. He had never in all his life felt so totally isolated, not even when he'd been alone, because loneliness is not rejection. Behold: he was despised by his own, an outcast.

And then this: he was learning a cruel lesson. Against his will he was admitting a truth which destroyed every good and dear belief in the world and which called every holy thing a lie. Everyone cut, cuts back and double. Then love is a deception. Chauntecleer was mourning the loss of his innocence, and of love, and of his God.

This is why he never crowed the crows again, though he never ceased to cherish them.

And this is why the lonely Rooster wept.

Heaven is empty.

Forty-five

Besieged

Animals began to desert him. Chauntecleer was not surprised. It was in their natures to be self-serving. Only, he hadn't truly believed that there was an organized conspiracy until now. He had denied that thought as an exaggeration and paranoia. But the Goats came to him in a body.

"Here!" they brayed with the tremulo of the insulted. "Look here!" they bleated, their eyes on high for having suffered such an affront. "We're leaving, see?" They stamped and shook their beards. "Little Mice to govern us, of the tribes of Hophni and Phinehas, *haw!*"

Chauntecleer looked down on them, the thing itself, bare, unaccommodated selfishness: Beasts. They were no friends of his. He knew it. It was all one.

"There's a problem?" he said.

"Food's the problem!" they brayed back at him. "Fraud's the problem! We're not such as likes to be lied to. And we had a peek at your marvelous stores of food. It wasn't a sweet thing in it. Not a tasty bite for any Beast, and surely not for the Tribes—roots, rinds and grasses, *haw!* Till then we believed you had our interests at heart. Till our little peek. But now we're going to the Wolves. How do you like that?"

Chauntecleer narrowed his eye at them. "What is this?" he said. "What do you mean?"

"Mean *gawn,*" said the Goats. "Gaw-aw-awn! We shake off the dust of this place. Mean going where we get some dignity. Respect!"

"What do you mean, the Wolves?" said Chauntecleer.

"Haw! Everyone knows what Wolves means, Lord-and-General-of-All, *haw!"* They took a thoroughly nasty delight in news he didn't know. It was their superiority. "When the change comes, it won't be a Rooster high and mighty. Oh, niggardly gets its come-uppance—that's what Wolves means. Starve a stomach, pay the price. No one oppresses the salt of the earth forever. They rise when there's nothing to lose. That. That's what Wolves means."

Chauntecleer leaned forward from his branch, worms sliding from his tear ducts, worms causing a contumely within him: *conspiracy!*

"You made it up," he hissed.

"Oh," they said in mock surprise. "We didn't know we had such powers. Out of our heads comes Wolf-howls all night long, to scarify the stupid Creatures round us. Or maybe that's just tummy-rumbles, from being hungry."

"Wolves howl. That means nothing!" hissed the Rooster.

And the Goats were positively gleeful. This distress was beyond their expectations—yet every bit what they deserved. "Wolves howl," they brayed. "Wolves talk, and only the ignernt don't know what they say. And it ain't *our* names in the night wind, Rooster. They don't fling *our* reputations abroad, *haw!* Two guesses who!"

Chauntecleer's silence, then, they took for defeat. Oh, they had brought him down. And as they trooped away, they nattered loudly, "Cut me from here to here, *haw!* Puncture my neck, *haw!* Bold is as bold does."

At the woods they turned for one last jeer: "The name is Chauntecleer!"

So! The Wolves, then. It's the Wolves will rebel against him.

Not everyone who cuts was cut first. Some just take advantage where they can. So! But he would meet them, if it came to that. Let them try their cut, then he would show them the law of the universe.

Chauntecleer thought that he would wait on them, grim under a hard grey sky, resting until he had to fight—and then he would glory in the use of Gaff and the Slasher, finally. The righteous fight would feel so good!

But while he hunched into an attitude of wary patience, another Creature came with the temerity to talk to him. There was no scorn in her voice. There could never be. She was a Hen of humility. And the talk was not easy for her. Therefore, the worms had nothing to say regarding her, and behold: he listened!

But she, too, mentioned the Wolves.

And since he was allowed one final moment of affection, Lord Chauntecleer determined to be not altogether passive, but to enact a love, even if it had no purpose whatsoever.

He would go, even now, and bury Mundo Cani. He would honor that Dog, he alone: the separated Dog, the separated Rooster. It was right.

Ah, thought little Chalcedony as she crept to the hemlock, he was a gaunt Rooster after all. And he seemed to her eye so terribly tired. He fairly hung across his limb. He glanced at her, and she fell instantly into a curtsy. But he looked away again. His comb clutched one side of his head like a dead leaf. The traveling had ruined him. Then how could she talk to him?

But she thought, Brazen it through, Chalcedony. Speak or leave.

She spoke.

"Animals said 'twould do no good, me talking to you," she hollered. "But I made bold to say, It couldn't do no harm neither. And I made bold to come—"

Hoo, this was a trial for her. The Rooster did not acknowledge her presence, and she found herself jacking up and down in endless curtsies.

"It's that important," she said. "And why? Well, you know there's hardly no food no more," she said, popping up and down. "But I don't never mind that. I can skip snacks, sir. But the others has needs, and their needs are increasing, and they scratch the ice from hunger, don't you know—but I guess you know. But I never mind that, neither, and they can go their ways, and I'll go mine—"

She was nearly out of breath, and still he wasn't looking at her, and still she hadn't made her point. She'd come to make a point.

"It's the Wolves, sir," she muttered, casting one-eyed glances at the Rooster. She had to keep him in the half-vision left to her, which meant that she kept cocking her head sideways, a fumbling way to talk.

"The Wolves are coming round where the child and me stand a sort of watch on her father. There's one that glares with a red eye. It's an ungodly red. No, I don't like that red. And it's Black-Pale he's looking at—"

Suddenly the Rooster lifted his head and fixed her with a stare. This was not better. This was worse. The stare made her so self-conscious, and she was a gimpy Hen and blind in one eye, unworthy to bring her suit to him.

But the point was so important.

She found herself shouting: "But I don't even never mind the Wolf, sir. A Wolf's no devilment in himself. It's the tooth. He's got a tooth with a fracture that runs from the cusp to the gum, a drooling, yellow tooth, sir, and what does he mean to do with it? There's the question."

The Rooster was focused on her now, was looking intensely at her, and that's what she wanted, but what a trouble it caused in her heart.

He whispered, "Chalcedony—" He said, "My Hen. My poor, anemic—"

She shouted on: "I don't never mind the tooth, neither. Oh! It's the egg! For once in her life Chalcedony has a child to love. One poor egg made it to hatching, don't you see? One baby made it to me. But what kind of loving is it if Chalcedony can't keep the horrors away, don't you see? Please see. The Fawn shouldn't cry no more, not any more in the whole wide world, on account of, she has cried enough because, I don't know why, but her papa died. There shouldn't be a Wolf come troubling her now. There shouldn't come that tooth to frighten her. Her papa died, sir. Died! And do you know what sadness it is to see the poor Fawn sad?"

The Rooster spread his wings and sank to the snow in front of Chalcedony, still gazing at her.

"Crow, sir! Crow, sir!" she cried. "Please give a crow, sir, as'll send a Wolf away—"

He silenced her absolutely with a touch to her face. "My own, my own, my own Chalcedony," he whispered. He flummoxed her. He turned her head until she could not see him, for he took the blind side. And then she almost slipped to the ground, because he put the tip of his tongue to her eyeball. She felt both breath and the warmth. Blind eyes can feel.

As quiet as the snow and mortally tired, he said, "What happened to your eye, Chalcedony?"

Blind eyes can also cry. What could she say to such a question, and all the feelings rushing through her? Nothing. She covered her face, both eyes between her wings. And she cried.

"Does it hurt?" he whispered.

She shook her head.

"Is that why you are crying?" the Rooster whispered.

She shook her head.

"Then why are you crying?" It was the old, old voice of her Lord Chauntecleer; and it waited her answer.

Oh, why was she crying—such no-account behavior—*now?* Because she had not made the Rooster to understand, for all her trying, and she blamed her tongue that couldn't keep on course. Because, if the Rooster wouldn't know, then there was no help nowhere in all the world for little children, and there were horrors to come, and none to stop them. But why was she crying? Because she could hardly bear the weariness in her Lord, nor the sight of his suffering, nor his touch—

She whined as truly as she could, "I don't know why I am crying, sir."

The Rooster whispered, "My poor, poor Hen Chalcedony."

She looked, and in his eye too was a tear. That was a marvel.

For a moment the crippled Hen and the Lord of the land looked upon one another in perfect understanding, and they were equal. All of their ghosts stood back. All of the furies fell silent. Chalcedony felt that she was lovely. Chauntecleer felt at peace. One moment. One tranquil moment. This moment was for both of them a benediction, and they loved each other.

But the Wolves howled. The light was dying around them.

Chalcedony went to her child and the need that wanted her there.

Chauntecleer dislodged the skull of Mundo Cani and bore it away to bury it.

Forty-six

They Asked His Name and He Said, "No One."

Ferric Coyote had no intentions of waking up. In a half-stupor it seemed to him that he could choose to stay oblivious forever, to shrink and shrink to nothingness. He could be the candle flame that blew out. This father had no right to be.

But someone was nuzzling his body, and he began to feel his own ribs truly, and he resisted. He groaned, "No. No." That's how he resisted. He was helpless to do any more than groan.

The nuzzling, warm and moist, the nuzzling grew stronger against his side, and he felt himself to be turned onto his back. His forepaws drooped to his chest. His lower knees flopped wide apart. He squeezed his eyes shut and groaned piteously, "No. No."

Please, just let him pass away.

But then a gentle flesh touched his lips, and his senses quickened there. The flesh just brushed below his nose, asking to come in. Ferric held his breath. Something so intimate and holy was happening that he woke with tingling, though his eyes stayed shut. He parted his lips. Lightly, deliciously, as soft as kindness, the living flesh slid into his mouth and lay upon his tongue, waiting. Ferric closed upon it. Immediately his stomach cramped with a painful hunger. And this is what Ferric did: he sucked.

And the flesh gave forth a wonderful, abundant fluid.

And Ferric moaned with a new sound now. He sucked hungrily. He swallowed milk sweeter than honey, thick and good; and the milk filled every hollow of his being; it ran in streams from the flesh in his mouth to the wastes inside of him. He grew breathless. He grinned. He buried his face in the whole pillow of skin above him, and he smelled the smell of straw, and he heard a gentle lowing in the air, and he drank until he was content.

As the flesh was drawn from his mouth, he opened his eyes. He saw the ample udder of a Cow and the one nipple that had been his own. And then he saw the face of the Dun Cow herself. She swung round to look at him. He smiled like a silly baby, and then he shuddered almost to weeping. For her eye was a deep pool into which the whole of Ferric Coyote might sink. Oh, what a dear and loving thing, to be gathered into that gaze! She had filled him with her intimate gift. Now she embraced him with her sympathy, and he was warmed within and without, and he did not know what to say. Ferric trembled and wept.

Was he worthy so to be healed by such a Holy One?

Down she lay beside him. Against his neck she nudged her muzzle, and he felt it and he sighed. Then she bathed him. Stroke for stroke she washed him with her tongue as though he were new born. From the corners of his eyes, down his sides, to the joint of his tail and everywhere private upon him, she cleansed the Coyote, and he was not ashamed. Infants are never ashamed. Ferric lay small, in a perfect infancy, loving with all his heart the tongue and the touch of the Dun Cow. He wept tears of absolute relief. These, too, she licked away.

It was the night.

At the beginning of this night, Ferric Coyote had admitted an utter helplessness, and that was a terrible thing, like death. Despair, defeat, and death. But see what the dear Dun Cow had done to helplessness? She consecrated it. She turned it into infancy, and that is a hopeful, holy thing, like the beginning of life.

It was the night. And he worshiped the lowing of the Dun Cow.

When she lay still beside him, he said, "Did you ever know Rachel?"

With an infinite eye she looked at him. Yes, she had known Rachel.

He said, "Ah," in speechless gratitude. Then he said, "Benoni? Did you know Benoni, too?"

She had known Benoni, too.

"He was my son," said Ferric.

He was your son.

"He loved me."

He did. And you loved him.

Ferric said, "Ah. Yes. Yes, yes." And then the soul of the Coyote rested indeed, and he was comforted. For if his wife and his child were known of this Holy One, then they were safe forever.

It was the night.

Presently the Dun Cow heaved herself to standing and she walked toward the steps of the canyon and she descended, going toward his home. Ferric, too, stood up on his unpracticed limbs. He followed her.

Twill stood back in childish awe when they came down, not

wagging her tail. She let her mouth drop open. But the Dun Cow lowed to her, and she squeaked to be spoken to. The child gave an instant trust to this figure with one horn on her head, and Ferric was glad.

The brown Bird popped from the Den, questioning things by the switching of her bill. The Dun Cow paused a long time in front of her, and both of the women went quiet. They communicated, neither one using a tongue. Ferric felt the sacred sigh of their communication, like a covenant slowly compacted, though he could not understand it nor interfere. Then the Dun Cow did an uncommon thing. One by one she bent her forelegs underneath herself and so bowed down before the Bird. Ferric shivered. If this was veneration, then that Bird of the broken wing was one of the Holy Ones too. Little Ferric! What revelations he was privy to this night!

And finally she did what she had come to do.

Hopsacking was sleeping. The Dun Cow drew her from the Den and ministered unto her, and this was more mercifulkindness for Ferric than all the ministrations that he had himself received, because he said, "She's Rachel's daughter." If Hopsacking did not die, then Ferric was forgiven. He was given a daughter again in spite of himself and his neglect. He was given a daughter for the *first* time, again. And with Hopsacking's life came Rachel's. Because he said, "This is Rachel's child."

He would never doubt the darkness again, nor death in that darkness.

And what could be dangerous, if it could not kill?

Nothing.

With what yearning, then, he watched while the Dun Cow turned the poor limp body to its back, its forehead and nose on the ice and its mouth agape. Then down lay the Cow, to curve around the child. And since one thigh was on the ground, her udder spilled out. One nipple touched the baby's tongue. Ferric waited. Then Ferric praised the instincts of babies. She closed her mouth and began to suck, and Ferric knew what she was feeling. He giggled. He laughed out loud. He said, "Did I tell you that this is the daughter of Rachel?" He laughed with an aching gladness. And when the baby dropped the nipple with a smack and a spasm of sighing, and when he saw that she was truly sleeping—because it was a milk of remarkable nourishment—that's when he began again to cry.

The Dun Cow washed the stringy body of Hopsacking, causing her fur to stand up and making her look ridiculous. And then she fed Twill, and she washed her, too; and Twill helped. She was the only one awake to know what goodness she was receiving from the angel of God.

Ferric slept soundly the rest of the night, his snout stuck out of the Den. That was so that he could watch. No one else was in the Den with him. The women had gathered together in the hill which was the Dun Cow. Two Cubs, a Bird, a Cow: the women. Finally it was the women and the children who shared by nature the foundation of a faith, because faith begins in weakness, and though every Creature is weak, it is the women who are willing to admit it.

All night long the Dun Cow lowed in a voice as deep as the planets.

By morning she was gone.

By morning, too, they were a family again, flushed with sudden good health, and it seemed to Ferric that the sun might shine.

"She talked to you, didn't she?" he said to Twill.

"It's two that talk to me now," Twill said happily.

"What did she say?" he said. "What did she tell you in the night?"

"That she loved you, Papa."

Ferric said, "Ah." Ferric grinned like a silly baby and said, "Ah."

"And that she loved another one as well as you," said Twill. She screwed her face up in a trouble of not understanding. "She said he's sick now. She said he's terribly sick. But she

wishes he was well. She said that if you go to him—you, Papa
—and forgive him the same way she forgave you, then he
would be well, just the same as you. Mostly she said that she
hoped that you would go. No—she said she *knew* you would,
on account of how brave you are."

"Ah," said Ferric Coyote, overwhelmed to be entrusted
with such a duty.

"Papa?"

"What."

"His name is Chanty-clear."

Forty-seven

Red in Tooth and Claw

Night.

Black-Pale's body was cool to the touch; the Fawn De La
Coeur's, too hot. She would stretch her neck toward her father
even as she backed away, part of her wanting to lick him, part
of her frightened of the thing inside him, death. The Stag lay
still. The Fawn could not settle. She could not sleep. His eyes
were knit shut. Hers rolled in bewilderment.

Night, and the Hen Chalcedony could only watch the halt-
ing drama, waiting for the child to tire. She stood in the
darkness apart because she didn't belong between them. This
was private. What could she do? This was a private and personal struggle.

And it was the night.

Suddenly she felt that they were not two living Creatures on
the Liverbrook, but three. What was it: a snort? A breath? The
heat of another body, or deadness in the sound behind her?

Chalcedony whirled and stared with one eye into the blackness, looking for form or some sort of motion. But all of the shadows merged, falling, falling into the dark.

Then all at once she saw him, and the thought skimmed her mind: *He wasn't howling! I didn't hear him howl!*

She would have screamed, but there wasn't time.

Charging up the Liverbrook on sock-feet like the Cat, but his head low down and his tail, too, and his lips curled, fangs clashing between them, came Notos the midnight Wolf. He was silent now! His eyes were mad-red, bleeding greed.

Immediately Chalcedony flew in the face of the Fawn, making her flinch backward. So the Fawn and the Hen sprawled in the snow. But the Wolf, in one smooth leap, sailed over them and landed at the Stag's belly.

De La Coeur said, "Aunty, what—?"

But Chalcedony knew what instantly. She screamed, "Leave us alone!"

But Notos spread his jaws and sank his teeth into the flesh of the great Stag. His throat emitted a savage, wretched snarling, and she could see his snout wrinkled by the hugeness of the bite. He jerked. He gathered his paws beneath him and jerked backward: now! Now! Now—trying to rip the skin free.

The Stag slid toward the Wolf, his great head turning up.

"*Papa!*" shrieked De La Coeur.

"*Aiee!*" sang Chalcedony in a perfect delirium of rage. Absolutely mindless of herself, the little Hen took to her wings and threw herself at the Wolf. She beat his head with her wings. She scratched at his eyes with her claws. She caused a furious inconvenience all round his face. But he only shut his eyes behind thick fur and yanked the harder.

When she heard skin pop and tear, and when it seemed to her that the dead Stag groaned, the blood shot through her temples.

Up on her wings the poor Hen rose, horrified at the abomination. Down she came on the Wolf's rump. And for once in her life the claw was not crippled. *Both* claws, *eight* nails, like the talons of the Eagles, pierced Wolf-butt and fastened to him.

Notos brought his head up with a little woof, truly surprised. It was as though he hadn't realized that anyone else was near him. For a second he whined like an innocent, then anger flooded him, and he twisted his head left and right to snap at the Hen.

She was silent. She was only just hanging on.

The Wolf bucked twice, whipping her head backward. But Chalcedony hung on.

Round and round he ran, chasing the affliction at his tail, howling both hurt and anger.

Chalcedony was afraid, now, because this body was so much stronger than she'd anticipated. It was a lethal engine dragging her into dizziness. But there was no letting go now. She concentrated only to keep her claws in the Wolf muscle, and she hung on.

Suddenly he bowed his head and ran flat out, southward into the blackness. She felt the wind. She cracked with the kick of his hindlegs. She heard a distant De La Coeur wail, "Aunty!" And she came to the cool conclusion that she was going to die. Her toes ached. The nails were slipping. She said, in the still part of her mind: *Soon. Soon, now.*

In a field of ghostly snow, Chalcedony let go. She somersaulted like a clumsy Hen then lay still.

The Wolf hurtled twenty yards before digging himself to a stop. He turned. It was a purely malevolent eye that he laid on her, red at twenty paces; and the growl that played in his throat made the whole world clear: he was going to bite, kill, and eat a Hen, and that was the way she was going to die.

Chalcedony did not so much as move. There was no protest in her, nor did the prospect seem all that wrong. Life had grown too troublesome for a crippled Hen. Then, let it go. Just: let it go.

At the instant he launched himself, she thought of the Fawn and sadness swept her. She began to say aloud, "But why mayn't Chalcedony have a child like—"

Snow blew up like smoke around the Wolf's lunging. One could hardly see the other lean black body between Chalcedony and him. One could barely hear the utterly fearless threat: "John gives *you* what-for—" As in a dream the Hen watched John Wesley Weasel flatten himself to the ground, directly in front of Notos. When the Wolf drove over him, then, the Weasel thrust upward like a dagger for the throat, in a flash taking his own bite, closing his jaws on the windpipe. And the Wolf ran on, a black strap hanging from his neck.

As in a dream Chalcedony saw the Wolf's red eyes pass over her, widened now with their own knowledge, and the mouth gaping and soundless and breathing nothing. Dreamlike, Notos spun into a dance of horrible beauty, leaping, leaping, leaping, beseeching heaven, finally lying on the earth as though that were the place for him after all—actually curling down for sleep! Three separate spasms for air, and then the black Wolf Notos was still.

The Weasel let go.

The Wolf sighed long, but it was only the giving up of the ghost.

When John Wesley came toward her, Chalcedony saw with a certain wonder that the Weasel was limping, too, that his left hindleg was useless.

He put his small eyes near her, sniffing the scents. Belatedly she began to tingle as the events crashed in on her, and she thought she was about to cry, but still she did not move.

"Hey, Chicky!" said the Weasel. "Is Chicky okay, what?"

She simply fell to shivering.

The Weasel whispered in a darker voice, "What-a-hell's a matter here abouts?" And he said, "Why-come a Chicky, she's gots to fight Wolfs? Why-come a Wolf, he'd fight a Chicky? And why-come John, he gots to be a murderer?"

She shook her head. She didn't know. She didn't know. It was all too troublesome to understand—too, too many for Chalcedony.

"Hey, Chicky," he whispered. "Is okay, Chicky. No, don't be worried, Chicky, on account of John."

Two crippled Creatures in a field of snow—and in the night, and wordless in ignorance. Two who felt so tiny in the universe. . . .

When they rose to limp home they saw the grey Wolf, Chinook, watching them.

Poor John sighed and raised his back to combat posture all over again—

But Chinook of the blue eye said, "He was the maverick." As fateful as the wheel she said, "He deserved the execution, Weasel." And she said, "If you came to us, we would not turn you away."

John Wesley said with honest feeling, "But why-come John, he gots to be the executioner. John fights. But did somebody thinks that John, he likes to kill buggars with fur like him own self? No. No. No."

And so they passed her in sorrow.

Forty-eight

John's Solution

"What is?" said John Wesley. "What is? What is? Oh, Lady Hen, what is?"

One last time the lesser company of Animals were gathered in a homely place, all sitting under the Hemlock: Pertelote, the Mice, Chalcedony, Jasper, the Hens and their bewildered brood, and John Wesley Weasel. No Dog among them. No Fox. These had died the death with the Wee Widow Mouse and the three Pins, Chauntecleer's children. And no Chauntecleer.

In silent sorrow John had heard what Chalcedony had to say

of the days and their deterioration. He'd met the Fawn. He'd stood in honor beside the Stag Black-Pale-on-a-Silver-Field. He'd passed the violated food bin.

And then the Brothers Mice had run to meet him, calling him "Uncle" and "Dear Uncle" with devout relief at his return.

And why was he so slow coming, they had asked.

"By-cause John lost him one leg," the Weasel had said.

But how was that?

But John didn't explain how the warrior lost his leg.

And the Mice had skittered all around him to bring him, like glad tidings, to Pertelote, under whom they were spending the night. And Pertelote had met him gravely, with unspeakable graciousness, a Lady to her roots, but mortally sad. It had stung him to see the depth of her sadness. Some could be sad in the world and John wouldn't spend two pennies on it; but Pertelote was not fashioned to be sad. Why, Pertelote had endured the horrors of the summer war more faithfully than any other, so that all others took their faith from her! Then if Pertelote was sad, the world was dying indeed.

Therefore he had sat down, gazing at her. And the Hens had dropped like fruit all around them from their roosts. And he had finally put the question:

"What is, Lady Hen?"

He truly wanted to know.

Pertelote smiled at her beak, not in her eyes, and didn't satisfy him. "How good it is to see you again, John," she said.

He said, "Goats, what? Goats bustered them butts out of here? Goats gone to Wolves by-cause it's *sides* atwixt us now?"

The Brothers Mice kept Pertelote from answering. From Wodenstag to Samstag they told their sins to the Weasel, how that they had managed the food too poorly, and so the Goats probably had cause, because they fed them like Mice and not like Goats. They were willing to take blame for everything of "what is."

Pertelote said, "All those who went north returned unhappily. Not just the Goats."

John Wesley lowered his head. Then he was no help. This is the way he returned, too.

Pertelote said, "Why, John? Was there no glory in killing Wyrm?"

He said, "No'm. No glory."

She said, "But it's what Chauntecleer went to do."

And he said, "Yes'm."

"So then Chauntecleer accomplished *something* of his purpose."

And the Weasel said without thinking, "No'm."

Pertelote swallowed. "John!" she whispered, and the Weasel felt wretched for not holding his tongue. "Didn't Chauntecleer kill Wyrm?"

Miserably, "No, ma'am."

"Then how?—"

"Oh, Lady Hen," said John, sick to carry such news. "Wyrm, he was dead already, dead when the Rooster come to him. Dead."

"Oh!" Pertelote put her wing to her face. *"That's* why—" She couldn't finish the sentence.

"Why what?" John shot the return with a narrow eye. "What, Lady Hen. *What is?"*

She looked at him as from another continent. Bleakly, willing to hear every hurtful word, she said, "Black-Pale came back so troubled that he lay down and died, John. Is there a reason for that?"

Now none of the Mice spoke a word. Samstag had begun softly to weep. Wodenstag patted the youngest brother for comfort. This was not a happy reunion after all.

John said, "Is."

Pertelote said, "And do you know the reason, John?"

The poor Weasel suffered under the weight of his knowledge. It was mortal on his back. "Yes," he said.

Pertelote had to press him for every piece of it. "What is the reason, John?"

"By-cause," said the miserable Weasel. "By-cause he stepped on a baby, and the baby died. John saw. John knows."

"John!" her voice cracked with sharpness. "That isn't all, is it? Or why do you hang your head? Don't cheat me, John. Don't think so low of me as to protect me. What else did you see?"

Wodenstag patted and patted his brother. Solemn were the faces of the Mice. Some news is so cosmic that it can only be heard in solemnity, as though one were praying.

"John saw," said John, urging his reliability. "John knows." He was making nothing up. "Is a Rooster what stabbed a Stag, what made him kill the baby." And there was more: "On account of," said John, "Rooster, he was mad to kill John. On account of, Rooster, he wasn't John's same Rooster what John found underneathings the earth, no. Lady, for what and for what, John doesn't know. But is blood on a Rooster now."

There fell upon the little company a cold, despairing silence. No one looked at another. Some news makes looking impossible and must be held in the private heart. Samstag stopped crying.

Pertelote prayed a prayer. "For what and for what," she said. "But I know. Wyrm took his worth. Wyrm took his life. Wyrm left him the thing that he most hated—and when he looked for the one whom he loathed most of all, he saw himself. So how could he be himself thereafter? Ah, Chauntecleer. Ah, my my Chauntecleer."

John Wesley looked on her, finally, with slow awe.

"Lady," he repeated his question again, for who would know but her? "What is? John, he killed a Wolf tonight. Why-come? Lady, she is so sad. Why-come?"

And Pertelote, closing her eyes against the universe, answered him. "Not 'what is,' John. What is not. My husband is not. Your Rooster—he is not. He doesn't crow the Crows nor discipline the Animals nor feed them nor comfort them. He is haggard. He gives no space for mourning in. He is haunted. Infested. And he—" The next word was not for John nor for any of them. It was spoken into her own soul, said because it had to be said. "He doesn't—" She swallowed. "I see. I know. He isn't the same Rooster who rode out. He doesn't love me any more."

John Wesley hissed his shock. John's blood ran hot at that. Then what hope was there for the future, if the Rooster could cease to love this Lady? What healing ever, ever could come from him, or for him, once he was dead at heart? None. There was no hope left whatever. None.

So: do and do. Do somethings on his own. And is only one thing left to do.

John Wesley stood up, his face changed utterly.

He said harshly, "Forget John, okay? Never thinks on John again, okay? Mouses, wipe John Double-u from the memories. Not Uncle no more, no. Gone. Nothings. John, he's nothings now. Lady Hen, you can hate John, too, if you want to—"

The poor Mice were stunned by this speech, and Samstag's eyes burst water, though he made no sound. The whole world was changing all over again, and they panted, gazing at their dear uncle.

Pertelote's attention rushed back from its great distance and sharpened on the Weasel's face.

The Weasel kept blinking and shrugging, suffering a violent shame. But his mind was made up, and it was a Weasel's mind, tenacious, bitterly determined.

"What are you saying?" said Pertelote.

"Well," said John. "Well, well and well. See, John, he knows where the Rooster is, on account of Chicky here tells him. So."

"So?" Pertelote had stood up as well. She glared at him. He stared at the ground.

"So," he said, "Rooster, he's gone to the Coop, what, to bury a Dog bone."

"So?"

"So what is that!" John Wesley suddenly cried. "Burying Dog's bone? What? Is crazinesses forever, is what! Rooster is ruined. John saw, John saw that. But Rooster, he's ruining all of the Critters now, one by one and all together, and some-

body's sad and somebody dies and then what? Oh!"

"And we should forget *you* for this?" she gasped. The world was spinning loose.

"No, not for this!" roared the Weasel. The Mice flinched. "But by-cause of what John, he's going to do. Oh, John—he's wicked, yes. Yes, John is wicked, is the all and the end of it. John, he's going to the Wolves. And John," he shouted at the top of his lungs, filling himself with roarings so that he would not be filled with tears. "John is going to say, 'Come, Wolves. Come and all your teeth, Wolves. Come see where the Rooster is.' And then—" the Weasel was bellowing. Samstag was shaking with his sobs now, uncontrolled. And Freitag, eyes wide open, was crying too. And no one patted anyone now, because their paws were wringing at their breasts. What had they come to? What had good-hearted Creatures come to?

"And then," bellowed the Weasel, "John will say, 'We'll kill him together.'"

"Oh, John, *no!*" cried Pertelote. "Betray my husband?"

But that was talk too dangerous for him to hear. It might persuade him from the wrong that had to be.

"Lady Hen, yes!" he said. And he said, "Mouses, *please* don't cry. Just hate John now, and then the Mouses, they won't cry." He said, "Goo-by. Goo-by."

And he was gone.

Pertelote looked here and looked there. Her eyes flew from the Mice to the Hens to the tree trunk, the empty branch and the limitless night. "Well," she said. "Well," as though speaking to herself about a keepsake she'd mislaid. "Well, then. Then what? Then I've got to tell him, of course." She looked with such profound meditation on the Brothers Mice that it seemed to hammer at them till they were helpless at the heart. They merely nodded. "Yes!" declared Pertelote. "I can't do otherwise, can I? It's right. It's the only right. Yes. I'll go now. He's my husband. I'll go to warn him."

She stepped into the night and paused.

Then she turned back to the Hens and the Mice together with wild agony in her eyes. "But he's tired!" she pleaded. "He is so tired. *What can he do against Wolves?*"

Forty-nine

Lazarus

In this way the web was shredding. Keepers who could not keep one another were no Keepers of the Evil any more.

Somewhere Darkness was smiling that night, and Coldness curled in a Cat's repose, content. Because Wyrm had been right: he could not have invaded the Animals frontally, but only by entering at the heart. There had to be complicity of one, then two, and then two thousand. They had to choose for Evil themselves and then, to protect and nourish it within, to justify their choices. Let wrong be right and right wrong. And how? By letting every living Creature believe his choices to be right simply because *he* chose them; then let him, as in a holy crusade, fight for the right against any who threatened it—who were wrong simply because they threatened it. Set Keepers against each other. Then, when the clash began at night, when things began to fall apart because the center could not hold, then Wyrm no longer lurked below the earth in his own sole sphere, oh, no. Then Evil had taken up dwelling among the Keepers themselves. *Spiritus Mundi.* The smell of rot arose from them, and *their* society stank to heaven. And they were Wyrm.

Somewhere Darkness was smiling. The spell was nearly done, the net asunder, and Chaos almost come again.

Oh, God, sang Darkness, soon I will *be* the separation among your Creatures and the void among your stars. I am coming to destroy you. Because who can remember your name in the bowels of Chaos? And if any do, how else shall they speak it except in a curse?

Lazarus makes a ticking sound when he digs. It sounds like time, like the passage of time, like something no one could dispute, and therefore gives pause to the hearts that hear him.

The Beetle Lazarus, digging graves for the bodies of the dead, whether in earth or ice or stone, ticks like time. Nor does it matter whether the body is large or small, the reputation high or low: the ticking is always unrushed, perfunctory, unvaried. Like time.

And he is himself both slow and predictable. Close on every death, the Beetle Lazarus shall come to cover the corpse. It is assured. He will come in a decent sadness, with his head hooded; but he'll never allow the sadness to overwhelm his duty nor hinder the digging. Even so did he quarry two pockets in ice and limestone despite the particular pain of a wife struck dead, a mother and her child. *Tick-tick:* he cut the stone while the rest of the family watched him and little cubs wailed.

Even so is he traveling south to bury the larger body of a father.

Lazarus makes a ticking sound when he digs. It isn't the way he feels; it is the motion of his labor; his *laboring* ticks, like time.

And now he goes to round a great hole for a Stag recently dead. Family will watch him again. He will endure their mortal eyes. He always has.

Yet—

This time as Lazarus approaches the land of the Rooster, the dreadful sense grows within him that there comes a death too huge to hide in the earth, a dying so universal that it threatens instead to cover earth.

He pauses. He waves his feelers to understand this enormity. Lazarus pauses in his progress, and it is as though time hesitated—

Fifty

And Fallen, Fallen Light Renew

The dirty light of the dawn slowly makes visible old battle plains between woods on the north and Wyrmesmere on the south, the naked stand of timber, the ice-grey sea. The snow on the plains, too, is old and hard.

Upon those plains, like an arm crooked, lies part of a wall —ancient, so it seems, because it crumbles at both ends and gives back a stubborn light, like stone.

On the ridge of that wall stands a solitary figure.

He stands cold and still, as though conscious that his is the only life in all that region, that he is alone and there is no other. Yet he stands commanding. The tilt of his head is proud, as though it says, *Very well, then I will rule the wastes,* and his posture so resolute, so indisputable that he himself, his very body seems the center: from him, both east and west and south on the sea; from him the long and level snows stretch far away.

He turns by slow degrees, surveying the emptiness. No living Creatures. No voices crying "Amen." No Animals of any disposition, either loving or hating. No one. Only the bare grey wilderness called forth and called flat by the dawning. Silence.

This is Lord Chauntecleer the Rooster. Lo: there is in him a tragic glory, that he can still seem sovereign even of a barren, uninhabited land. *Very well, then I will rule the wastes.* This, from a shattered visage.

Bound tightly to his shanks are the wicked weapons, Gaff and the Slasher. As tight as those thongs, so tight are all his muscles. He is rigid on the earthwork. His beak is a spike and his claws like grappling hooks—

But finally he's one lonely Creature, small in the vastness. Finally, he is just Chauntecleer. That sad truth becomes evident when someone else appears far east of him, running raggedly on snow, and she is no smaller than he, but she seems so tiny and so lost and so overwhelmed by the bleak expanse.

She is a Hen, coming as fast as she can. But the distance mocks her speed, and she seems to move slowly. She stumbles and falls sometimes, then lies still to catch her breath before she gets up and runs again.

"Chaunte—" she cries. It's Pertelote. He can't yet hear her. But she's been crying his name through the night and into the morning. "Chaunte—!" And she runs.

Chauntecleer turns on the brow of the wall. He fixes his eye in her direction and waits. He doesn't go to her, and he does not acknowledge her with a call.

She closes the last length of the distance, then collapses fifty yards from the earthwork, and the Rooster stands on top of it.

Pertelote thrashes the ground. She wants desperately to talk, but she hasn't the breath.

He watches the woman passively.

"They—" The words come out of her like dry rags. "They are— Oh, Chauntecleer, they're coming to kill you!"

The Rooster doesn't move. His expression stays the same. He looks at her as at a curiosity.

Pertelote cries, "Did you hear? Me?"

"Yes," says Chauntecleer. "I heard you. You're screaming."

"Well! Well!" She strikes the ground in her frustration. "Well, *do* something. Fly. Escape this place. I'll go with you. Or go without me, I don't care. Chauntecleer, they're going to *kill* you! It's no accident. And it isn't just Goats or rabble. Chauntecleer, it's their cold intent!"

Chauntecleer says calmly, "I knew that."

"It's the Wolves!" she wails the cruelest information. "Oh, Chauntecleer! The Wolves!"

On his hilltop, imperturbable: "Pertelote, I knew it. You won't shake my faith any more."

This defeats her. "What?"

And suddenly the Cock declares in a loud crow, as though it were a decree: "Everyone cut, cuts back, woman! This is the way of the world. Everybody, *everybody* protects himself. Your kindness is exposed as weakness and damned for a futility. And if I haven't succeeded until now, it's because I believed in lies till now. But I've got a clear head, woman. And I've got clear eyes and the strength to stand the truth—and I know precisely whom to protect—"

"Chauntecleer!" whispers Pertelote. "Who are you?"

"Did you think you'd break me down with your message?" There spreads across the Cock a certain triumph. He straightens in pride. "Why, you build me up, woman! You think I should be as shocked as you. But all you're doing is proving the truth. This is no shock. Only children are shocked, and the blind are shocked. Of course they want to kill me. I am more powerful than they are, I! I am a danger to them, I!"

"Chauntecleer!"

"O soft voice! O meek-hearted woman!"

"I love you!"

"Don't, Pertelote!" Chauntecleer stamps the earthwork with his claw. "Don't tangle me in that lie!" Now he is raging. "When I believed it I was as soft as you and full of guilt and impotent. But I've seen *through* it, woman. And I may be alone, now; but I am not deceived, now. Oh, you woman! All that time of misery, why, it was needless. It was needless. It came of a contemptible deception. Get away from me!" roars the Cock, trembling in his fury.

Pertelote shrinks, but stares at Chauntecleer in disbelief and does not move. White and worn and lost, she does not move.

"Get away! Get away! Get away!" the Rooster thunders, throwing himself in broad strides back and forth on the wall.

Each cry strikes Pertelote across her face, beating her down into the snow. She whispers, "Oh. Oh, my husband." But she does not blame him. She suffers, gazing at him high above her.

"Rooster!" Suddenly the challenge bursts from the northern wood, and Chauntecleer spins to meet his enemy.

In as wild a howl as he was called, he calls in return: *"Boreas!"*

So the warriors name each other. And so the battle plains are prepared, and all the world holds still.

The White Wolf emerges from the trees, walking slowly and in perfect control. Behind him, three more Wolves appear; and then, along the entire line of the wood, the Animals step out. Chauntecleer's watching is grim and unsurprised. Goats and Cats and the great Deer, hooves and claws in assembly. And there is but one Rooster—he on the earthwork—but he is assessing the enemy, and he is not afraid.

"Woman," he says, "behold the truth."

But then he glimpses among the Animals one Creature low down and long, limping; and for an instant the hardness passes from his countenance, and he *is* surprised.

"John?" he says. Bewilderment makes him look weak. "John Wesley? What are you doing there?" It is a whine. The Rooster is whining.

The Weasel must have heard his name. He drops his face and paws the ground.

Chauntecleer cries, "What did I ever do to you?"

Then the Weasel steels himself. He gathers himself into a posture of belligerence, and he cries in return, "Tries to kill me! Tries to kill John, what! But that's nothings." And then the accusation is called into the face of the universe, and nothing is hidden any more: "But Rooster, he doesn't tries to kill some baby, no. Rooster, he *kills* that baby! He kills that baby's mama too!"

Chauntecleer staggers. The naked indictment hits him like a rock, the personal sin that he had refused to know; and for an instant the Cock is vulnerable, hanging on the air.

But he is protected now. He is armed with convictions now that shield him from guilt: there is no sin. There is no sin in all the bloody world. There is only self-defense and survival and the right to be alive. Chauntecleer knows the truth; John Wesley has nothing on him!

The Weasel chose the stronger side. That's all.

Then out of the wood comes a thin Coyote, crouching, creeping, and the Rooster barks one sharp laugh. *There* is the truth made manifest.

"Everyone cut," cries Chauntecleer in a voice so cold and sneering that it confuses the Animals, "cuts back! Holy Weasel—come to kill your Lord. Wounded Coyote—come to take your vengeance. And one of you justifies the other. Ha! Woman!" he shrieks from the top of the earthwork. "Watch them attack me, and behold the truth. This is the way of the world!"

John Wesley shrinks before the diatribe, ashamed.

Pertelote weaves her head back and forth.

The Animals falter at the edge of the plains—

—because the Rooster seems only to swell into a grand nobility, solitary before the forces ranged against him, and unafraid. Horrible is the power in his stance, solid in the truth; and iron is his eye; and stinging the laugh that issues from his beak.

Only the Wolves prowl forward, their heads slung low, their eyes narrow. They separate themselves and begin to circle the Rooster's wall.

With an icy, godlike grace, he revolves to watch them.

Here it comes.

And a sound goes up that shivers the hearts of the Animals, a long, inarticulate siren: two notes, *A* and *Ah*. The faster that the four Wolves circle, the shriller becomes that sound: *A, Ah! A, Ah!* Whole choirs in heaven, the hosts of the air, are singing at crescendo, deafening the Animals who bleat and bray and rub their ears as though the Whirlwind is coming and there's no place to hide. *A! Ah! A! Ah!* But who can tell, because of its volume, that it ascends from the place of the Rooster? And who can know that the siren is a single word to pierce the world:

CHAOS!—like the screaming of the wind.

CHA-*OS!*

Suddenly the White Wolf barks. The whole pack strikes in new directions. Pertelote cries, "Wait!" The Rooster sucks a serious breath. And here it comes.

Favonius the Wolf has curved his run. Fleet, he angles up the earthwork, charging Chauntecleer with a curled lip, snapping his fangs. But the Rooster leaps from the ground, and twice before the Wolf has passed beneath him, he stings the skull with accurate cuts of the Slasher. Down the wall Favonius tumbles. Blood springs behind his ear.

But Eurus is dashing up the other side.

Chauntecleer drops and meets this attack sideways, spinning away. He doesn't lose his balance. Gaff, quick as scissors, slits flesh from the eyelid to the lip, and immediately the grey bone shows within two flaps, and blood is spreading like lace between his teeth when Eurus hits the plains again.

Pertelote, dry-eyed till now has begun to cry. John Wesley is creeping round the battlefield toward her. Ferric Coyote has begun a howling, but none can hear it; it is only the rounding of his mouth. The more tremendous sound drowns him out. The wind-scream. The *CHAOS!*

Three Wolves, now, from three sides, but perfectly together: Eurus, Favonius, Chinook lunge up the earthwork. Muscle and tooth and bone, they attack relentlessly, their legs spread, their necks curved for the pounce. Their snarls are uttered at the base of their throats.

Chauntecleer's eye is level, his motion sudden and adroit, his mind pure calculation. He counts his enemies one at a time, one by one by one—

Eurus is shredded about the eyes by a flurry of Rooster-claws, pierced and blinded and bleeds tears.

Favonius whines and collapses, finding his foreleg tendon sliced. He seems to bow.

Again and again Chauntecleer thrusts at the throat of the

grey Wolf, but she has a thick collar of fur. He can't find the flesh. The failure frustrates his fighting rhythm, and he feels the more pressed on several sides. One tooth rakes his own back. He stumbles. Then all at once the three Wolves divide and retreat, two crippled, one still in her strength. Chauntecleer tries to regain his footing, but all four Wolves are working in concert. As if he came through a curtain parted, Boreas the White Wolf streaks toward the Rooster at a terrifying speed. He catches Chauntecleer in his jaws and with a mighty whirl of his head flings him far from the wall. Chauntecleer spins and flutters through the air, can't find his wing, falls and hits the ground with a crack as sharp as stone.

Pertelote screams and leaps up. Whenever could a Rooster stand four Wolves?

And still they work in concert. In the instant the Cock hits earth, Chinook drives down on him, striking a blow to the back that doubles him over, and on she runs.

John Wesley is holding Pertelote now, restraining her. The Hen is struggling to get to her husband. His beak's spread wide in silent pain, his tongue thrust out. So is hers.

And now comes Boreas, closing a circle upon the Rooster, running steadily. Favonius may be lamed and Eurus blinded and three held back by the single Cock; but Boreas the White Wolf is mightier than them all. The ice reports when his paw comes down. His brow is as massed as the glacier, and his eye as white.

Pertelote freezes at what is to be. The Animals, all along the wood, have fixed a perfect attention upon the point of impact. Here comes Boreas. The winter, the world stands still—

—except that siren: *CHA-OS!*

At the very last instant Chauntecleer vaults into the air. He somersaults backward; the Wolf has no choice but to run under him; the Rooster lights on the neck of the Wolf, then binds himself with his claws, and Boreas has a rider. Chauntecleer's head snaps hard at the sudden jerk forward; but run he never so fast, Boreas has a rider, and he cannot lose him.

Now grimly Chauntecleer sets to the business of killing. At high speed across the plain, he leans forward and grips the neckbone in his beak, just behind the skull, and fastens the bite. His body rolls with the running of the Wolf. He draws the Slasher free. And while the White Wolf races, the Cock begins to stab him at the neck. Boreas, astoundingly, increases speed. But the blood bursts out and is snatched by the wind. Blood streaks the sides of the Wolf. The Animals are stunned by the display. Where does the Rooster get his strength? What reserves? Boreas has a brute power in his legs. But the Cock's a cold machine. And the one is running for his life, and the other is digging it out of him.

It's a ragged sheet of blood that wraps them both. It's a running trail of blood that stains the snow where they have gone. It seems an eternal contest, as fast and as slow as mortality.

Suddenly the Wolf throws up his head and launches himself into the air. He twists violently to loose the Rooster, turns over, and slams shoulders-first into the snow. They slide full thirty feet, the Rooster caught beneath the Wolf. They smear the snow with a brilliant red. The Wolf reaches up. The Wolf, on his back, stretches one paw as high as it will go, grinding his skull in the ice and bending his body upward still to reach the higher, all of his weight on Chauntecleer. And then he sighs. And the paw comes down. And the white Wolf slumps to the side. The Wolf is dead.

SSSSSSS! OSSSSS! CHA-OSSSSSS!

Chauntecleer drags himself apart from the corpse and staggers to stand. He stumbles three steps to the left, his wings trembling. They crutch him on either side, and he stands. He stands. He raises his head like a battle-flag; slowly he lifts his eye from the bloody snow to the long audience of the Animals, and they stare at one another, and he stands. Oh, the figure of that Rooster, gored and gory! In their eyes sits horror. In his, pure spite.

"Everyone cut, cuts back again."

Pertelote no longer tries to come to him. She does not know him any more. That countenance has hardened into a hatred triumphal, and therefore firm, inflexible. Pertelote merely lies down. In all the world, there is nothing left for her.

But for Chauntecleer—everything.

The field is his, now, and he takes it. He walks toward the Animals, gathering strength as he goes, his eye lancing a wicked light.

"Everyone cut, cuts back again. You came to kill me, and what shall I do about that? What," he whispers hoarsely, "is the righteous thing?"

The Animals know no stopping him. They shy backward.

But the worms within him find a voice. And the worms hiss, *Finish it!* And Chauntecleer nods once, briefly. And the Animals shudder at the alien noise: *Finish it!* It sheds from him like water. *Finish it, and then I shall be free. There will be no truth among the Beasts but me. Finish it! Finish it! Make me the Spiritus Mundi, and free.*

Chauntecleer struts toward the Animals.

The closer he comes, the more restive they grow, mewing and whimpering. They stamp the ground. They shift. They roll their eyes to the side. "O Lord Chauntecleer! Take your weapons off! We didn't mean— We only meant—"

Finish it!

The Goats break and run, kicking smaller Animals as they go. Birds explode in a panic. Like fire, terror leaps from heart to heart, and the bodies collide, and the bodies press to impossible knots, mounting each other, trampling each other. "O Lord Chauntecleer—"

But then the Coyote steps out in front of them all, so frightened that he skulks. By the sheer force of his will, he moves to meet the Rooster.

The Animals seize any savior. They back into the trees, but they watch.

And Chauntecleer pauses.

"You. I know you."

Ferric Coyote, as thin as sticks, raises his narrow face and, slowly, smiles.

"You," says Chauntecleer. A crooked delight of his own begins to smear his face. He chuckles. "You." His breast swells. The blood of the Wolf shines on him. Then, harsh and horrible, he damns the day with laughter. He frowns and he laughs at once, sharply, like the cracking of an icicle. "And I know why you have come. Ha! Ha! Ha!"

Chauntecleer the Rooster addresses the Animals with killing scorn: "Is *this* your reason for rebellion? John Wesley Weasel! Your papa with a baby dead? Your husband and his wife is dead? This justifies your treachery? Murder me? Murder me and satisfy yourselves that it was done all righteously? Oh, don't tell me. *I* know the right. *I* know the only law at bedrock in the universe. WOMAN!" Chauntecleer crows, and there is no laugh in him now. That crow splits the air like yellow lightning. "WOMAN! BEHOLD THE TRUTH! EVERYONE CUT, CUTS BACK AGAIN—AND DOUBLE!"

There is no laugh in him now. His voice descends to the level of dust. "Vengeance," he whispers to Ferric Coyote. "I know why you have come. For vengeance. I am the bitter gorge you cannot swallow, so you came to spit me up. Well, you are the gorge that I can't swallow. You stand at the cause of my own torment. Come. We are the last two in the world. Attack me, so that I can kill you and finish it."

But Ferric Coyote shakes his head. He is trembling in fear; yet he manages to save the smile; and by the truly gentle look in his eye, he gives the smile as a gift to Chauntecleer.

"Don't do that! Why do you do that?" The Cock grows angry. "Why are you smiling at me? Fight me!"

Ferric shakes his head. He murmurs, "No," and the smile peels back to his cheeks as though he can't help it. He dips his head to show that he means well.

Chauntecleer strikes the snow with his claw. "Fight me!" he demands. "I warn you, I will not be mocked. I will not be laughed at!"

Ferric says, "I'm not laughing at you," but the smile expands nearly to silliness. All the rest of him shivers; but the smile fairly blooms on his snout.

"Fight me!" cries Chauntecleer.

"I won't do that," says Ferric.

"Craven! Coward!" cries Chauntecleer. "Worthless! Nothing!"

"Aye," says Ferric. "I am. But that's not why I won't fight you."

"Why?" shrieks the Rooster.

"Because," says Ferric, embarrassed, "I love you, Chanty-clear."

"What!"

"Because I love you, Chanty-clear."

"Oh, you liar!" Chauntecleer explodes. For one instant he hesitates; then he hurls himself forward; and with the Slasher, red in Wolf's blood, he gashes Ferric's leg.

The Animals send up a groan.

The Coyote grunts and goes down.

Chauntecleer whirls into an attitude of defense, awaiting the counter attack.

Finish it! hiss ten thousand voices.

But the Coyote is rising to his feet again, and there is a difference in him, but it is only this: that he's no longer nervous nor afraid. He seems relieved by his pain. He looks, in fact, apologetic; and still he keeps his smile. He says with greater certainty, "I meant it, Chanty-clear. I love you."

"No!"

Chauntecleer brandishes his claw, four naked nails. "No, you don't!" And he strikes the Coyote's face. He rakes that smile so that it bleeds in three parallel lines.

But Ferric was prepared this time and does not fall. Neither does he wipe the blood. His eyes tear, but that's only a reflex to the stinging, and he smiles to prove it.

"Love! You don't love me," cries Chauntecleer. "That's some trick. You can't love me. How can you love me?

You don't know me. Do you know me?"

"Yes."

"Ha! Do you know what I did?"

"Yes."

"What?"

"You killed Benoni. He was my son—"

"*Ah!*" The words in the father's mouth are more terrible than ever Chauntecleer imagined. They burn him like fire.

"—and you killed Rachel. I know that. She was my wife—"

"Cut back! Cut back! Fight me—"

"No," insists the Coyote, smiling still through shredded lips. "But I love you—"

"*Aiee!*" shrieks Chauntecleer. He throws himself upon the little Creature, ripping furiously his flank and his haunches and his shoulders, a Cock cutting the other to the bone. And Ferric's legs buckle underneath the beating. He goes down, bleeding. But he does not, he does *not* protect himself, nor does he make the first effort to strike back. So then an extraordinary reversal takes place: the Rooster's slashings seem slashings at his own heart, upon his own flesh, and he feels them every one because the Coyote so calmly *allows* them. Ferric bleeds, but Chauntecleer is in pain, screaming. This is madness!

Finish—

Chauntecleer throws himself backward, as galled as if he *had* been cut.

"You— You—" He cannot think of the word.

And though he's unable to stand, the bloody Coyote lifts his face and smiles with an ineffable sadness. "I don't blame you, Chanty-clear," he whispers. "Not for this either."

But that, precisely, is the torture. "God damn it!" cries Chauntecleer. "Do I want your kindness?"

"No," whispers the Coyote. "You didn't ask. I give it anyway. On account of, we're alike."

"Oh, no. Oh, no, we're not!" the Cock growls with revulsion. "I am like nobody— I am the only— I alone—" He strikes the ice in confusion.

The Coyote whispers, "It's okay, Chanty-clear."

"I cut you!" cries Chauntecleer. "Look at you. I cut you! *Will you stop smiling at me?*"

"But it's okay," the Coyote repeats. A section of his jowl is loose and hangs like a tassel. "Truly, on account of, I understand you. On account of, we're alike. Truly. We hurt the same, because we hurt others the same. It's only that you're hurting, Chanty-clear."

He is. He is! And he groans pitifully in the torment.

"Oh, Chanty-clear. I hurt Rachel so many times. Then how can I blame you for hurting her, too? I can't."

"Ah!" The Rooster slumps to the snow, seeing the woman dead in her canyon. His beak spreads wide against the snow. He makes a gargled, wretched sound.

"And what did I give Benoni his whole life long? Only misery, Chanty-clear. This is the truth. Hunger and worries and fears for his papa. And I wasn't there at the end, and I didn't protect him from dying—"

"Ah! Ah! *Ah!*" The Rooster twists. It is an agony.

But Ferric doesn't mean to make it an agony. They are only just two wounded Creatures, lying in the snow together.

"Then how can I blame you? I can't," whispers the Coyote. He crawls closer to the Rooster, using his elbows. "Chanty-clear, I came to forgive you. We should be the same in this, too, don't you think?"

During the next words of the little Coyote, a remarkable change seizes Lord Chauntecleer the Rooster. He lies very still, listening. And then he seems to shrink, curling in on himself, his eyes and his face compressing nearly to nothing. Then, helplessly, he bursts into tears.

"Oh, Chanty-clear, there is a beautiful Cow. When I was hurting the most, this beautiful Cow came to me. And somebody maybe should have punished me, on account of all the troubles that I caused. But she loved me, Chanty-clear. Isn't that a mercy? She touched me, she fed me, she washed me, and that is how she loved me. Then this is how she forgave me: she did the same thing for my daughter Hopsacking. All of the hurts, every one of the hurts, she took away from me with her eyes and with her tongue, and there was no reason for that, but she did it, Chanty-clear. Do you know this beautiful Cow? One horn on her head? She knows you, Chanty-clear. She said that she loves you, Chanty-clear. You especially— Shh, don't cry, Chanty-clear, poor Chanty-clear. You didn't listen to her when she came to you, but that's okay, too, because look: she sent me. This is the main reason why I came. To forgive you. Don't cry. Don't cry. See? I forgive you—"

Chauntecleer the Rooster has delivered himself to grief. He is gulping the air and sobbing like an infant. His tears drill the dirty snow.

So Ferric Coyote pulls his own poor body forward until he is next to the Rooster. Then, like a mother and a newborn, he begins to lick Chauntecleer, stroke and stroke and stroke, nodding his head with every stroke, beak and neck and back and breast, washing him clean of a winter's filth—and smiling.

And Chauntecleer burns. The tongue of that Coyote seems to scorch his very flesh, too hot to endure, and he wails the louder with every stroke.

"Oh, God! Oh, God!" howls Chauntecleer. "Oh, dear God, how can I stand this?" Every stroke of the Coyote's tongue wakens a wickedness in the Cock, draws it through his memory in order to wipe it away. It is a poor, pitiful life he remembers. No, this is no soft tongue. It is as rough as gravel and scours the Rooster, but he does not deny it, because it comes in kindness. Kindness. *Kindness* is the reason it burns so much. And kindness is his Keeper.

There comes the moment when Chauntecleer opens his bleary, humiliated eyes to look upon the Coyote so close to him. He looks. He sees the final horror and he draws back, roaring the final pain of all.

Crawling all over Ferric's tongue, and hanging from his snout, are the thin, thread-like worms, twisting obscenely.

"*No!*" roars Chauntecleer. "No more! It ends here! It is finished here! Oh, no more, no more!"

Wildly he falls to sweeping Ferric's face with his wings, and where the worms fall he punctures them, precisely in the middle. He is a blizzard of activity. And in the midst of it he lifts his voice and bellows, "Pertelote! Pertelote! Where are you, Pertelote? Oh, Pertelote, come to me! Please hurry, hurry, Pertelote, and come to me!"

A madness has seized Chauntecleer. He whirls, darts, cuts, bites and kills worms even as they rain from his feathers and coil on the snow. "Oh, Pertelote, hurry!" It is as if time has run out. So desperate is his thrashing that he seems to be fighting the night itself, to keep it back.

"*Pertelote!*"

And when that Lady—carefully, uncertainly—steps into his vision, poor Chauntecleer is overcome with gratitude, and the words pour out of him, and he sets himself immediately to a new task. With one weapon he begins to slash at the thongs of the other, the thongs so tight that they bite bone.

"You came! Oh, thank God, that you would come. You have to see this, Pertelote," chatters the Rooster, while the Hen only gazes at him and flinches from what he does. Gaff is cutting his leg together with the thong, but that doesn't matter. "You have to understand, dear Pertelote. It was me. I know it was me did these things, all these things. But there's a division in me, can you understand that? It wasn't *all* of me. No. They were liars in me, and it wasn't you who lied, Pertelote, Pertelote, I know that now. They lied, and I believed them, and that's why it was me, truly. This is the sadness, that I believed them and not you—" The Slasher suddenly pops free and falls into the snow. Chauntecleer grabs it backward in his claw, then grows very still, gazing deep, deep into Pertelote's wary eye. "You must know, you must see and believe, that they were liars only. Because I love you. And I need, I need—Oh, how I need you to love me, too, dear Pertelote."

Before any Creature can stop him, Chauntecleer the Rooster puts the point of the Slasher to his own breast—

A scream goes up above the plains. A scream ascends between the wood and the ice-grey sea. One scream of perfect grief flies lonely over the battlefield and dies away.

The Animals all along the trees shuffle and utter moans because they are, every one of them, made lonesome by the dying of that scream, and they have no understanding.

John Wesley Weasel is stung. "Why-come," he cries. "Why-come he make her scream again? Rooster, he should be done with hurting her now!" He creeps three-legged across the snow to save Pertelote from ruin. But there is nothing that he can do.

Chauntecleer has cut his stomach open.

Pertelote is staring down with unspeakable emotion.

It might be the Rooster's own bowel that slithered long and moist from the wound in his gut. But it isn't. It's a thousand threadlike worms all braided into one worm, squirming and contracting on red snow.

And Chauntecleer is quiet, now, serenely lying on his side and smiling up to Pertelote. "See?" One drop of blood sits in the corner of his beak. "Do you see the thing that lived in me? Wyrm. And can you love me, Pertelote, now that he is out?"

Epilogue
Pertelote's Song

"Love you," Pertelote protested. "Oh, Chauntecleer, I have never ceased to love you."

She held his head upon her breast, where her feathers still remembered a crimson color, though faded now. The beauty of younger days, that color. Today, this evening, in the dusky light, someone might say, " 'Tis brown, no more than a patch of dun at her throat. Why do you call it beautiful?"

Pertelote rocked her husband, gazing toward the nighttime coming from the east. "I loved you," she said. "I only lacked the means to tell you and to persuade you that I did. Ah, Chauntecleer. In the night I've thought of nothing but your suffering. In the morning I've seen nothing but your dear face. And sometimes," the Hen admitted with a sigh—a gentle sigh because this was not complaining, and he shouldn't think that it was complaining—"sometimes I remember the days that were so good for us, a Hen, a golden Rooster, and their three good children—"

Ferric Coyote lay beside them, content to see this closing at the end of the day. Quietly he licked his lacerations. They would heal.

John Wesley Weasel crept furtively near, as though uncertain whether he should be present, but knowing nowhere else to go.

The Animals were a broad, dark company in the background, Creatures of the earth caught for the last time in a universal assembly, all the breeds and tribes and tongues and nations under heaven. Perhaps they would lie down and sleep right where they were. Perhaps they would travel home in the morning.

And Chauntecleer lay on his side, bearing a mortal wound from the breast to the thigh, his eye unsteady, his wings in disarray.

He said, "John, is that you?"

The Weasel muttered, "By-cause," and, "Well," and "Yump"—by which he meant both Excuse me, and Yes.

Chauntecleer said, "Good, friend. I am glad. Will you do something for me?"

This was a pure kindness for the Weasel, who sat down as though he *should* be there.

Chauntecleer said, "Will you bite Gaff from my leg? The

spring is coming, John. When the spring comes, will you take both Gaff and the Slasher, and stand at the rolling sea, and throw those weapons as far as God gives you the strength, so that they sink forever? John?"

John Wesley said, "Yump, Rooster. John, he can do somethings."

The Rooster sighed in gratitude. He said, "Wait a little while." And then he said, "The spring will come."

Pertelote put her neck beside his face. In a distant voice she murmured, "Have you thought of the three Pins lately? Have you thought of our children, Chauntecleer?"

"No," said Chauntecleer. "It's a fault that I haven't."

"Shh, but I have," she said. "And this is what I have thought: long or short, what does it matter? They lived in this world under the love of a wonderful father—the only father that ever they knew—and any time is some time, and some time is time enough. This is what I've thought," said Pertelote, "that under the everlasting stars all time is short and the length of it foolish to measure. *Is* is enough to say. And *was* is a fine enough memory when it is done." She hugged her husband close to her throat. "Right, Chauntecleer?"

There spread a smile across his beak, though his eyes stayed closed. "I hear you, woman," he said.

John Wesley said, "Wee Widow Mouse, she was."

"Right," said Pertelote. "As lovely a *was* as any of us can expect to have. Cherish it, John."

"And Rachel," said Ferric Coyote. "And little Benoni the oldest Coyote."

Pertelote nodded peacefully, saying, "Right. Right. Keep them close to you."

Chauntecleer whispered from the darkness, "The children were brave, dear Pertelote, because you are. Ah, my beautiful Pertelote. All these years, and all these happenings, and all your patience. Oh, woman, I love you with all my heart."

Rocking, rocking him, she said, "I love you, too, Chauntecleer."

But nobody wept. The time of weeping was over. They knew better, now. They knew to say *Is* and *Was* in righteous separation, to sit in the *Is,* to remember the *Was,* and themselves merely to *be.*

So they sat until the midnight.

Then Chauntecleer began to chuckle, a low thrumming in his throat, and still his eyes were closed. He saw his own visions.

Pertelote traced a line along his brow, acknowledging the joke.

"Do you know," he said. The chuckle turned into weak laughter, shaking his body like hiccups. "Do you know that I couldn't even bury Mundo Cani's head? Oh, the poor Dog!" he laughed. It seemed a marvelous irony. "Oh, poor Mundo Cani, marooned wherever he is. I couldn't make a hole big enough for his nose. Pertelote, Pertelote, what do you think of such a nose?"

She didn't answer him.

For, in the middle of his laugh, he died.

Pertelote lifted up her voice and began to sing on the battlefield. She sang as though she walked the rim of the universe, like the moon, a pale and lovely presence everywhere on earth.

While she sang, the grey Wolf Chinook left the form of Boreas and came to Pertelote and bowed her head and listened, and then there were two women together to make a common memory of the ones they loved. The women bore the same things in their hearts.

While she sang the Animals lifted their heads from sleep and looked at the sky and saw the stars, and these became the blanket for their beds, and they resolved never to forget the song nor the singer.

And far, far away the Brothers Mice pulled their noses from the circle in which they slept. "Listen," they said. "Do you hear that? The dear Lady Pertelote is singing Compline. Oh, she remembered us with a Compline."

And Pertinax Cobb told his wife that the winter was breaking up. She asked him how he could know such a thing, and he answered that he heard the spring. He heard it singing in the air.

And Chalcedony the crippled Hen touched the Fawn to waken her. "Listen, listen, child," she said. " 'Tis seldom in a lifetime you shall hear an angel. 'Twould be a pity if you missed the blessing. Listen."

But Pertelote stood in her solitude, singing one thing only, one thing only ringing in her soul:

> "He woke me from my slumbering;
> He taught me how it was to sing
>   The songs;
> To him my mornings and that part
> Of me most holy—oh, my heart!—
>   Belongs.
>
> "And who was bolder on the ground?
> Or who more golden sailed around
>   The sky?
> Remember thee? Oh Lord, I will
> Remember none but thee until
>   I die.
>
> My dear. My dear.
> My Chauntecleer—"

Here ends the fifth and final part of the last book of the Bestiary.
Domine, exaudi orationem meam. Amen